Options and Futures Markets, Uses, and Strategies

Options and Futures Markets, Uses, and Strategies

FIRST EDITION

Richard Rosenthal

cognella

SAN DIEGO

Bassim Hamadeh, CEO and Publisher
Mieka Portier, Senior Acquisitions Editor
Tony Paese, Project Editor
Susana Christie, Senior Developmental Editor
Abbey Hastings, Production Editor
Emely Villavicencio, Senior Graphic Designer
Greg Isales, Licensing Coordinator
Natalie Piccotti, Director of Marketing
Kassie Graves, Senior Vice President, Editorial
Jamie Giganti, Director of Academic Publishing

3970 Sorrento Valley Blvd., Ste. 500, San Diego, CA 92121

Contents

Preface

This book has been in gestation for longer than I can remember—and I have a pretty good memory. I wanted to create a book on options that was both academically sound and approachable by students and, for that matter, the public at large. Call me an optimist, but I think such things are possible. The academic reader may snort and guffaw at such pretension, but the gnarled prose of academia often obfuscates when it should enlighten. (Parenthetically, sometimes I am led to believe that the obfuscation is deliberate—just to show students that the professor is still the boss.) No reason exists *not* to consider the usefulness of a book simply because its prose style wasn't truly academic enough. My hope is that readers, academic or laic, will consider its informal nature readable, usable, and applicable. Concurrently, information will reflect current academic thinking as well; rest assured, the text will be academically sound. Otherwise, what really is the point of academia?

By the same logic, options and futures must be presented accurately, without fluff and exaggeration. Options in some ways are indeed esoteric and ponderous; this leads many to misunderstand and simplify both their original purpose as hedging instruments as well as their newer uses as instruments of risk management and income. But despite some option complexities, options are approachable by the layperson: it is not necessary to be a statistics maven or licensed astrophysicist to understand and successfully employ options. Too many popular books pretend that options offer entry onto a surefire, high-speed highway to wealth and influence. Let's all join the real world: options should never be considered riskless and high-speed wealth generators, but neither should they be a source of fear and loathing. Futures suffer similarly. Too many popular books "dummy-down" the basics to the lowest common denominator, clearly a way to bolster market size, without being honest about the risks involved in futures trading.

Concurrently, options and futures are not *a-b-c* simple. Some thinking and/or analysis is a prerequisite. I know that sounds snarky, and it is, but experience shows that at any mention of options and/or futures, investors' eyes frequently widen and their jaws slacken as though they have seen some specter from the underworld. The option mystique is inadvertently furthered by brokerages that require new clients to demonstrate a certain level of investment experience—frequently as much as five years—before clients can even *think* of merely buying a put or call. And this is just to buy them! The act of writing options requires "experience" trading long option positions, even though the process of option writing is without doubt the most profound and flexible—if arguably most likely profitable—of actions that the investor can undertake. (Much more on option writing is forthcoming on the pages that follow.)

Almost 60 years have passed since the establishment of the first options exchange, the Chicago Board Options Exchange, and yet options are still treated as an investment pariah. Why is this so? Despite thousands of books on the subject, many investors still do not have a firm grasp of what these derivative instruments can do, how they are priced, traded, or even their legal terms and conditions. Perhaps an educated investment community will impart a more honest and reasonable treatment than extant in the retail investment community today. The very word *options* can strike terror in the hearts of many investment neophytes and veterans alike. Maligned by the retail investment community for years because retail clients tend to lose millions of dollars employing them, these derivatives have nonetheless been deployed by a multitude of hedge funds, pension funds, and mutual funds to great effect. Options can provide so much flexibility to the strategic investor that—*used properly!*—they can enhance portfolio returns while not necessarily adding much risk. Note the previous phrase: they do not necessarily add *much* risk. But understand: *they do add risk*. For this reason, if used carelessly, they can be ruinous to your equity. So be forewarned, and proceed carefully.

Yet the bad rap is here to stay simply because many investment newbies lose money on them. End of story. I am not certain if this anti-option bias is due to an overarching ignorance of the attributes of options, but I am reasonably certain that if ignorance is the reason options have such a poor reputation, education is the cure. Toward that end, the purpose of this book is to educate; to demystify options, as it were, so that you, the reader, can use options in the manner they were designed to be used. I passionately believe that an antidote against perennial option losses for the option-shy investor is an intimate knowledge of what options are, what they can do (and what they cannot do), how they should be used and not used, and the dynamics of option pricing.

Futures have a much longer history and are vigorously used by end-users such as food processors to effectively hedge against severe price disruptions in the marketplace. Without futures, the price of food products you buy at the grocery store would be much more volatile. But thanks to technological advances, accessibility to the futures market has widened exponentially, gaining a stalwart company of adherents to electronic or algorithmic futures trading. This accessibility has also lured in too many who view futures as a quick road to riches. There are those out there who have indeed made a fortune trading in commodity futures, but these individuals are rare exceptions. I would even venture to say that the proportion of successful commodities futures traders is roughly the same as those who have made a fortune playing a professional sport, compared to all of those who have seriously played that sport in high school, college, and the minor leagues. Understand this: the use of futures contracts as a speculative vehicle requires more than a casual understanding of contract and pricing mechanics. If, for the average investor, option contracts have a reputation for a high proportion of capital losses relative to gains, futures contracts have a *deserved* reputation for the same—only worse. The reason for this is twofold. One, futures are highly levered investments. That means that a small investment can either create disproportionate profits or catastrophic losses; even small price moves that, from a broader perspective, would be regarded as simply market price "noise" can destroy the value of an account. Two, unlike an option contract which has "value" only if price levels of the underlying asset allows its exercise logically, a futures contract pricing represents an actual physical position in the underlying commodity: thus, for example, when you buy a futures contract, you have agreed to pay for and to take delivery of a large amount of the commodity at the time stipulated in the futures contract. The value of the position in your account rises and falls with changes in the underlying commodity and could result in a loss *greater than the initial amount in the account*, leading to the dreaded "margin call." Without the addition of more cash to the account, the contract position will be *automatically liquidated* by the broker, and you, the client, will be responsible for any losses—especially if those losses exceed the capital balance in the account. Therefore, unlike options, futures must be used as an investment vehicle only by those who thoroughly understand the markets in which they are investing.

I have been an investor of both options and futures contracts for a very long time; for options, since 1979, and for commodities, since 1994. I was in my second year of B-school at UCLA when introduced to options and could not wait to trade them. I was smitten by these seemingly exotic instruments. Having already been a 14-year veteran of equities,[1] I could see at once the value of options. Alas, I was too young to really appreciate their strategic importance or their astonishing flexibility, and, aside from a smattering of thick academic articles, explanatory books on the subject had not yet been published. I soldiered through the Black-Scholes model and over time developed sufficient expertise to become a profitable *user* of options.

My personal trade history with options goes back to the prehistoric age when both equity orders and option orders were placed by phone (landline, no cell phones then) to a

---

1   I opened my first stock account at the age of 14 at a normal brokerage house, not some two-bit online firm. Happily, online research was unavailable for about 25 years afterward; I did my research the old-fashioned way.

broker, who then cabled the order to a floor broker who executed the trade. Maybe a quarter hour later, the client received a return call from the broker to advise the client that the trade was made. A confirmation would be received by mail (that is, the US Postal Service) a few days later. Options were traded almost exclusively at the Chicago Board Options Exchange (CBOE; pronounced *SEE'boh*, rhymes with *oboe*) and were priced in fractions such as quarters, eighths, and sixteenths.

Changes to the options marketplace have made them much easier to buy and sell, and the number of resources available to the average investor is now vast. This has not necessarily brought greater profitability to the average investor. Trade execution speed does not translate to profitability. In fact, fast transaction speeds lead most investors to act impetuously when they should be taking their time, analyzing the trade, before the buy/sell button is pressed. As for the plethora of advice, some of it is simply wrong, some bad, and some misleading. Sometimes a little information is worse than none—for example, when investors think they know what they are doing when in fact they do not.

Thus, simply stated, this book is intended to fill the gap between the highly technical academic text and the overly simplistic, popular "how-to" text. It can safely be used in an upper-division undergraduate options and futures class. The plan for this book is to approach important academic concepts (i.e., option and futures price theory) with a jaundiced eye by covering what needs to be considered as a means of reinforcing an understanding of why options exist, understanding what function and role they have in the financial marketplace, and providing examples of how flexible they can be by offering actual historic examples. Any detailed discussion of difficult subjects, such as the mathematics of the Black-Scholes model, is relegated to an appendix. This approach provides the student with the proper amount of detail without getting bogged down in minutiae.

This book is structured so that an understanding of the characteristics of options are mastered first, before specific strategies are discussed. Therefore, the text is designed to be read sequentially. The first chapters introduce and explain the origin of options and their legal and physical attributes. The next set of chapters discusses the factors that determine their pricing and functions used to assess potential option price behavior. This section will contain theory and mathematics, but do not allow your brain to freeze. I will be as erudite as I can and will explain in plain, understandable English what the theory means and its relevance to the option user.

The middle section describes the various performance statistics currently in use by option traders, collectively known and referred to as the Greeks. These must be clearly understood because understanding them enhances the probability of successful option employment. In my opinion, no investor should consider investing with options unless they have mastered the Greeks. That is how important they are.

The last section is a compositum of option strategies. This is a rigorous section, populated with examples and real-life case studies taken from my actual experience, using real data. Together with these examples are advisories on what to do if a trade moves away from its expected path.

Now, let us take the first step.

Chapter 1

Introduction: Options

From Whence Options?

Where did these marvels of finance come from? Who invented them? The truth is, no single person, nation, or culture can lay claim to being the "inventor" of options. Like all other financial instruments, like coinage, paper money, bank accounts, insurance, and stocks, options have evolved over time as needs and technology have changed over the years. However, although it is likely that option contracts (or option-like contracts) have a long history possibly dating back to the Shang Dynasty of China or the civilizations of Mesopotamia, the basic structure of the modern option contract was created by some pretty smart people in the Netherlands during the mid-17th century. At the time, Amsterdam was what London and then New York City would be in future years, the capital of global finance, and for similar reasons; because it was a comparatively open, commercial city. Amsterdam was the site of the first stock exchange and had become the center in Europe for merchant banking and insurance.

Options first arose because there was a dire need to find a way of risk transference. Option contracts were originally (and remain) a species of insurance contract (hence the term *premium*, referring to the cost of an option contract). It has been stated that options arose as insurance against wild speculation manifest in the infamous "tulip mania" of 17th-century Holland, but the reality is more mundane. By the early 17th century, so-called joint stock companies were becoming more widespread among mercantile societies, but particularly in the Netherlands and England. Joint stock companies were the great-great-great-great-grandparents of the modern corporation and were involved in exploration, agriculture, trade, manufacture, and insurance. (Banking maintained a partnership business form for another century or so.) Although primarily the playground of the landed aristocracy, as industrialism advanced and feudalism declined, the bourgeoisie became much more involved and company ownership more widespread. These individuals were actually more risk-averse than nobility

1

and were inclined to seek out ways to manage the risk of their holdings in these joint-stock companies, which tended to be relatively illiquid and risky.

To hedge risk against business reversal, these investors began to protect profits with put options. All of these options were private contractual agreements between the option (policy) writer and the option (policy) buyer. It would be as though there were no insurance companies today and any insurance you needed—car, health, fire—was negotiated between you and another person or group of people. Each option contract was therefore tailored specifically to the needs of the particular client, a fact which rendered their tradability moot. To help you understand more, we now define puts and calls.

Put Option: This is a contract which **allows the owner of the contract to sell assets** at an agreed price on or before a particular date, solely at her or his discretion. The fact that the contract owner is not required to buy, but merely has the **option** to buy, should ring a bell in your mind: it is the reason these contracts are called **options**. However, the option to perform is only given to the *contract owner*. These **contingent put option rights** (i.e., the ability to sell an asset on or before a prearranged time in the future) are what give these put contracts monetary value, and it is why an investor would be willing to pay a premium for it. For example, imagine you have just purchased a share in the Dutch East India Company for 10,000 Dutch guilders. You recognize the potential in the enterprise, but its purchase represented, say, 50% of your personal wealth. You want to protect it against loss of value, so you purchased a put option which gave you the right to sell the asset at a price of 10,000 Dutch guilders anytime between the date of purchase and, say, 10 years after the date of purchase. Now you can sleep at night because you know that if the company becomes insolvent, you can still sell your investment for the price you paid for it. By buying the put, you have in effect insured your investment against loss of value. You have transferred value risk from yourself to the contract counterparty—the individual who wrote that policy contract and sold it to you for a premium. That counterparty, who wrote the contract and then sold it to you, *is obligated to perform* under the contract terms at the sole discretion of the put option owner. This means that if your investment becomes worth only 5,000 Dutch guilders, **if you exercise your put option contract, the writer of that contract must buy your share** of the Dutch East India Company for 10,000 Dutch guilders, even though the current market price is only 5,000 Dutch guilders. Clearly, the option writer never expected the price to decline, but even if he or she did, that individual collected a premium, which in the least offset any value loss incurred by the option exercise. (*Much* more on this later.)

Call Option: Contrary to a put option, a call option is a contract which allows the **owner of the contract to buy** assets at an agreed price on or before a particular date, solely at her or his discretion. Again, the right to perform under the terms of the call option contract rests solely with the option owner, just as the case in put options. If the owner of the call wishes to exercise his or her rights, then the seller of the call is obligated to perform under the terms of the contract. Again, these contingent call option rights (i.e., the ability to buy an asset on or before a prearranged time in the future) are what give these call option contracts monetary value, and it is why an investor would be willing to pay a premium for it. Let us consider a new example. You are interested in investing in the Dutch East India Company, but maybe you are truly risk-averse or maybe you have committed capital to other ventures so you just don't have the funds to purchase at this time. However, suppose you would be willing to buy the share of the Dutch East India Company for 10,000 Dutch guilders anytime between the date of purchase and, say, 10 years after the date of purchase, if the investment looks more favorable. Accordingly, you agree to buy a call option, which stipulates that you can **buy** that share of the Dutch East India Company under terms of the call option contract. This is an interesting arrangement, because it seems to only benefit the option holder (the option buyer) because the call option holder would only exercise the call if the price of the share of the Dutch East India Company has gone up (assuming the option holder is a rational actor). Meanwhile, the individual who wrote the call option contract and then sold it to you *is obligated to perform* under the contract terms at the sole discretion of the call option owner. This means that if that investment becomes worth 20,000 Dutch guilders, a ***call option exercise means the writer of that contract must sell her or his share*** of the Dutch East India Company for 10,000 Dutch guilders, even though the current market price is 20,000 Dutch guilders. Furthermore, suppose that the share price of the Dutch East India Company declines by 50%, to 5,000 Dutch guilders. The owner of the call does not need to buy the shares. He or she is not obligated to perform. He or she could do nothing, allow the option to expire, and the only loss they incur is the cost of the option. Not bad for the option holder!

Why would anyone want to sell such a call option? This is a topic that will occupy our attention in future chapters. In the meantime, suffice it to say that ***it all depends on how much premium was earned by him or her when the option was sold***! Suppose the option writer sold it for 5,000 Dutch guilders: The option seller has thus netted a very solid 50% return on capital and has reduced their exposure on the asset they own by the amount of premium received. They would have been very happy indeed.

However, in this instance, there was a fly in the ointment: What if one of the parties to the option contract *refused to abide by the terms of the contract*? This condition is called a ***default***. In theory, that party is liable, and the injured party can find recompense through tort action. With standardized option contracts, in today's structured market environment, such a default is extremely unlikely, as we shall see in Chapter 5. But in 17th-century Holland—without an organized, structured, and disciplined marketplace—defaults could, and did, occur. In 1638, the Dutch economy slipped into recession. Put option defaults were widespread as the prices of listed equities in Dutch markets declined sharply. Facing mounting capital losses, many put option writers were either unable or unwilling to fulfill their obligations and could not or would not buy underlying securities at their agreed-upon strike prices. This in turn further weakened equity prices, which led to more put defaults.

Analysis suggests that this dynamic is neither unusual nor unlikely given the laxity of regulation (even self-regulation) and market illiquidity in Amsterdam at that time. One could easily suppose that a lack of moral hazard was manifest by the false sense of price security brought about by widespread put writing. If buyers generally believed that their price risk was fully mitigated by put writers, then that fact by itself would stimulate further buying and thereby contribute to an "overbought" market, with prices rising above perceived fair value. Overbought markets are inherently unstable and always—eventually—lead to massive sell-offs. In 17th-century Holland, this led to an avalanche of put defaults.

Post-crisis thinking in Holland and elsewhere banished puts (and calls) for use *only* by well-capitalized and sophisticated investors. Thereafter, options established its reputation as a dangerous investment vehicle, only to be used by sophisticates and with the utmost discretion. During the next two centuries, options remained esoteric and rarely employed.

But as the United States experienced rapid growth and the need arose for massive amounts of capital to fuel that growth, options were once again being used as hedge devices. Railroad issues, in particular, experienced a surge of protective put buying. Indeed, by the late 1800s, broker-dealers began to place advertisements in financial journals on the part of potential option buyers and sellers. Within a few years, option prices would be regularly quoted, although volume and interest remained very thin. The formation of the Put and Call Brokers and Dealers Association, Inc.[1] was the earliest American effort to systematize options trading, albeit entirely by means of an informal over-the-counter[2] network. However, options remained non-standardized and lacked a centralized clearing agency for trades made. The stock market crash of 1929 was a watershed moment when Congress determined that self-regulation failed and that government needed to intervene in the financial marketplace. The Securities and Exchange Commission (SEC) became the regulating authority under the Securities and Exchange Act of 1934. By 1935, shortly after the SEC began regulating the over-the-counter options market, it granted the Chicago Board

---

1   The principal self-regulatory organization for the conventional (unlisted) stock option market in the United States through the early years of exchange-traded options. It still exists, but has no real purpose or function.

2   Over-the-counter (OTC) is a term describing a decentralized market in which market participants trade stocks, commodities, or other financial instruments directly between two parties, without a central exchange or clearinghouse. These markets do not have physical locations and are contrasted with an auction market system. Before electronic networks were possible (i.e., before the early 1970s), OTC markets dealt with thinly traded unusual, small, or exotic instruments. With the advent of NASDAQ, these markets have gained a stronger following.

of Trade (CBOT) a perpetual license to register as a national securities exchange if it so chose. Acting on that perpetual license grant, almost 40 years later, the CBOT established the Chicago Board Options Exchange. In contrast to the informal over-the-counter options market, which had no set terms for its contracts, this new exchange set up rules to standardize contract size, strike prices, and expiration dates. They also established centralized clearing, initiated strict financial standards for market makers and dealers, and strong ethics and pricing standards.

The impetus for the establishment of the CBOE was the 1973 publication of the classic article "The Pricing of Options and Corporate Liabilities" in the *Journal of Political Economy* of the University of Chicago, by Fischer Black and Myron Scholes.[3] This article described what has become known as the Black-Scholes model, the first and most important pricing model specifically designed for derivative instruments in stochastic (so-called "random walk") pricing environments. Suddenly, the pricing for esoteric financial instruments—in particular, options—became relatively simple for dealers to institute. Instead of operating in a black box, dealers could establish prices with substantially more confidence than before. (We will revisit Black-Scholes again in Chapter 7.)

Modern option trading began on April 26, 1973. In the beginning, the scale and sophistication of option trading was nowhere near what is today. There were only a few monthly option expiries, and only calls were traded on 16 of the 1200 underlying stocks then listed on the New York Stock Exchange. Total volume that day was just over 900 contracts. The entire listing of *all* option issues fit on a single page of the *Wall Street Journal*. Also, that year, the Options Clearing Corporation (OCC) was established as a wholly owned subsidiary of the CBOE. It was created to ensure that the obligations associated with options contracts would be fulfilled in a timely and reliable manner. For those who wished to be brokers and/or dealers in options, contract default was not an option (no pun intended). The establishment of a well-funded, organized clearinghouse was a game-changer for many. Now it was possible to write, sell, and buy options without the fear of third-party default.

After about a year, daily volume had grown to over 20,000 contracts, with further exponential gains in the years to follow. In early 1975, the Philadelphia Stock Exchange and American Stock Exchange opened their own option trading floors, increasing competition and bringing options to a wider marketplace. Listings of options increased to 43 issues by 1977, and for the first time, put options were also traded.

This explosive growth compelled the SEC to conduct a complete review of the structure and regulatory practices of the new option exchanges. A moratorium was instituted on

---

3   For their work on option pricing, Myron Scholes was presented with the Nobel Prize in Economics in 1997. Fischer Black was awarded the prize the same year but posthumously; he had passed away two years prior.

listing options for additional stocks while a debate focused on the viability and desirability of a centralized options market. Within three years, during the first years of the Reagan administration, the SEC published new regulations to increase option market oversight by establishing audits, compliance standards, and systems at brokerage houses, as well as new option-user protection protocols. The CBOE, with the moratorium lifted, added options on 25 more stocks.

The next few decades witnessed an explosive growth in the options market, and the CBOE has been the primary driver of changes to the options market. Today it represents the largest and most sophisticated options market in the world. Selected CBOE innovations to the options market are shown on Table 1.1 below.

TABLE 1.1

YEAR	EVENT
1978	First automated order-routing with new limit-order protocols.
1983	Introduction of options based on the S&P 500 (SPX) and S&P 100 (OEX) indexes.
1983	The first fully automatic trade execution system (the RAES).
1987	Introduced automatic routing of complex option combinations.
1989	Introduced the first interest-rate futures options.
1990	Introduced LEAPS®, which feature expirations of up to three years.
1992	Introduced options on sector and international indexes.
1994	Created the Volatility Index® (VIX®)—a measure of market volatility.
1998	Introduced the first options on the Dow Jones Industrial Average℠.
1999	Rapid Opening System; reduced time to open all series in a class.
2001	Introduced CBOEDirect state-of-the-art electronic trading platform.
2004	CBOE Futures Exchange℠ opens.
2005	Volatility Index (VIX) futures begin trading.
2005	Weekly option expiries introduced.
2006	VIX options introduced.
2010	CBOE goes public with IPO.
2015	CBOE launches global trading hours for SPX and VIX options.
2017	Acquires BATS and expands into European equities, ETFs, forex products.

The emergence of computerized trading systems and the internet has created a far more viable and liquid options market than ever before. Because of this, we've seen several new players enter the marketplace. As of this writing, the listed options exchanges in the United States include the Boston Stock Exchange, Chicago Board Options Exchange, International Securities Exchange, NASDAQ OMX PHLX, NASDAQ Stock Market, NYSE Amex, and NYSE Arca. There are also option exchanges on every continent. Daily option trade volume in the United States currently averages **over 1 billion contracts in volume each day**.

Introducing Some Important Basic Terms

Before we dive further into the text, let us learn some basic option facts and terminology. The following terms are noted here because we will use them immediately going forward; get used to them now. This group is nowhere near exhaustive. More terms will arise as needed.

Definitions

Option Contracts: Options are indeed contracts drawn between two parties which—at a cost—allow the transfer of an asset between the parties at a prearranged price, solely at the discretion of the option holder (owner). The specific terms of these contracts will be discussed in Chapter 5.

Option Premium: As a note of acknowledgment to their initial purpose, option price is referred to and synonymous with *option premium*. In theory, one wouldn't ask, "What is the *price* for option XYZ?"; one would ask, "What is the *premium* for option XYZ?" In reality, many market participants refer to price and premium interchangeably. The amount of premium paid to acquire an option is *the* central theme in options trading.

Option Quotes: Options are priced in *dollars per share of premium*. Since most options represent a contract for one-hundred-share lots, a premium quoted at 2.10 means the purchaser will pay $2.10 times 100, or $210.00 for the contract. A quote might look like this:

	LAST	BID	ASK	NET CHANGE	VOLUME	OPEN INT
18 Jan 2017 XYZ 65 Call	2.14	2.01	2.10	– .04	2100	565

Notice that if you buy a contract *at market*, the quote is based on the **ASK**. If you are selling the contract at market, you will be selling at the **BID**. This factoid is often lost on a rookie. You may rightfully ask, "Doesn't the BUYER usually bid a price?" And the answer is, yes. What one doesn't realize is that the quotes are made by the ***dealers*** (market-makers) of options, so they are the ones actually doing the buying and selling of option contracts. We, the customer, buy and sell to a market-maker. Consider it this way: from the standpoint of the dealer, you are buying from her, so you are paying the premium she is asking. If you are selling to her, she will bid a price that, at market, you accept. ***You sell—she buys at her bid. You buy—she sells at her ask.***

Strike Price (or simply Strike): This is the preconditioned and accepted price at which the asset exchanges ownership; not one penny higher or lower.

Expiry (also called Expiration Date or simply Expiration): This is the date after which the option is no longer tradable. Terms of the contract usually expire the next day. After expiry, the option becomes worthless and privileges attendant to the option are null and void.

Volume: This is the number of contracts that passed from dealer to customer during the trading session from all exchanges ("consolidated" volume).

Open Interest: This number equals the total number of contracts for that issue (strike and expiry) in existence in the entire universe. (Well, in this world at least. It is not impossible that other worlds in other galaxies also trade options.)

Moneyness: This term refers to the degree by which an option is "in-the-money," "at-the-money," or "out of the money."

In-the-Money (ITM): This means that the option can be exercised rationally: the current market price of the underlying is higher than the option strike for a call, or lower than the option price for a put.

At-the-Money (ATM—not to be confused by the initialism of a famous cash machine): This means the underlying is trading at, or very close to, the option strike.

Out-of-the-Money (OTM): This means that the current market price of the underlying is higher than the option strike for a put, or lower than the option strike for a call. These options would eventually expire worthless and unexercised if the underlying price relationship to the option strike remains the same.

Underlying: This is the official jargon that refers to the asset that would be transferred if an option is exercised. One could surmise that it was in fact initially referred to as the "underlying asset" but has been shortened to simply "underlying" by market players, who always seem to be in a hurry.

Option Class: The puts *or* calls of all strikes and expiries for a particular underlying asset. Puts are one class and calls are the other class for a given asset. Example: The call class for IBM is the set of all calls (all strikes) of all expiries for only IBM and the put class for IBM is the set of all puts (all strikes) of all expiries for only IBM.

Option Series: An option series is a subdivision of a class, constituted of *all* the calls *or* puts (but not both calls and puts) for an underlying asset that expire in the same month and which have the same strike. Example: IBM has *a call class* of options *composed of 14 expiries and with approximately 100 different strikes.* Therefore, IBM has approximately 1400 different option series in its call class. All options in the same series will have the same price.

LEAPS: (Acronym for *L*ong-term *E*quity *A*ntici*P*ation *S*ecurities) These are options issued with expiries at least one year in the future when first issued. They are generally issued for more liquid option classes of companies and indexes. If LEAPS are issued, they will always have a January expiry, but there are on occasion March, June, or September expiries as well, as in for example the option classes for the S&P 500 ETF (SPY).

Summary and Conclusion

Options are comparatively modern financial instruments whose socioeconomic value has been demonstrated for almost 400 years. Their evolution from the illiquid and esoteric financial instruments of the relatively near past to the extremely liquid and flexible instruments of today has been remarkably rapid. This demonstrates in full their popularity among all market actors—from sophisticated hedge funds, mutual funds and investment institutions, banks, and others who seek ways to transfer exposure of risk to a counterparty; to the retail investor seeking income or capital gain. Options have been a particular beneficiary of technological change, which has enabled investors of modest size easy access to these instruments.

Options should be treated with respect, however. They are legally binding contracts that are designed to enable the transfer of an asset—and its risk—from someone who has a specific asset to another who wants it. Accordingly, there are two types of options, puts, and calls. In its most popular form, call options are designed to allow the call holder to buy 100 shares at a predetermined price called the strike at any time before the option's expiration. A put allows the put holder to sell 100 shares at a predetermined price called the strike at any time before the option's expiration.

Now worldwide trading of options are used (and misused) by multimillions. Some believe that fortunes can be rapidly built with options, but those individuals without patience will be frustrated in their efforts to do so. The reality is that all options are wasting assets; they gradually lose their value until by expiration, they are valueless, unless the option is ITM. It is that risk that has given options a very bad reputation, but if properly understood, options can serve investors very well as a strategic component in a risky portfolio.

Going Forward

In the next chapter, you will be introduced to a more mundane form of derivative: the futures contract and its cousin, the forward contract. There are similarities between options, futures, and forwards, as well as important differences, as you will see. The most important difference is that options are contingent assets which may expire worthless, but futures represent an outright ownership interest with possession occurring at a designated time in the, well, *future*. You will find that futures contracts have challenges that are unique to their purpose and structure. Therefore, the arithmetic of futures contracts will be of foremost concern.

After the next few chapters, we once again return to the world of options for a detailed and clinical look at their pricing mechanics and uses.

Chapter 2

The Futures Market

Introduction

Take a moment and think about how your food ended up at the supermarket. Think all the way back: the pallets of goods go back on the truck, the truck goes back to the distributor, the distributor sends its stuff back to the processor, the processor sends it back to the producer. Now stop. Where is price in all of this?

The bedrock upon which this massive and complex system rests is the price of the product that the farmer receives for its goods. After all, the producer takes on all the risk; it has to get some reward for doing so. Where does this price come from? Good question. My personal library contains many volumes on the subject. The usual pablum is that it is supply and demand; it is the capitalization of costs of production; it is the dissemination of knowledge, knowhow, and information; and for the more politic of the authors—it is governmental interference and regulation or its mirror opposite, insufficient regulation. So many words have been dedicated to this fearsome subject that an honest reader should have little choice but to conclude that no one knows. The movement of price is mysterious, and probably contains a little truth from all theories and hypotheses. But it is the reason we have futures markets and futures contracts.

Background

Commodity markets are probably as old as civilization itself. It seems to have emerged globally as soon as the differentiation between "city" and "farm" life became distinct and separate.[1] To be sure, these ancient contracts were not the highly liquid futures contracts known today, but they carried many of the characteristics that today we would characterize

---

1   What is meant by *market* is a single location where parties come to exchange goods or items representing value (i.e., coinage).

as a "futures contract."[2] Great strides were made by the Romans, who traded wheat and barley over long distances across the Roman Empire. Over time, Roman contracts had become the closest to a modern commodities contract in terms of content and purpose.[3]

Evidence exists that robust rice futures exchanges were established in China before the common era and more recently in 17th-century Japan. In the West, it wouldn't be until the early Industrial Revolution—more than a thousand years later—that standardized, tradable commodity contracts would resume that level of importance.

The first stock exchange in the world, in Amsterdam, originated as one of only a handful of commodity exchanges in Europe; it was chartered in 1530. The Dutch were remarkable innovators of financial derivatives and even early trading of commodities in Amsterdam frequently used newly invented instruments such as short sales, forward contracts, and options. The reasons that such robust financial innovations were invented in Holland are unclear. But at that time, Holland was the single most important center for commercial activity. Known for their obsession with work and tolerant and open to new ways of thinking, the Dutch had the temperament and the resources at their disposal to lead. With their mastery of maritime commerce, the presumption is that the reestablishment of global trade linkages, plus a massive increase in scale of demand and production, necessitated the invention of new and efficient means of finding price. The Dutch apparently invented what they needed to invent. These necessities, combined with the technological ability to bring millions of metric tons of product to market safely and quickly, were the catalysts that spurred the enormous growth of physical commodity markets after the start of the Industrial Revolution.

The development of North and South American agricultural lands—and in particular the production of grains—during the early 1800s wrought the development of commercial storage sites to serve farming regions within an ever-enlarging radius. Notably, in the United States, a confluence of geographic advantages drew Midwest and prairie grains to Chicago for storage before distribution to the East Coast. Because of the perishability of agricultural products, the quality of the stored items would often deteriorate while in storage. The price chaos that ensued required the creation of the first domestic *forward contracts*, which allowed a buyer to *pay for a specific commodity of a specific quality prior to taking delivery* rather than

---

2   Clay tablets reflect some commoditization of grain delivery from agricultural sources outside Sumer and other Mesopotamian urban centers. Cf. Edens, C. (1992). Dynamics of trade in the Ancient Mesopotamian "world system." *American Anthropologist*, 94(1), 118–139.

3   Kessler, D., & Temin, P. (2007). The organization of the grain trade in the Early Roman Empire. *The Economic History Review*, 60(2), 313–332. http://www.jstor.org/stable/4502066.

immediate payment while waiting for delivery. These *forwards* were the direct precursor to futures contracts.

- <u>Forward Contracts</u>: A forward contract is *a customized (non-standardized) contract between two parties to buy or sell an asset at a specified price on a future date.*

- <u>Futures Contracts</u>: A futures contract involves *standardized quality, amounts, and delivery dates of commodities* **previously traded under forward contracts**.

As the delivery of grains and livestock to Chicago grew, the first American commodities exchange, the Chicago Board of Trade (CBOT), was established in 1848. Its establishment was a significant step toward the establishment of a more efficient, standardized method of purchasing goods, with payment by means of *futures contracts*. Instead of managing customized contracts between interested parties, markets streamlined the process of buying and selling goods for future delivery at a present-day price by using standardized contracts, identical in description of asset quality, delivery time, and payment terms. Soon afterward, commodity exchanges were established in Kansas City, Minneapolis, Winnipeg, Milwaukee, New York, St. Louis, San Francisco, Memphis, and New Orleans. The two main Chicago-based exchanges, the Chicago Mercantile Exchange (CME) and the Chicago Board of Trade (CBOT), however, remained the innovators and the largest commodity exchanges, even as many of the regional exchanges closed.

Throughout its early existence, the CBOT was entirely unregulated. It was as late as October 1865—almost 20 years after the founding of the exchange—that the CBOT wrote and published its own exchange rules and bylaws. These dealt primarily with margin and delivery procedures, another step in the evolution of standardizing them for greater contract-clearing efficiency. Throughout the course of the late 19th and early 20th centuries, rule-making was mostly *ad hoc* as either a means of curbing trading abuses or as a reaction to the threat of federal intervention. For example, acting on the recommendations of a report from the Federal Trade Commission during the 1920s, CBOT defined futures contract specifications of grains and livestock, and as a response to unusually high speculative volume, established exchange-based position limit rules.

Nonetheless, despite the laissez-faire attitude of the Coolidge and Hoover administrations, federal oversight began to be implemented. The Grain Futures Act (enacted 1922) established the first federal oversight of the commodities markets by means of a new Grain Futures Administration, established as an agency of the US Department of Agriculture (USDA), as well as the Grain Futures Commission, which consisted of the secretary of agriculture, the secretary of commerce, and the attorney general. The authority to suspend or revoke a contract market designation was then vested in that commission. Soon, the extraordinary collapse of grain prices during the Great Depression led to the first direct federal intervention in grain market pricing. In 1932 and again in 1933, the secretary of agriculture temporarily suspended futures trading in grains in a vain attempt to prop up sagging prices.

The exchange gradually added more commodities to its trading floor after congressional approval of the Commodity Exchange Act,[4] including soybeans in 1936, cotton in the 1940s, and livestock and meats in the 1950s. After the collapse of the Bretton Woods system in the 1970s, a whole new variety of futures in currencies as well as gold were instituted. This important transition, while gradual, reflected the fundamental change in the nature of the American economy from agrarian to manufacture and financial services. Instead of *delivery* as a means of contract settlement, *cash settlement* became an alternative to physical delivery of goods. Now price levels were as vital as physical goods, and throughout the 1980s and 1990s, futures contracts in non-consumable products, including stock market indexes like the S&P 500 and government debt instruments, were added to the list of tradable futures.

Then, in the first major commodities legislation since the Depression, the Commodity Exchange Act of 1968 enhanced reporting requirements, increased criminal penalties for manipulation and other violations of the act, and enacted a provision allowing for the suspension of contract market designation of any board of trade that failed to enforce its own rules.

- Cash Settlement: A settlement method used in nonagricultural futures and options contracts where, upon expiration or exercise, *the seller of the financial instrument transfers the cash equivalent value of the position rather than the actual (physical) underlying* asset.

- Commodity Futures Trading Commission (CFTC): An independent *industry-based, self-regulatory organization* designed to maintain order and discipline among commodity industry participants.

---

4 The act (approved in 1936) provides federal regulation of all commodities and futures trading activities and requires all futures and commodity options to be traded on organized exchanges. In 1974, the Commodity Futures Trading Commission (CFTC) was created as a result of the Commodity Exchange Act, and in 1982, the National Futures Association (NFA) was created by CFTC.

Despite efforts to curtail direct market intervention, further federal oversight was enacted with the passage of the 1974 Commodity Futures Trading Commission Act. The bill created the Commodity Futures Trading Commission (CFTC), an independent agency which was granted complete oversight of all traded commodities. With the establishment of the CFTC, no additional federal oversight was necessary or established. Indeed, all of the contracts and instruments now traded on any United States commodity exchange is under CFTC supervision, and the introduction of new contracts is overseen by them as well. This includes introduction and oversight of options on commodities, introduced in 1981. The CFTC was empowered to perform many regulatory tasks; also in 1981, the CFTC established the National Futures Association (NFA), a self-regulatory organization (SRO), to supervise all commodity trading professionals, all of whom needed to become members of the NFA if they chose to remain in the futures business.

Meanwhile, wireless and/or digital technology was being applied to both equity and futures markets. By early 1989, futures markets entered the Information Age when the CFTC unanimously approved rules proposed by the Chicago Mercantile Exchange for their new all-electronic Globex system, the first international electronic trading system. Trading began in June 1992.

- <u>National Futures Association (NFA)</u>: A self-regulatory organization (SRO) established to *standardize qualifications, licensing, and regulate behavior of commodity trading participants.*

- <u>Globex</u>: The *CME Group–owned and operated electronic trading platform* that directly linked buyers and sellers without the use of open outcry auctions.

Globex proved to be a resounding success, particularly for its electronically traded stock S&P Index e-mini contracts. Encouraged by their S&P Index products, similar futures were established for the Dow Industrial Index, the Russell Index, and the NASDAQ 100.

By the early 21st century, a new turf war was building between the CFTC and the SEC: which organization would be better suited to regulate these new equity-based futures products? By 2001, the Securities and Exchange Commission and the CFTC jointly adopted their first set of rules enabling trade of single-stock futures and futures on narrow-based stock indexes. Additional rules are adopted in subsequent months, and the forthright cooperation between the SEC and CFTC continues to this day. Within a year of publication of these rules, two new small electronic trading platforms were launched specifically to trade single-stock and index futures: the NQLX[5] and OneChicago.[6] Neither exchange would last very long.

Meanwhile, the Commodity Futures Modernization Act of 2000 (CFMA)—the law which legalized single-stock futures (yet prevented the oversight and regulation of exotic swaps and other financial derivatives)—was signed law by President Bill Clinton in December 2000. The intent of the law was to streamline and modernize commodity futures trading in much the same manner as the Financial Services Modernization Act of 1999 modernized banking. As with most far-reaching legislation, the infamous "law of unintended consequences" soon began to play out. The first noticeable trend was an immediate consolidation of the commodities business, accompanied by a frenzy of mergers and acquisitions in the commodity exchanges. By mid-2007, the Chicago Mercantile Exchange and the Chicago Board of Trade announced the completion of their merger, forming the world's largest futures exchange, the CME Group. Subsequent mergers also affected NASDAQ, the Intercontinental Exchange, and other lesser exchanges in the United States, Europe, and Asia. Commission and exchange fees were diminished to paltry sums, and the popularity of electronic markets doomed open outcry markets. As of this writing, only the Eurodollar pit remains as the sole remnant of an obsolete exchange system.

Digital and electronic technologies have escalated the rate of change in commodity markets since the early 1990s. One change has been the "democratization" of commodities and futures trading. The enormous increase in volume experienced by most commodities since the early 1990s is a direct consequence of a newfound convenience and ease of online accounts for use by others besides experienced industry professionals. Electronic markets revolutionized futures trading by permitting anyone with a computer to trade—anywhere, anytime. The obvious advantages— in cost and efficiency—have massively increased the breadth of markets globally. Trading now occurs almost 24 hours per day, beginning in Asia (their Monday morning; Sunday afternoon in New York) until 4:15 p.m. Friday afternoon New York time. Anyone in any part of the world can trade any commodity provided the trader has a computer and access to the internet.

Market Structure

Market structure is another story. The commodities market structure is an evolved neces- sity that started simply and continues to change as technology, scale, culture, and needs

---

5   NQLX was a joint venture between NASDAQ and the London Financial Futures Exchange (LIFFE). It closed in 2004.
6   OneChicago was an electronic futures market that dealt exclusively in single-stock futures. Jointly over- seen by the CFTC and the SEC, it ceased operations in September of 2020.

change. For those seeking stability and consistency, commodity markets are not for you. As of this writing, all markets—once a crazy, frenzied scene of yelling and physical gestures—are non-places, merely screens of digitalized data. Nonetheless, the administrative superstructure has remained more or less intact because it still seems to function very well. That is not to say these institutions haven't also evolved; it is merely to say that their function in the marketplace hasn't changed that much. This "administrative superstructure" is constructed with few parts: the broker/dealer, the exchanges, regulators, and clearing organizations. That is all.

> - Commodity Exchanges: Commodity exchanges in the United States today are *platforms upon which traders can buy or sell various commodity contracts.*

Exchanges

Most commodity markets around the world trade in agricultural products and raw industrial materials, but some of the largest exchanges today also deal in financial instruments such as interest rate and foreign exchange futures, as well as other instruments such as ocean freight contracts and environmental futures such as weather and carbon. Trading includes various types of derivatives contracts based on these commodities, such as forwards, futures, and options, as well as spot trades for immediate delivery. Some of these exchanges also trade financial derivatives. It will be surprising to note that as of this writing, there are just over 100 commodity exchanges in the world (14 in Africa, 19 in the Americas, 46 in Asia, 20 in Europe, and 3 in Australia). The significant exchanges in the United States that are all electronic are:

- **CME Group:** by far the largest, and includes all digital trading—no open outcry—for a very broad range of commodities, including grains, energy, treasuries, equity indexes, precious and industrial metals, meats, currencies, Eurodollars, bitcoin. The group was formed by the acquisition or merger of the Chicago Mercantile Exchange, the Chicago Board of Trade, and the New York Mercantile Exchange.
- **Globex:** the electronic platform for the CME.
- **Intercontinental Exchange (ICE):** energy, emissions, grains and meats, biofuels.
- **Kansas City Board of Trade:** grains and meats.
- **Minneapolis Grain Exchange:** grains and soybean oil.

As discussed above, all US-based commodity exchanges are self-regulatory, with broader oversight from the NFA and the CFTC.

Dealers/Brokers

Historically, commodity brokers traded grain and livestock futures contracts. Today, commodity brokers trade a wide variety of financial derivatives based on not only grain and livestock, but also derivatives based on foods, "softs," metals, energy, stock indexes, equities, bonds, currencies, and an ever-growing list of other underlying assets. Ever since the 1980s, the majority of commodity contracts traded are financial derivatives with financial underlying assets such as stock indexes and currencies. One would expect a sharp uptick in the number of commodity houses, given the rich tapestry of futures-based products now widely available. Further stimulus for new firms should have come from the congressionally favored implementation of the Volcker rule in 2014.[7] Yet the number of commodity trading houses and individual brokers has dwindled. Despite this decline—or maybe because of it— by October 2019, five federal financial regulatory agencies, including the CFTC, announced finalized revisions to simplify all firms' compliance requirements relating to the Volcker rule.

The dealer/broker space is composed of several main actors, including:

- **Floor Broker/Trader:** an individual who trades commodity contracts on the floor of a commodities exchange. When executing trades on behalf of a client in exchange for a commission, he is acting in the role of a broker. When trading on behalf of his own account, or for the account of his employer, he is acting in the role of a trader. Floor trading is conducted in the pits of a commodity exchange via open outcry. A floor broker is different from a "floor trader": he or she also works on the floor of the exchange, makes trades as a principal for his or her own account. This role is evolving rapidly, with the near-extinction of the open outcry trading pit.

- **Futures Commission Merchant (FCM):** an entity that solicits or accepts orders for commodity contracts traded on an exchange and holds client funds to margin. Most individual traders do not work directly with an FCM, but rather through an IB or CTA.

- **Introducing Broker (IB):** an entity that solicits or accepts orders for commodity contracts traded on an exchange. IBs do not hold customer funds to margin: client funds to margin are held by an FCM associated with the IB.

---

7   By statute, the Volcker rule generally prohibits banking entities from engaging in proprietary trading or investing in or sponsoring hedge funds or private equity funds.

- **Commodity Trading Advisor (CTA):** an entity that, for compensation or profit, advises others on the trading of commodity contracts. They advise commodity pools and offer managed futures accounts. Like an IB, a CTA does not hold customer funds to margin; they are held at an FCM. CTAs exercise discretion over their clients' accounts (they have power of attorney) to trade the client's account on its behalf according to the client's trading objectives.
- **Commodity Pool Operator (CPO):** an entity that operates commodity pools advised by a CTA. A commodity pool is essentially the commodity equivalent to a mutual fund.
- **Registered Commodity Representative (RCR) or Associated Person (AP):** an employee, partner, or officer of an FCM, IB, CTA, or CPO, duly registered and licensed to conduct the activities of an FCM, IB, CTA, or CPO.

All of these entities have similar counterparts in the securities business and in particular the options trading universe.

Clearing Agencies

- Clearing: The *process of transferring assets* from a selling party to its buying party.

In the commodities universe, clearing is the process whereby the ownership of a commodity derivative is accurately and smoothly transferred from one party to the other after a trade. The first clearing organization was established in 1883 to clear CBOT contracts.

Considerable confusion arose between the Chicago Board Options Exchange and commodities exchanges when options on commodities started to trade in the 1980s. Jurisdictional confusion was laid to rest by late 1991 when the CFTC and the SEC concurrently approved rule changes by the Options Clearing Corporation (OCC) and the Chicago Mercantile Exchange. The changes were intended to improve coordination in the clearance and settlement of futures and options by settling boundaries of supervisory and transactional oversight and clearing. Ultimately, the rule changes expanded the cross-margining programs between the OCC and CME and permitted clearing members to include intermarket futures and option positions held in various nonproprietary accounts.

Unlike the options market, which is almost exclusively cleared by the OCC, commodity transaction clearing is accomplished through a *Derivatives Clearing Organization* (DCO). A DCO is an entity that "enables each party to an agreement, contract, or transaction to substitute, through novation or otherwise, the credit of the DCO for the credit of the parties; arranges or provides, on a multilateral basis, for the settlement or netting of obligations; or otherwise provides clearing services or arrangements that mutualize or transfer credit risk among participants."[8] Any party can become a DCO by registering with the CFTC. To obtain and maintain registration, a DCO must comply with strict criteria outlined in the Commodity Exchange Act (CEA), including:

- **Financial criteria:** Demonstration of adequate financial, operational, and managerial resources; adequate and appropriate system safeguards, emergency procedures, and plan for disaster recovery

- **Oversight of client capability:** Development and adherence to appropriate standards for participant and product eligibility; composition of governing boards to include market participants

- **Risk management:** Adequate and appropriate risk management capabilities; efficient and fair default rules and procedures; well-founded legal framework for the activities of the DCO; standards and procedures to protect member and participant funds

- **Operational integrity:** Ability to complete settlements on a timely basis under varying circumstances; adequate rule enforcement and dispute resolution procedures; obligation to provide necessary reports to allow the CFTC to oversee clearinghouse activities: maintenance of all business records for five years in a form acceptable to the CFTC; publication of clearinghouse rules and operating procedures; participation in appropriate domestic and international information-sharing agreements; governance arrangements and fitness standards; rules to minimize conflicts of interest in the DCO's decision-making process.

Regulators Today

Commodity markets, similar to options markets, are generally self-regulated today. No direct federal agency is vested with trading oversight, with the authorship of rules and bylaws having been largely passed to the exchanges themselves. However, the responsibility for oversight, discipline, and introduction of new contracts and instruments remains firmly within the CFTC, while disciplinary actions of exchange members, advisers, and account managers are administered through the NFA. (This approach echoes the regulatory

---

8   Source: CFTC. https://www.cftc.gov/IndustryOversight/ClearingOrganizations/index.htm.

structure of equity markets, which also feature self-regulatory exchanges, subject to federal oversight, and self-administered disciplinary actions for members and agents through FINRA—Financial Industry Regulatory Authority.)

The CFTC and Jurisdictional Boundaries

Later that year, the CFTC and the Securities and Exchange Commission jointly announced an agreement which clarified regulatory responsibility of each agency for financial instruments that appear to contain elements common to either or both agencies, in particular stock index futures. This agreement was known as the Shad-Johnson Accord and later became part of the Commodity Exchange Act. With the advent of products that appear to cross jurisdiction, such as commodity ETFs or stock index futures, drawing boundaries has become a cottage industry during the 21st century. Examples abound:

- **September 14, 2000:** The CFTC and Securities and Exchange Commission announce an agreement providing for joint jurisdiction over security futures products; that is, single-stock futures and futures on narrow-based stock indexes.

- **November 13, 2008:** The CFTC, the Board of Governors of the Federal Reserve, and the Securities and Exchange Commission (SEC) enter into a Memorandum of Understanding (MOU) to establish a framework on regulatory issues related to central counterparties for credit default swaps.

- **October 16, 2009:** The CFTC and SEC issue a joint report identifying areas where the agencies' regulatory schemes differ and recommending actions to address those differences.

- **December 10, 2013:** Five federal agencies, including the CFTC, issue final rules developed jointly to implement section 619 of the Dodd-Frank Act (the "Volcker rule"). The final rules prohibit insured depository institutions and their affiliates from engaging in short-term proprietary trading of certain securities, derivatives, commodity futures, and options on these instruments for their own account.

These examples show that regulatory authority becomes muddied when new products evolve that overlap the jurisdiction of imbedded institutions. The nature of the broad base of commodities almost guarantees policy and regulatory conflict. The problem is amplified when some commodities attain a status that impacts constituencies. For nondemocratic nations, this is less of a problem, but for those with a democratic orientation, these conflicts are typical. Not surprisingly, oversight policy sometimes clashes with political procedures.

A recent example involved the impact of biofuel mandates on the prices of commodities that are also used as an important food source. Policy mandates seem innocent enough, but the complexity of the systems today inherently create conflicts, which no doubt influence pricing of commodities. Indeed, it has been demonstrated that biofuel mandates do have an impact on corn prices, in the 5–6% range.[9]

The NFA

The other commodity trading regulatory organization is the National Futures Association (NFA), which is the self-regulatory organization (SRO) for the US non-equity derivatives industry, including exchange-traded futures, retail forex trading activity, and OTC derivatives such as swaps. To formalize exchange and broker self-regulation, the CFTC in 1981 granted registration to the National Futures Association as a self-regulatory futures association and approved its articles, bylaws, and rules. The commission's authority to issue rules derives from the Commodity Exchange Act of 1974 (later extended by the Dodd-Frank Act in 2010). Formed by statute in 1981, the NFA began its regulatory operations a year later. The NFA is governed by a board of directors elected by its members. It is headquartered in Chicago with a satellite office in New York.

Margin[10]

> • <u>Margin</u>: The *minimum amount of capital that must be available in an account to trade futures contracts. Capital* refers to cash (or cash equivalent) as well as the value of contracts held in said account.

Commodity contracts are highly leveraged. Unlike options, which represent a "contingent ownership interest" as discussed in Chapter 5, commodity *futures contracts represent an actual ownership interest* that has not been delivered and paid for until delivery. When a trader buys a futures contract, the trader must in the very least have sufficient funds to pay a small good-faith payment. This payment represents a relatively small amount compared to the total value of the commodity. An analogy might be the down payment made

---

9   Zhou, X., & Babcock, B., Using the competitive storage model to estimate the impact of ethanol and fueling investment on corn prices. *Energy Economics*, Volume 62, 2017, pages 195–203, ISSN 0140-9883, https://doi.org/10.1016/j.eneco.2016.12.017
10   This section refers only to margin as it is used in commodity trading accounts.

toward the purchase of a residence: it is necessary to retain an ownership interest in the home until terms of the contract enable full payment and delivery of the residence to the buyer's possession.

Margin balances have two thresholds:

- **Initial Margin:** This represents the minimum amount of cash or equity in the account before a position in that commodity can be attained.

- **Maintenance Margin:** This represents the minimum amount of cash or equity in the account per position that must be available. The amount is less than initial margin to permit some market price leeway.

Each exchange sets initial margin, which must be equal to or greater than the margin policy established by the CFTC and range from 2% to 12% of the value of the underlying commodity, dependent mostly on the volatility and price of the commodity. For examples, see Table 2.1.

TABLE 2.1 Examples of typical margin requirements.

COMMODITY	QTY	$/UNIT	VALUE	INITIAL MARGIN	% OF $ VAL	MAINTENANCE MARGIN	DAY TRADE
AUSTRALIAN $	A$100,000	$0.7413	$74,130	$1,760	2.37%	$1,600	$1,600
GOLD	100 trOZ	$1,7316.60	$173,166	$8,575	4.95%	$7,500	$1,875
CORN	5,000 Bu	$5.32	$26,600	$1,725	6.48%	$1,725	$1,725

Initial and maintenance margins can change based on market conditions, including a surge in volume or price volatility. These changes may result in higher margin requirements to accommodate increased risk. If the funds in the account drop below the maintenance margin level, the broker may either (1) communicate a margin call requiring the immediate deposit of additional funds to bring the account back *up to the initial margin level*; (2) require the trader to reduce position(s) if the client is unable to provide immediate margin rebalance; or (3) immediately liquidate positions automatically once it drops below the maintenance margin level.

Brokers are absolutely uncompromising regarding margin balances. If a client is not forthright, the account will be liquidated, regardless of how the client feels about it. Any losses to the firm will be collected from the client, period. That is the *raison d'être* for margin: an account with any broker is considered to be a reasonable tradeoff of interests—accessibility of markets to the client in exchange for a small "entrance fee" called commissions—and the broker won't accept client irresponsibility as an acceptable risk.

Market Participants

It is remarkable how little the average person knows about the commodities market, despite their ubiquitous importance to our society. The reality is that commodity markets are composed of rules and regulations composed by people, administered by people, and physically created and maintained by people. This is the reason markets are both fascinating and exhausting at the same time. So, who are the people who *actually use* commodity markets? We now consider who these folks are—not by name, of course, but by category. The categories of futures market users are enumerated below.

Producers

> - <u>Producers</u>: Entities that *extract raw commodities from the earth*, thus increasing societal wealth.

The first group consists of those who produce and wish to sell their product. This may consist of farmers, agribusinesses, mining corporations, or oil drilling corporations or refiners. Any entity that produces wealth out of, or on, the planet is a producer who is anxious to sell its raw material to those who will use it. From their standpoint, it is immaterial as to whom it is sold or for what purpose. They produce something that must be sold, and markets are the perfect place.

Consider why they use markets. We will use a corn farmer as an example because it is relatively easy to comprehend. Imagine a farmer with 5,000 acres of recently planted corn. The farmer opens his Microsoft Excel spreadsheet and sees that breakeven for the crop is $5.03 a bushel. The farmer estimates a yield of 100 bushels per acre, with an estimated yield to sell 500,000 bushels of corn. The farmer faces a lot of risk from weather, insects, and disease. Any of these forces could ruin the crop altogether. The farmer isn't concerned about that; the crop is covered by federal crop insurance. However, the biggest risk of all is the potential for a bumper crop (an excess of corn) which could drive the price below cost but above federal price supports.

The farmer mitigates these risks by selling his crop in the futures market. A quick glance at the market reveals a spot price of $5.35 per bushel and a futures price for September delivery of $5.65 per bushel. The farmer sells 100 contracts at $5.65 a bushel. Now its only risk is the amount it can actually harvest for delivery. *By selling in the futures market, the producer has transferred price risk to the buyer.* This motivation holds for all producers and is the primary reason futures markets exist.

End-Users

- End-Users: Organizations that *take delivery* of commodities for their own use.

The interesting irony is that end-users have similar concerns as the producer with a slight twist. Consider General Mills (GIS), who needs enormous amounts of wheat, corn, oats (Cheerios), soybeans, and other raw grains for its multitude of finished goods. Their motivation is twofold: (1) they want a stable price so that their profit margins remain stable; and (2) a stable supply so that their production need not be adjusted down in the event of shortfall. These two motivators are obviously linked; GIS will enter the futures market to mitigate both of these risks. Purchasing futures contracts assures the supply of raw materials at a known price. The firm can plan production schedules with fewer unknowns; risk is reduced. The use of the futures exchange therefore allows less risk for both producer and end-user while still permitting flexibility, as we will see in Chapter 4.

Hedgers/Arbitrageurs

- Hedge: An investment intended to *reduce the risk of adverse price movements* in an asset. Normally, a hedge consists of taking an offsetting or opposite position in a related security.

- Arbitrage: the simultaneous buying and selling of securities, currency, or commodities in different markets or in derivative forms in order to take advantage of differing prices for the same asset.

A sizable portion of futures trading is dedicated to protecting their financial interests against losses in any number of investment areas, from agricultural products, to minerals, metals, and even assets such as stocks and bonds. This *hedging* process is complex and a subject unto itself, covered in Chapter 4. In general, hedging involves the simultaneous purchase or sale of an opposite contract position, which offsets any undesired price movement.

Consider a trucking firm that consumes large quantities of gasoline. These firms buy futures contracts to assure them of a future supply of gasoline. They aren't concerned about a rise in the price—they have already purchased their inventory—but they are very much concerned if the price declines, because the added cost of having bought gasoline at higher prices reduces their operating profit margins. Rather than calmly accepting fate, truckers will hedge their long position in gasoline with either a long put or by selling futures against their long position. The dynamics of hedging will be discussed further in Chapter 4.

Speculators

Individuals and investment companies have poured hundreds of millions of dollars into the commodities and futures markets. The development of electronic trading platforms and exchanges such as Globex has revolutionized commodities trading by greatly broadening the potential number of futures traders by making these markets accessible to a broad swath of potential speculators who would otherwise never have been able to buy and sell futures contracts.

Prior to the 1990s, futures contracts were indeed esoteric. At the early outset of electronic trading, in September 1997, the CFTC introduced e-mini contracts (exclusively trades electronically) for indexes such as the Dow, S&P 500, NASDAQ 100, and later, even the Russell 2000. These contracts represent one-fifth of the value of the original index futures, allowing smaller investors access to these important instruments. In 2019, the CME Group had even introduced the *micro-mini index contracts*, which are *one-tenth the size of the e-minis*.

These instruments have been so successful that the CME has introduced mini and micro contracts for agricultural, precious metals, and energy futures as well. The immediate success of both e-mini and micro-mini contracts has opened a floodgate of a new generation of speculators. This influx of new third-party traders now has a significant impact on the prices of commodity-based goods. Speculator interest is not necessarily securing the price of goods for delivery. These are individuals who use *speculation* about buying and selling behaviors to predict a futures contract's value. These new players seek to make profit through price movement. The jury is still out: we don't yet know whether this has proven to be a gambling parlor or an instrument for price discovery.

Summary and Conclusion

Commodity markets are critical to the smooth price discovery process. Their practical value is such that futures—or mechanisms similar thereto—have been in existence for hundreds of years. Futures are instruments that transfer price risk, assure supply, and motivate production. Their importance has inspired constant refinement as technological advances permit, while also being able to process the enormous productivity growth of underlying finished goods.

The importance of futures and futures markets to society appears self-generating, reaching a level critical enough to warrant oversight and regulation. In general, broad policy to control risky speculative behavior only became a national priority in the 20th century, although self-regulation of exchanges and market participants has been extant since the mid-19th century. Even today, hands-on regulation is conducted almost entirely by the industry itself through the NFA and CFTA, with some "prompting" from Congress in 1922, 1936, 1974, 1999, and 2010.

Futures markets have consolidated in recent decades so that only a handful of exchanges are now capable of handling trillions of dollars of commodity trades annually. As volumes continue to rise each year, obsolete or inefficient processes such as open outcry die off. But what remains are the cadres of producers and end users who rely on market liquidity to help them sense price structure and demand for what they ultimately produce. Other participants, speculators, hop on board the train to squeeze out profits if they can. Overall, these individuals help "lubricate" the pricing machine: they expand the number of trade prices that help producers and end users sense the actual value of what they produce and manufacture. Hedgers, meanwhile, are the worriers; their concern is stability in a random world, but in the short run, they, too, bring liquidity to the markets.

Going Forward

This chapter provides important basic information on the function and purpose of commodity markets. Chapter 3 discusses details of the futures contract itself, including the accounting processes for positions in place, contract specifications, and delivery and payment procedures. Chapter 4 focuses on the process of hedging, for which a large part of futures trading is done.

Chapter 3

The Futures Contract

Introduction

The futures market is in flux, since it reflects the consumer demand of the age. Various contracts have come and gone throughout the century-and-a-half of the existence of futures markets in the United States. It might surprise some, for example, that pork bellies, once a mainstay of the commodity trading pit, was retired as a trading contract in 2011. This raises several questions: who decides what items become tradable? What are the criteria for listing? What exactly are futures contracts? And finally, what are contract specifications? This chapter will answer those questions.

Requirements for Futures Contract Designation

Procedures for the definition and listing of tradable contracts was originally nonexistent. The chaos that ensued necessitated a national standard that was first established by the Futures Trading Act of 1921. Approved on August 24, 1921, by the 67th United States Congress, it was intended to standardize grain futures contracts and set minimum standards for futures exchanges that traded them. The act was challenged and found to be unconstitutional by the US Supreme Court in May 1922, which spurred the creation of a substitute bill in late 1922, the Grain Futures Act, which was ultimately upheld by the Supreme Court. Although some of the Grain Act's provisions were superseded in 1936 by the Commodity Exchange Act (CEA) and again in 1974 (the Commodity Futures Trading Act), its standards for contract listing are still valid today.

Contract Listing Procedure

> - <u>Designated Contract Market (DCM):</u> *A commodities market approved for trading any listed or unlisted commodity or derivative contract.*

The CFTC has ultimate authority to approve or disapprove the continued trading of any commodity futures contract, but a *Designated Contract Market*[1] (DCM) may list new contracts for trading by filing a *self-certification* with the CFTC that declares that the new contract complies with the Commodity Exchange Act (CEA) and the commission's regulations. An alternative communication may merely request CFTC review and approval. The review process is usually requested for unusual products (e.g., bitcoin futures) or products that may cross jurisdictional boundaries. For contracts filed under self-certification procedures, the DCM filer is "expected to assume primary responsibility for ensuring that the contracts meet, on a continuing basis, the applicable statutory and regulatory requirements."[2] The self-certification application must contain:

- **Rules** concerning the contract's terms and conditions;
- **Explanation and analysis** of the product and its compliance with provisions of the Commodities Exchange Act (CEA) and CFTC regulations;
- **Declarations** that the product is a "legal security" as defined by the CEA, that the DCM can properly execute and clear trades in the new contract;
- **Any additional information** that the applicant deems relevant or as requested by the CFTC.

The CFTC then has 45 days to approve or disapprove, with an additional 45-day extension also permitted by declaration of the CFTC. If the request is not approved, the DCM may attempt again with a modified application. Thus, considering the potential complexity of these contracts, the process is relatively straightforward.

---

1   Designated Contract Markets are entities that have been approved to open futures exchanges by the CFTC.
2   https://www.cftc.gov/IndustryOversight/ContractsProducts/index.htm.

Characteristics of Futures Contracts

Contract Specifications

Each futures contract must provide specific information regarding all aspects of a contract's terms, including these important attributes:

- **Quantity** of the underlying commodity being traded.

- **Quality** of the underlying commodity being traded (called the *trading unit*).

- **Trading schedule**, which includes the exact time that a contract no longer trades. (Any trades at or during the noon bell must be completed within one minute with price deemed to be the last printed quote at noon.)

- **Price increments**, which constitute the *minimum amount* the contract value can change; also called the *tick value*.

- **Daily price limits** (if any), which specify how much the value of a contract can change—up or down—during a trading session. Exchanges are at liberty to halt trading if it deems it is in the interests of its customers or the exchange.

- **Position limits**: the maximum number of contracts which can held by a customer at a given time, if any.

- **Delivery and payment**: exact locations, times, and procedures for those taking delivery of the commodity. For those commodities that settle in cash, the exact nature of cash transfer and clearing of the transaction.

- **Storage**: specific storage locations, storage charges, and billing procedures if delivery is not immediate.

About the Symbols

Like equities, symbols are used to identify which commodities are being bought and sold. The quotes identify the commodity first, then the month of delivery, and then the year of the month of delivery. This is an example:

ZW N 22

What this represents is CBOT wheat (there is a different symbol for Kansas City wheat or Minneapolis wheat because those contracts specify a different type of wheat), for delivery in July of 2022.

TABLE 3.1 Contract specifications for a sample of futures contracts.

COMMODITY	EXCH/ SYMBOL	CONTRACT MONTHS	SIZE	MIN TICK	$/TICK	INITIAL MARGIN/ CONTRACT	MAINT MARGIN/ CONTRACT
Wheat	CBOT/ZW	H,K,N,U,Z	5,000 bu	¼ cent/Bu	$12.50	**$1,897**	**$1,725**
Gold	COMEX/GC	G,J,M,Q,V,Z	100 troy oz	10 cents/oz	$10.00	**$8,250**	**$7,500**
Live Cattle	CME/LE	G,J,M,Q,V,Z	40,000 lbs	¼ cent/Cwt	$1.00	**$1,760**	**$1,600**
Crude Oil	NYMEX/CL	MONTHLY	1,000 bbl	1 cent/bbl	$10.00	**$5,610**	**$5,100**
S&P e-Mini	GLBX/ES	H,M,U,Z	$50 X Index	0.25 points	$25.00	**$12,650**	**$11,500**
Euro	CME/E6	MONTHLY	€125,000	0.00005 pts	$6.25	**$2,420**	**$2,200**
Cocoa	ICE/CC	H,K,N,U,Z	10 Met Tons	$1/m ton	$10.00	**$2,090**	**$1,900**

Month Code	JAN	FEB	MAR	APR	MAY	JUN	JUL	AUG	SEP	OCT	NOV	DEC
	F	G	H	J	K	M	N	Q	U	V	X	Z

Cash Settlement

In cash settlement, the purchaser of a cash-settled futures contract is required to pay the price difference between the spot price of the commodity and the futures price, rather than having to take ownership of the physical commodity. In physical settlement, delivery of the actual underlying instruments or commodities occurs. Although it is a choice for some commodities, other contracts can only be cash-settled, and this condition is specified in the respective contract specifications of the commodity being traded. Equity option contracts, however, are always settled with delivery of the subject securities, and never cash in lieu.

In practice, many contracts today either must be cash-settled (bonds, currencies, stock index futures), or may be cash-settled at the discretion of the contract buyer. Cash settlement has proven to be a more convenient—and less expensive—method of transacting futures and options contracts. One unintended but positive consequence of cash settlement has been the entry of speculators who bring more liquidity to commodity markets. Furthermore, clearing agencies have found that cash settlement reduces clearing time at contract expiration and/or delivery. In addition, the chance of default is reduced to zero because cash-settled accounts (all retail commodity trading accounts) must be margin accounts. Thus, ability to pay is constantly monitored, and positions are closed out if there is any chance of customer default.

Order Types

> - OCO (One-Cancels-Other): a pair of conditional orders stipulating that *if one order executes, then the other order is automatically canceled.*
>
> - OSO (One-Sends-Other): a set of conditional orders stipulating that *if one order executes, then the other order is automatically entered.*

Futures contracts may be bought and sold with the same familiar order instructions used in equity markets. However, on electronic platforms, speculators who adopt "scalping"[3] strategies often employ order brackets after entering a position. This means the trader, after the position is filled, places a simultaneous buy and sell order—one being a limit order to close the position for profit, the other being a stop order for risk management. This order pair is entered as a *one-cancels-other* (OCO) order. An OCO order will fill either order, whichever first occurs, and then automatically cancel the unfilled order.

In contrast, a one-sends-other order (OSO) is a set of conditional orders stipulating that if one order executes, then others are automatically entered. These are usually bracket orders: upon entry into a position, the OSO will enter a new OCO order. This type of order system manages risk effectively.

Another commonly used order technique is the trailing stop. All electronic platforms are designed to accept this order strategy. A trailing stop is a risk management order system that will automatically raise (lower) a stop as new position highs (lows) are reached. The degree by which the stop is raised or lowered can be customized in a variety of ways, including percent of price move or target gains. The riskiness of commodities is such that a trade placed without a stop borders on financial suicide. There are those who don't use them, to be sure. However, the more prudent investor *always* uses them. Further, stops should *never* be arbitrarily changed.

Contract Dates, Volume, and Open Interest

Volume and open interest are calculated exactly the same as in option contracts. Volume is the measure of the physical number of contracts that were traded that day. Open interest represents the number of contracts available for trading, similar to what in equities is

---

3   Scalping is a trading practice whereby a contract is bought and sold intraday at small tick intervals for a small profit. This day-trading technique may involve several trades per day, each of which incurs separate commission fees.

called "float." One distinct feature of commodities is the rollover, which is the process of closing out a contract during its last days of trading and moving to the next (or another) contract month.

Unlike options, which expire with no further value or rights, a commodities contract doesn't expire but instead achieves several key dates, which eventually lead to settlement and/ or delivery. The important dates to note are: (a) first notice day; (b) last notice day; (c) expiry date; and (d) physical delivery date (settlement). These dates were of enormous consequence when physical delivery was the norm. At that time, no speculator would own a contract past first notice day. These days, however, with the preponderance of cash settlement, these dates do not have the same impetus. Nonetheless, unless the account holds sufficient cash for settlement, any long position should be closed prior to FND.

First notice day (FND) is the day after which a long-contract holder *may be required* to take physical delivery. The first notice day varies by contract and is subject to exchange rules and bylaws. A delivery notice was at one time a written notice only by the holder of the short futures position to inform the clearinghouse of the intent of delivery. The **clearinghouse** subsequently sent delivery notice to the long-position holder of pending delivery. With electronic trading now the norm, all notices are emailed directly to the client. Further, online trading firms will not accept any new buy orders for commodities posting FND. Firms today permit *liquidation orders only* after first notice day.

The last notice day is the *last day the seller can deliver commodities to the buyer*. The **last trading day** is *the day after which commodities must be delivered* for any futures contracts that remain open. Hedgers pay attention to this date, after which they can sell delivered product at the spot rate if desired. The expiry date is almost always the last trade date. It is usually the Friday before delivery or settlement. *Any contract holders who do not wish to take delivery have this last opportunity* to dispose of a contract before settlement. However, a prudent speculator should be out well before expiry.

Forward Roll

One common method of closing a futures position and avoiding physical delivery is to execute a **forward** roll, which extends the contract's maturity. A forward roll is a simple transaction whereby the trader sells to close their current-month long position and simultaneously buy the same commodity for future month delivery. There is no legal limit to how often the trader can roll the same commodity. Although there is likely to be a price differential between the two (see *Basis Risk*, below), no additional initial margin is usually required.

The nature of the commodity market means there are a few risks inherent in futures contracts. One of them has been discussed above, the risk of unwanted delivery. This simple fact is all-too-simple to mitigate: pay attention! Others are addressed below.

Special Risks of Futures Contracts

Leverage

Although not unique to futures contracts, leverage is a significant and often misunderstood risk. Price moves are not clearly understood by novice traders in regard to how leverage affects their impact on an account. It is imperative that a futures trader fully comprehend the risk of even small price fluctuations. Therefore, they must be completely knowledgeable about and familiar with contract specifications. Consider the following positions in Table 3.2.

TABLE 3.2 Margin account equity balance after day T_1.

POSITION	SYMBOL	ENTRY PRICE	QTY	EOD PRICE	%Δ	INIT MGN	Δ VALUE	%Δ
NYMEX GOLD	GCN	$1,858.70	1	$1,809.20	–2.7%	**$8,250**	–$495	–6.0%
EURO	E6Z	€1.1752	1	€1.1622	–1.1%	**$2,420**	–$1,625	–67.4%
LIVE CATTLE	LEU	$128.112	–2	$126.04	–1.6%	**$3,520**	$406.60	+36.2%
WHEAT	WZN	$699.79	1	720.12	2.9%	**$1,897**	$1,015.5	+53.6%
CASH						**$1,041.50**	**$1,041.50**	EOD Cash Bal
				EOD EQUITY T_1:		**$16,802.10**	**–$697.90**	For the Day

This illustration shows the effect of leverage. Relatively small changes in commodity prices result in disproportionately large changes in wealth. The account incurred a loss of $697.90 on the day, and the end-of-day (EOD) balance reflects this loss. This also represents a loss of roughly 4% on the account, despite the loss of less than 2% on average for the underlying commodities. The new equity balance reflects changes in the value of the contracts. It is important to note that maintenance margin on this account is $14,625.[4] (A statement

---

4   Maintenance margin for the account equals the sum of the maintenance margin for all of the contracts held. Even if one contract falls below maintenance, no margin call occurs, provided there is sufficient equity to support the loss.

showing similar data is emailed to the client a few hours after close of business every day, although the format is very different.)

Now suppose that the next day gold again declines by 0.29%, live cattle rise by 0.45%, the Euro closes down 250 ticks, and wheat is down 1.8%. What is the impact on the account? Table 3.3 shows the individual impact of these price changes on the account.

TABLE 3.3 Account balance change after one day. Account equity now below maintenance margin.

POSITION	SYMBOL	T_1 PRICE	QTY	T_2 PR	BEG BAL	Δ VALUE	END BAL
NYMEX GOLD	GCN	$1,809.20	1	$1,803.9	$7,755.00	−$53	$7,702.00
EURO	E6Z	€1.1622	1	€1.1450	$785.00	−$1,625	−$840.00
LIVE CATTLE	LEU	$126.04	−2	$126.61	$3,926.60	−$454	$3,472.60
WHEAT	WZN	$720.12	1	$707.16	$2,912.50	−$648	$2,264.50
CASH		$1,41.50		**Loss on Day:**		−$2,780.00	$1,451.50
EQUITY T_1:		**$16,420.60**		**EOD EQUITY T_2:**		**$14,050.60**	

The next day, the client receives a margin call because equity has fallen below maintenance. The client must now place $ into the account to avoid liquidation. This amount brings the equity balance back to initial margin, not maintenance margin, and the account is free from liquidation threat—for now. These moves are not particularly large. Indeed, without a broader context, these moves almost constitute market noise. And this is the problem with leverage: small moves, usually of no real concern, become very important because of *leverage*.

Margin Risks

An adequately financed account will not undergo financial stress. What constitutes an "adequately financed" account? There is no simple answer to this query. It all depends on the risk aversion of the account holder, the volatility of the underlying, and the prudence of the broker/dealer. Certainly, the account should be able to withstand a move by any single contract to maintenance margin, a condition which may endanger all of the assets in the account. Some traders use, as a rule of thumb, a 25% cash cushion at trade initiation. This requires account holders to be cognizant of price ranges that the underlying commodity can experience during the expected holding period.

Basis Risk and Price Convergence

> - Price Convergence: The tendency for *futures prices* to have a time premium that *gradually converges to the spot price* as holding period of the futures contract approaches delivery.
> - Basis: The arithmetic *difference between the spot price and the futures* contract price.
> - Basis Risk: A hedge risk whereby *offsetting positions will not change price at exactly reciprocal rates.*

All futures contracts carry some time premium which gradually erodes as the contract nears delivery. This gradual price erosion is the source of what is known as *basis risk*. Basis is the difference in value of the spot price of a given commodity and its futures contract equivalent.

Basis risk is the financial risk that offsetting investments in a hedging strategy will not experience **price changes** in entirely opposite directions from each other. This imperfect correlation between the two positions creates the potential for excess gains or losses in a hedging strategy.

This risk is particularly real for so-called cross-hedging (Chapter 4 will discuss cross hedging in more detail). A cross hedge uses a futures contract to hedge against price changes in a similar non-contracted commodity, such as gasoline, which has futures, and kerosene, which does not. Both assets correlate highly with each other, but gasoline futures are subject to price convergence, whereas kerosene sells on the spot. Thus, there is a risk that the two assets will not move identically in price.

Summary and Conclusion

This chapter considered some of the essential information for a futures trader to grasp before they venture forth into the world of commodities. Commodities are the "real deal." It is no place to earn bragging rights (sports are designed for that). The market doesn't care if you are male or female, about your personality traits, your political or religious leanings, and especially not about your financial condition. It cannot be bought, seduced, or coaxed. Therefore, traders leave their ego at the door and focus on the task at hand—price and risk management.

Many individuals try their hand at commodities; few turn it into something viable. The professionals tend to be producers and end users, and these individuals feed on the foolish. Therefore, understand that these instruments are not for the stubborn or immature. Nor is there a "special technique" to make millions, regardless of the hype.

That doesn't mean at some point you shouldn't wade into those turbulent waters. Simply understand the risks involved. And a final word of caution: to be a professional trader with futures, it is imperative to "have a PhD" in the commodity; in other words, professionals know all about their commodity—they become specialists: where the commodities are produced, what risks face production, shipment costs, logistics, labor and other production needs, state of the market on the demand side, the factors involved in demand, and so on. If a person has no inherent intellectual curiosity about the commodity to be traded, it would be better for that person to go find a casino.

Looking Forward

The next chapter discusses how commodities are used by hedgers—probably the largest professional class of those who trade futures—and why they do what they do.

Chapter 4

Hedging with Futures

Introduction

Futures are popular vehicles for hedging either spot positions, other futures positions, or equity portfolios and is done regularly by using futures contracts, options, or swaps. (Swaps are a whole separate discussion, not discussed in this text.) Both producers and end-users use futures to hedge adverse price movements. For instance, Kellogg's actively hedges because it wants a stable production cost, while farmers hedge to protect the forward price captured in the sale of their produce via futures contracts. Banks also employ interest rate hedges either with interest rate swaps or with T-bond, T-bill, or other interest rate futures to protect their typically thin interest rate spreads and profit margins. Some corporations that are producers of commodities—such as integrated oil companies and mining corporations—use futures contracts to reduce the risk that an unfavorable price movement in the underlying commodity will result in the corporation experiencing unexpected expenses or losses later.

Hedging has been briefly mentioned in previous chapters. But this chapter will focus on procedures and terminology affecting hedging activities. By the time you will finish reading this chapter, you will find (a) an explanation of hedging theory and terminology; (b) an explanation of the procedures and techniques involved in hedging; (c) why hedges reduce risk; and (d) the various instruments used by hedgers, including forwards, futures, and options.

Revisiting Basis

We will now digress to discuss theory that will assist our understanding of the role of basis in hedging.

Basis

Recall that the basis is calculated by deducting the futures price from the spot price. Basis is an important factor in estimating the eventual price. Formally, basis is defined by:

$$b(t) = S(t) - F(t),$$ [Eq. 4.1]

where $b(t)$ is the basis, $S(t)$ is the spot price, and $F(t)$ is the futures price. The cost-of-carry model suggests that by predicting the basis of a commodity, the delivery price of a commodity can be estimated at the time the hedge is placed. This is based solely on the assumption that the commodity in question will maintain the same level of volatility and that there would be no supply or demand disruptions. We now introduce some new concepts, cost-of-carry, convenience yield, backwardation, and contango.

Cost of Carry

> • __Cost of Carry__: The *costs associated with holding physical commodities over time*, including storage costs, insurance, or haulage and transport.

The cost of carry (or carrying charge) is the cost of holding a security or a physical commodity over time. The carrying charge includes insurance, storage fees, opportunity costs, haulage, and other incidental costs. In interest rate futures markets, it refers to the differential between the yield on a cash instrument and the cost of the funds necessary to buy the instrument.

The cost-of-carry model expresses the *estimated* futures price as a function of the spot price and the future value of the cost of carry, as follows:

$$F = Se^{(r+s-c)t}$$ [Eq. 4.2]

where F is the forward price, S is the spot price, e is the natural logarithm base, r is the risk-free interest rate, s is the storage cost, c is the convenience yield, and t is the delivery time of the futures contract (expressed as a fraction of a year).[1] The equation is straightforward in this iteration: the futures price is equal to the spot price, compounded by the risk-free rate plus storage costs minus "convenience yield" over time held.

---

1   For currency markets, the model, as applied, is known as interest rate parity, demurrage, or carrying cost of currency.

Suppose a US investor is considering the purchase of an S&P 500 e-mini futures contract on Globex. The investor expects the cost of carry to be the one-year risk-free interest rate minus *expected dividends* paid by stocks in the S&P 500.[2]

If the contract is held long, the cost of carry is the cost of interest paid on a margin account. If the contract is short, the cost of carry is *the cost of paying dividends*—the opportunity cost of holding an alternative (but usually the risk-free rate earned on a comparably termed T-bill or equivalent). Physical commodities such as grains, meats, softs, energies, and metals incur actual storage costs, expressed as a percentage of the spot price, and is added to the cost of carry.

Cost-of-Carry Model

The cost-of-carry model is an arbitrage-free pricing model which builds upon the basic beliefs of the efficient market hypothesis; that a futures contract is priced to preclude arbitrage profit. It is the most widely accepted and used model for pricing futures contract.

Convenience Yield

- Convenience Yield: An *implied return from holding inventory*. Inventory provides a convenience to buyers who are willing to pay a premium for immediacy.

Convenience yield is an implied return on holding inventories. The implied return is gained from customers who need a certain commodity now, and are willing to pay a premium for that convenience. Users of a consumption asset may obtain a benefit from physically holding the asset (as inventory) prior to T (maturity), which is not obtained from holding the futures contract. These benefits include the ability to profit from temporary shortages and the ability to keep a production process running.

One reason that convenience yield exists is the availability of inventory. High inventories suggest relatively high supply of the commodity now versus the future. Thus, it should be expected that future prices would move higher as inventory is reduced. Futures or forward prices should be higher than the current spot price, *ceteris paribus*. When inventories are low, expectations shift to scarcity now rather than the future and the opposite reaction would prevail: *ceteris paribus*, futures prices would be higher than spot price. Consequently, convenience yield is inversely related to inventory levels.

---

2   Future dividends must be estimated since actual future dividends are unknowable.

Meanwhile, if $Fs_{t,T}$ is the *forward price* of an asset with initial price S_t and maturity T, and r is equal to the one-year continuously compounded risk-free interest rate, then the pricing formula would be $F_tT = S_t e^{r(T-t)}$. But a correction to the forward pricing formula is given by the convenience yield c. Thus, the equation is modified to:

$$F_tT = S_t e^{(r-c)(T-t)}. \qquad \text{[Eq. 4.3]}$$

Notice that Eq. 4.3 differs from the cost-of-carry equation, Eq. 4.2, in that the exponent for the natural log basis e is composed of two factors: one is the risk-free rate adjusted downward by the convenience yield, and the other reflects the holding period of the commodity only. Importantly, if convenience yield is greater than the risk-free rate, it becomes possible that the futures price is discounted relative to the spot price. This equation introduces us to another concept, backwardation.

Backwardation

- <u>Backwardation</u>: A situation *whereby the price of a forward or futures contract is below the spot price at contract maturity.*

Backwardation is thought to be a rare condition that describes the situation when the futures price is trading at a lower price than the spot price.

This condition usually occurs if there is a supply or demand shock that causes the spot price to rise above the futures price. For example, suppose the December holidays are approaching when an outbreak of hoof-and-mouth disease decimates live cattle herds. The spot price will rise, but the futures price may not necessarily rise as much, so that the spot price is higher than the futures price. This condition is usually temporary and dissipates as soon as it becomes evident that supply will soon return to normal conditions. This would be a demonstration of backwardation. The opposite of backwardation is *contango*.

Contango

- <u>Contango</u>: A commodities market condition where *the futures price of a commodity is higher than the spot price.*

Contango is the usual pattern for commodity prices. A contango market is also known as a normal market, or carrying-cost market.

We have already seen how commodity prices tend to converge on the spot price as delivery approaches. Certainly, for all interest rate futures, contango markets prevail (at least until negative interest rates become the norm). Contango is a situation where the futures price of a commodity is higher than the expected spot price of the contract at maturity. In theory, a contango is evidence that speculators pay more for a commodity future now as an expression of cost utility: pay a premium now to have the commodity in the future, rather than paying the costs of storage and carry resultant from a purchase today.

Convenience yield, backwardation, and contango affect the hedger on a number of levels. First, if the hedger looks to the futures market as a means to hedge their spot inventory, determination of an estimated future price has obvious importance, as does the understanding of inventory risk if the market is contango or if backwardation is present. Second, the choice of hedging instrument can change, depending on whether commodities are following a normal course or not.

We note that a trader can estimate future prices—and thereby find proper hedging instruments—by using Eq. 4.2. Consider a hedger that sees the nine-month (T) price (F) of corn futures at $5.45 per bushel, whereas the spot price (S) is $5.10 per bushel. Assume the one-year T-bill rate (r) is 1.25% per annum, and storage cost for corn is 1.5%. Given Eq. 4.3, we can derive the following relation:

$$F = S[1 + (r - c)T] \qquad \text{[Eq. 4.4]}$$

so that:
$$c = r + \frac{1}{T}\left(1 - \frac{F}{S}\right)$$

and by substitution, $\quad c = .0125 + \frac{1}{.75}\left(1 - \frac{5.45}{5.10}\right) = -.07897 = -7.9\%$ per year.

This means that there is *negative convenience yield*. How can this be, and what does this mean? It means that there is an insufficient difference in price between the spot and future price to offer any convenience yield. Let us now check Eq. 4.3 by substituting -7.9% into it. We should be able to calculate an expected futures price, one year out. And the result is a futures price of $5.46 per bushel, which is statistically equal to the current futures price: we confirm the efficacy of Eq. 4.2.

We see in Figure 4.1 the normal futures upward curve where contracts for further dates typically trade at higher prices relative to spot. (The curves in Figure 4.1 plot market prices

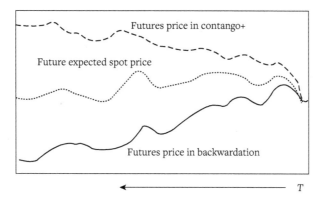

FIGURE 4.1 Spot, contango, and backwardation of commodity contracts—spread against spot price.

for contracts at different maturities.) Some theorists suggest backwardation reflects the market expectation of bearish future spot prices, and contango that they will move up. Thus, they maintain that backwardation is a leading bearish indicator and contango, bullish.

Types of Hedges

Now that we are aware of the fair-value variables in play, we turn to the practice of hedging itself. The *main advantage of a futures contract is that it removes the uncertainty about the future price* of a commodity, security, or a financial instrument. By locking in a guaranteed price for buying or selling a particular asset, buyers or sellers of futures contracts are able to eliminate the risk of any unexpected expenses or losses. There are three basic types of hedges: the long hedge, the short hedge, and the cross-hedge.

Long Hedge

> • <u>Long Hedge</u>: A strategy employed by buyers of commodities who are *protecting against market price increases.*

A long hedge is used when a commodity user plans on *buying a commodity such as soybean meal and wants to protect against prices increasing.* An example would be a hog producer who wants to protect against soybean meal feed prices. This is accomplished through the purchase of soybean meal futures contracts. This long hedge *protects against price increase of a commodity the user already had intentions of buying.* It is important to note that a long hedge only protects against price increases and is typically only used by those already committed to purchase the commodity. *It does not protect against price decreases.*

An example is indicated in Table 4.1a, where a farmer *wants to buy* soybean meal in October for March delivery. Table 4.1a indicates the financial impact of a long hedge: the farmer elects to buy the March futures contract rather than electing to buy the soymeal now. If the price of bean meal rises to, say, $350 a ton, the farmer gains $23 a ton, since it purchased a futures contract for delivery in March for $327 while the spot price is $350. Notice what happens with a decline: the farmer takes delivery and loses $15 on the trade, since the spot price declined to $312. The loss is smaller than the difference in the spot because the basis has moved from −$12 to zero.

TABLE 4.1A The purchase of a futures contract "locks in" the delivery price with the price of soymeal at the time the contract was purchased. The farmer wants delivery. However, if the price of the commodity declines, there is no protection against that loss.

FUTURES PRICE					SPOT PRICE	
COMMODITY	MKT PRICE	B/S	$ COST		COMMODITY	SPOT PR $
ZMH22 March Soybean Meal	$327/ton	B	−$327		SOYBEAN MEAL @ SPOT October	$335
IF PRICES RISE, FARMER TAKES DELIVERY OF CONTRACT, GAIN:						
ZMH22 March Soybean Meal	$350/ton	Del	+$327		SOYBEAN MEAL @ SPOT March	$350
Financial Gain:			*+$23/ton*			*+$15*
IF PRICES DECLINE, FARMER STILL TAKES DELIVERY, LOSS:						
ZMH22 March Soybean Meal	$315/ton	S	+$320		SOYBEAN MEAL @ SPOT March	$312
Financial Loss:			*−$15/ton*			

Short Hedge

- <u>Short Hedge</u>: A strategy employed by sellers of commodities who are *protecting against market price decreases.*

A short hedge is used to protect the producer against declines in the price of products it wants to sell. A hog producer will short (sell) a Lean Hog Futures Contract for hogs to be shipped at a future date. Just before the hogs are actually shipped, the hog producer will close the short position by buying back the futures contract. Any decline in the cash spot prices would be mostly offset by a gain in the futures transaction.

Note that a short hedge protects against price decrease of a commodity the user already had intentions of selling. It does not protect against price increases.

An example is indicated in Table 4.1b, where a farmer *wants to sell* lean hogs in November for the spot price at that time. Table 4.1b indicates the financial impact of a short hedge: the farmer elects to sell a November futures contract rather than electing to sell hogs now.

TABLE 4.1B The sale of a futures contract "locks in" the delivery price at the price of lean hogs when the contract was sold. The farmer wants to deliver its hogs. However, if the price of the commodity increases, there is no protection against that loss.

FUTURES PRICE				SPOT PRICE	
COMMODITY	MKT PRICE	B/S	$ COST	COMMODITY	SPOT PR $
HEU22 December Lean Hogs	$85.88/cwt	S	−$85.88	LEAN HOGS @ SPOT May	$84.25
IF PRICES FALL, FARMER DELIVERS ON CONTRACT:					
HEU22 December Lean Hogs	$72.60/cwt	Del	−$85.88	LEAN HOGS @ SPOT December	$70.40
Financial Gain:			*+13.28/cwt*		
IF PRICES RISE, FARMER DELIVERS, LOSS:					
HEU22 March Soybean Meal	+$88.20/cwt	B	−$88.20	LEAN HOGS @ SPOT December	$88.20
Financial Loss:			*−$2.32*		

In this instance (Table 4.1b), the farmer is able to deliver hogs at the futures price despite a price decrease: price risk was transferred from the grower to the buyer. If prices had increased, the *buyer would have been at advantage by $2.32 per hundredweight.* Is the farmer unhappy? Probably not, because the advanced sale was likely priced above its breakeven production cost. Contrarily, if the price of bean meal falls, the farmer is in "hog heaven" (pardon the pun) because he has delivered its hogs at the contract price, which is $13.28 per hundredweight higher than the spot price.

Cross-Hedge

> • <u>Cross Hedge</u>: A hedge strategy that *uses two different assets or commodities with a positive correlation* in the movement of their prices.

Cross hedging refers to the practice of hedging against price risk of an asset that is not directly traded in the futures market by using an asset with which it shares a positively correlated price relationship. The investor takes opposing positions in each asset in an attempt to reduce the risk of holding just one of the assets. However, hedgers recognize that assets are not perfectly correlated. Therefore, they must weigh non-correlation risks against the risk of no hedge.

For example, jet fuel is a major expense for airline companies. Profit or loss for airlines hangs in the balance, depending on the price of jet fuel. To mitigate this risk, airline companies should buy futures contracts for jet fuel. But what happens if there are no futures contracts for jet fuel (as is the case here)?

In that situation, companies are forced to implement a cross hedge, whereby they use the closest alternative asset available. Therefore, an airline would cross hedge its exposure to jet fuel by pairing the purchase with crude oil futures or gasoline futures. Even though crude oil, gasoline, and jet fuel are three different commodities, their prices correlate well. Therefore, they could be used as a "proxy" for jet fuel and would likely be adequate as a hedge. Note, however, that the success of any cross hedge relies on the continued correlative relationship between the two commodities.

One interesting attribute of a cross hedge is the *approximate* hedging; it will never be absolute because of two factors: (1) prices of divergent commodities are never 100% correlated; and (2) there is almost always a mismatch between quantities. Correlation factors are a given, but quantity mismatches can be at least partially mitigated by determining the proper hedge ratio, to which we turn next.

Hedge Ratios

Static Versus Dynamic Hedge

A hedge can be constructed as either a static hedge or as a dynamic hedge. In a static hedge, the number of hedging contracts remains unchanged over the course of the hedge, despite any price movement of the underlying contract or hedged asset. In a dynamic hedge, on the other hand, the number of hedging contracts changes to bring back the proper hedge protection. To determine the proper number of contracts to utilize, end-users employ the hedge ratio and calculate the optimum number of contracts.

- Hedge Ratio: A ratio showing *how much of an asset is fully hedged* against adverse price movement.

The hedge ratio compares the value of a position protected through the use of a **hedge** with the size of the entire position itself. A hedge ratio may also be a comparison of the value of **futures contracts** purchased or sold to the value of the cash commodity being hedged. A calculation of a hedge ratio determines how much of the asset is hedge protected.

For example, consider a currency dealer holding A$150,000 (Australian dollars), which exposes the dealer to **currency risk**. If the dealer enters into a hedge to protect against losses in this position, which instrument would provide the best hedge, and how much of the currency position would be hedged? If the dealer uses an Australian dollar futures contract to hedge, the dealer would be 67% hedged, since the contract size for Australian dollars is A$100,000. The dealer could say that its hedge ratio is .67, which is the same as saying that 67% of foreign currency exposure is hedged.

Thus, the hedge ratio is the comparative value of an open position's hedge to an overall position. A hedge ratio of 1, or 100%, means that full protection against price risk is in place for the open position—a complete hedge is in place. By contrast, a hedge ratio of 0, or 0%, means that no protection against price risk exists for the open position. Hedge ratios are easy to calculate. It is simply the ratio of the hedge value and the hedged asset value:

$$R_H = \frac{Q_a}{Q_h} \qquad [\text{Eq. 4.5}]$$

where Q_h equals the hedge value (the contract size of the hedge instrument) and Q_a equals the total size of the asset being hedged. An example is drawn from the airline scenario described above. Suppose a purchasing agent for an airline wants to hedge its inventory of 520,000 gallons of jet fuel. The agent determines that gasoline futures contract specifications are 42,000 gallons per contract. The agent is able to determine that the hedge ratio will be: $R_H = \frac{520,000}{42,000} = 12.38$. The hedge ratio tells us that each contract will only hedge roughly 8% of the total asset to be hedged. The purchasing agent will need about 12 contracts (12

X 8% = 96%) for an almost complete hedge.[3] However, this tells us only part of the answer. Perhaps the two assets don't correlate well enough to assume only 12 contracts are adequate. It may be necessary to weight the number of contracts by the correlation coefficient of the two assets. This realization brings us to the use of correlation statistics to determine the *optimum number* of hedge contracts.

Optimum Number of Contracts

> • <u>Optimal Hedge Ratio aka Minimum-Variance Hedge Ratio</u>: A method to calculate *the ideal number of contracts required to optimize the hedge* ratio.

Now we explore the *optimal hedge ratio* (also known as the *minimum-variance hedge ratio*). The minimum-variance hedge ratio is critical for **cross hedging** since it ultimately determines the *optimal number of futures contracts required to fully hedge* a position.

This ratio is calculated as the product of the **correlation coefficient** between the changes in the spot and futures prices and the *ratio of the standard deviation of the changes in the spot price to the standard deviation of the futures price.*[4] There exist several ways to calculate this number, but the most direct optimal hedge ratio formula is as follows:

$$R_{\hat{H}} = \rho \left(\frac{\sigma_s}{\sigma_f} \right)$$ [Eq. 4.6]

where ρ is the correlation coefficient of changes in the future price and spot price; σ_s is the standard deviation of changes in spot price, s; σ_f is the standard deviation of changes in futures price, f. After calculating the optimal hedge ratio, the optimal number of contracts needed to hedge a position is calculated by dividing the contract size of the hedge future by the units of the position being hedged by the size of one futures contract.

Consider this example. A commercial bakery is purchasing 7,800 bushels of millet, a wheat-like grain. It has been provided with daily closing spot prices for millet as well as nearest-contract futures prices for wheat. Using this information, the VP of operations calculated the correlation coefficient for the grains and determined it to be .735. The standard deviation

---

3   The result must be rounded down to the nearest whole number; there is no such thing as a partial or fractional contract.

4   Both of these statistics are easily calculated on Excel when the closing data is provided.

for both grains was also calculated and found to be .278 for wheat and .174 for millet. The optimal hedge ratio was then calculated as

$$R_{\hat{H}} = 0.735 \left(\frac{0.174}{0.278} \right) = 46\%$$

Because millet is considerably more stable than wheat, and since they correlate fairly well, about half, or 46% (approximately), of the millet needs to be hedged. Therefore, the bakery decides to use mini- and micro-wheat contracts to hedge appropriately. If the bakery is ordering 7,800 bushels of millet, then they need enough mini-contracts to hedge 7,800 x .46, or 3,588 bushels of millet.

With the hedge ratio, the VP is ready to set up his hedge, using this equation:

$$N^* = R_{\hat{H}} \times \left(\frac{Q_a}{Q_h} \right) = .46 \times \left(\frac{7,800}{1,000} \right) = 3.59 \qquad \text{[Eq. 4.7]}$$

where N^* equals the *optimal contract number*. This is calculated to be $N^* = .46 \times 7.8 = 3.59$. Again, no fractional contracts, so a portion of the millet cannot be hedged.

> • Optimal Contract Number: The precise *number of futures contracts required to optimize the effectiveness of a hedge.*

Using Options as Hedge Instruments

Options are frequently employed in hedging. Unlike futures, the holder of an option is not required to buy or sell the asset if they choose not to do so at **settlement**. There are options on futures as well as on stocks. Hedging stocks with options is a matter of balancing the deltas.[5] Since long position in stocks carries a delta of 1.00, puts would be used, using any combination of puts to equal -1.00. If this is accomplished, the portfolio is said to be *delta neutral*, and any upside move would be offset by losses in the puts and *vice versa*.

> • Delta Neutral: A condition where the *positive delta of a portfolio is completely balanced by the negative delta of the options* and vice versa for a short equity portfolio.

---

5   Delta is discussed in Chapter 9. It is a statistic that measures the sensitivity of an option to the price movement of a stock.

Delta Neutrality for Equities

Delta neutrality is difficult to maintain since option deltas change over time, whereas long-stock delta always remains at 1.00 and short-stock delta always remains at –1.00. A delta neutral long equities portfolio features an option delta of –1; the expression for this condition is **h = –1. H = –1** means that long put options or short call options[6] of equal magnitude to the underlying are needed to exactly offset moves in the underlying stocks. The number of exact number of options to buy or write, called the total delta equivalent, can be determined with this equation:

$$\Delta_{SE} = \frac{-(q_1 S_1 + q_2 S_2 + q_3 S_3 + \ldots + q_n S_n)}{100}$$ [Eq. 4.8]

where $q_x S_x$ is the **x** quantity of shares of stock S_x. In other words, since each share has a delta of 1, it is necessary to sum the number of shares owned in each position of the portfolio and then divide by 100, since each option is written for 100 shares. The number of total option contracts is equal to: $\frac{\Delta_{SE}}{\Delta_o}$, where Δ_o is the delta of the hedging option.

As an example, consider a position of 1,000 shares of SPY at $352 per share. The closest at-the-money put option has a delta of –.47. The number of puts needed to hedge the shares of SPY would be: $\frac{-10}{-.47} \approx 212$ at-the-money SPY put options.[7]

Delta Neutrality for Futures

The same principal applies to commodities, since commodity futures contracts also have options, whose deltas are calculated and listed in listed quotations. Hedge ratios are used in hedging every type of financial instruments. No matter what instruments are being hedged against, the same delta-neutral strategy applies, where the total commodity portfolio deltas are offset by their countermanding option positions. An important reminder would be the fact that if short positions are held in a portfolio, they can only be hedged with long call options or short put options—both of which have positive deltas.

Summary and Conclusions

Hedging is a significant activity in the futures market, accounting for a large portion of futures volume. No hedge is cost free, and the ultimate decision to hedge is to determine if

---

6   Short calls and long puts both have negative deltas. See Chapter 9.
7   The number is approximate because there are no fractional options contracts. The actual number is 212.766.

a hedge is worth the cost. Simple long or short futures contracts are a hedging mechanism unto themselves; the very purpose of a futures contract is price risk management.

The situation is somewhat more complex for those individuals wishing to hedge a product that does not have an equivalent futures contract. For cross hedgers, where the purchased good is not a listed commodity, the hedger needs to calculate the hedge ratio and then the minimum-variance hedge ratio optimal *before* the optimal number of contracts can be determined.

Options are frequently used in hedging because they are generally less expensive than futures contracts and for the simple reason that any loss incurred can only be as large as the cost of the option itself. To be effective as a hedge requires the achievement of delta neutrality, which is a condition of balance between the summed deltas of the item to be hedged and the summed deltas of the option hedge. A significant disadvantage to options is that they have a limited affective lifespan. However, this disadvantage can usually be overcome by buying or writing options with expiries that match the duration of the futures contract delivery dates.

Looking Forward

Since this discussion of hedging also concludes our discussion on futures and the last topic of this discussion was the procedures of hedging with options, it is only appropriate that we now turn attention and focus to options. Accordingly, the next several chapters will be dedicated to that subject. In Chapters 5 and 6, basic components and attributes of options are discussed. Chapters 7–10 discuss pricing mechanics and theory. Chapters 11–15 focus on option strategies.

Chapter 5

The Option Contract

- <u>Derivative</u>: A derivative is a financial security whose *value is derived from an asset* or group of assets such as a benchmark index. The derivative is often a tradable asset itself but is subject to expiration, after which it has no force or value.

Characteristics of Option Contracts

Option contracts are a form of asset called a *derivative*. Other derivatives include futures contracts, all types of swaps, including credit default swaps, and certain collateralized debt obligations (CDOs). When we discuss options here, we generally refer to *stock options*, but there are *commodity options* as well. As contracts, options have the characteristics of a legal contract with parties, rights, and restrictions attached thereto.

Stock options give the option holder the right, but not the obligation, to buy or sell particular stocks for a particular price (the strike price) within a specified time. Options are contingent claims in that the option holder needn't claim its rights unless the underlying price moves in a favorable direction. If a buyer of a $50 strike call finds the underlying price at $40, it is unlikely that the holder will decide to exercise the option and buy the stock at $50. But if the same holder has the same option and the stock is at $70, it is most probable that the holder will exercise its claim and buy the stock at $50.

- <u>Contingent Claim</u>: Put and call contracts are known as *contingent claim contracts. This means that they have no value whatsoever unless something, defined in the contract itself, occurs.* Put options allow the owner of the option to sell the underlying asset only if the price is less than the strike price. Call options allow the owner to buy the underlying asset only if the price is greater than the strike price.

Option contracts expire after a specified period of time, after which they have no contingent right whatsoever.

- Leverage: Leverage (called "gearing" in the United Kingdom) refers to situations where *small investments in equity benefit disproportionately from price movements* of securities that would either cost much more to own outright or would require a much greater risk. This is often accomplished by using debt, but options offer rights as though the investor actually owned (or shorted) the underlying.

Leverage is fundamental to options, but the option price must nonetheless be respected. Leverage is a double-edged sword (or for careless investors, the sword of Damocles). For instance, buying 100 shares of a $50 stock would require a $5,000 investment, but to buy a call contract for 100 shares of that same stock at $5 per share would only require a $500 investment. This sounds attractive, but just to break even (i.e., cover the cost of the option), the underlying must increase 10% in value during the holding period, since the premium for the option equaled 10% of the per-share price of the stock. If the stock rises 9.999% or less, you lose. If the probability of the stock reaching $55 or more is less than, say, 15%, then the purchase of this particular option was a bad idea. Furthermore, if the stock actually declines and closes at a price less than $50 a share by expiry, the option is worthless and you lose your entire investment. Thus, *leverage by itself is a terrible reason to purchase an option.*

Nonetheless, it is because of leverage that options are attractive financial instruments for hedging or for speculation, but which option to buy is critical and requires some mathematical analysis, which we will discuss later in the course. As for hedging, options are used extensively for this purpose, but once again, the cost of the option must be weighed against the probabilities of the option investment actually being viable. Some math is necessary to properly gauge effectiveness of options when used as hedges as well.

Besides common stock, there are also options for stock indexes, foreign exchange, agricultural commodities, precious metals, and interest rate futures.

Parties to the Contract

- Party and Counterparty: The *owner of an option contract may or may not act, whereas the writer (the seller) of the option must perform* if the owner exercises its rights under the contract. (This is why this instrument is called an option!)

All option contracts are created by legal individuals who are **_not_** legal representatives or agents of the underlying asset. In other words, unlike stock, which is issued by the subject corporation, no option contracts are written and issued by the corporations who are subject to the terms of the option itself. (An exception are employee stock options, which are similar but not tradable. Nor are they transferable unless directly stipulated in the contract.) *Standardized options are not a component of a corporation's balance sheet.*

There are no legal or physical limits to the number of contracts that can be written and sold by any party, except for market-makers and dealers, who have position size constraints placed on them by the exchanges with whom they are registered. The total number of contracts in existence at any given moment is referred to as *open interest*. Open interest will rise as new contracts are written and fall when a contract is either exercised or canceled. This term contrasts with the term *volume*, which refers to the actual quantity of a given option contract that changed hands that day.

Option contracts are written, sold, or held by two parties known simply as the *party* and the *counterparty*. These terms are interchangeable in regard to their function and are best thought of as "this person" and "that person." When a party has "written" an option contract (also called the *option writer*), the option is created *ex nihilo*. The process does not involve any physical activity today except the pressing of a key to confirm a "sell to open" transaction. When a contract is written and sold, the option writer automatically assumes the legal responsibilities and terms of that option contract, which are contingent upon the achievement of a price level stipulated in the contract. These obligations vary, depending on whether the option is a call or a put, as discussed below.

The option is immediately purchased (if it is a market order) by a counterparty for an amount called the *premium*. The entity who buys the option now has a contingent claim on the *underlying*, which remains in force until expiry. Therefore, the party that owns the contract *may act* based on the terms of the contract. The party who has written (and sold) the contract *is obligated to perform* per the terms of the option contract solely at the behest of the option owner.

The option holder, unlike the holder of the underlying stock, has neither voting rights in the corporation nor is entitled to any dividends paid by the corporation. Brokerage commissions are not stipulated in the options contract, but are set by each brokerage house. Commissions, which are currently very low (often less than $1.00 per contract purchased or sold), are paid by both party and counterparty when buying or selling options. (When assignment or exercise of option contracts occurs, commissions are not usually charged.) There are also trivial exchange fees charged per contract transaction, except assignment, amounting to $.01 or so per contract.

Other Miscellaneous Contractual Information

Settlement is the term that describes completion of a transaction. It represents the time when cash from one account is transferred to another and ownership of securities have transferred from seller to buyer. The settlement time for all option trades is one business day (T+1).

No options are marginable, regardless of their market value, and therefore their asset value cannot be used when calculating the amount of allowed margin of the account. To trade options, an investor must have a brokerage account approved for trading options and must also acknowledge receipt of a copy of the FINRA disclosure called *Characteristics and Risks of Standardized Options*. Furthermore, each new options trader is restricted to the type of transactions available to her. There are four trading levels:

- **Level I** allows the account holder to only buy to open puts or calls or to sell to close puts and calls.

- **Level II** allows the account holder to perform all transactions of Level I and also allows the account holder to sell covered calls.

- **Level III** allows the account holder to perform all transactions of other lower levels and also allows the account holder to enter into debit and/or credit spreads, but forbids naked option writing.

- **Level IV** allows the account holder to perform all transactions of other lower levels and also allows the account holder to sell naked options.

Generally, once access to an options trading platform is established, investors will be able to view the full listing of option classes for any underlying security that offers options. The entire set of classes and series of a particular underlying is referred to as an ***option chain***.

Components of the Options Contract

The elements of a standardized option contract specifies whether it is a put or call, its style as to when the option can be exercised, the underlying security, the strike price, the expiration date, and the number of shares of the underlying security for each contract, which is almost always 100 shares for equity options. (However, different countries may have different standards. For instance, option contracts traded in the United Kingdom on the London International Financial Futures and Options Exchange (LIFFE) is for 1000 shares.)

> - Components of an Option Contract: The option contract stipulates specific infor-mation such as the *underlying* security: *option type* (call or put), *style*, *class*, *strike* price, *expiration* date, and *quantity* represented.

Option Types

> - Option Types: There are only two types—*puts* and *calls*.

There are only two types of options. As discussed in Chapter 1, a *call* gives the holder the *right*, but not the obligation, to buy a specific security for a set price, called the *strike* or *exercise price*. A *put* gives the holder the right, but not the obligation, to *sell* a particular security for the strike price. As we learned above, the writer of the option is obligated to perform at the sole behest of the option owner.

Option Styles

> - Option Styles: All US exchanges that trade stock options offer only *American-style* options. Commodities generally have *European-style* options. Any other types are rarely used in the United States and often traded OTC, if at all.

There are many styles of options in existence today, but only American-style and European-style are standardized and traded in the United States. American-style options allow the holder to exercise the option *at any time* before expiration, whereas European-style options allow the holder to exercise *only for a short time before or on the expiration date*. The option style is not related to geography—most options traded in Europe are American-style options. All equity options are American-style options, but most foreign currency options, CBOE stock index options, and options on commodities are European-style options. A third less-common option, not exchange traded, is the Bermudan option, which is a hybrid-type between American and European exercise; where the right to exercise is allowed at several distinct times prior to expiry. There also exist at least 35 other varieties of exotic options with both standard exercise styles and path-dependent exercise styles such as "lookbacks," "barriers," "capped-style," or "Quantos." Although interesting in their own right, these varieties are esoteric and not pertinent to our current discussion.

Strike Prices

Originally, option strikes were set as follows:

- For stocks valued per share less than $25, in $2.50 increments.
- For stocks valued per share greater than $25 but less than $100, in $5 increments.
- For stocks valued per share greater than $100, in $10 increments.

Now, however, depending on the price and volume of the underlying security, option strike prices can be set at $0.50, $1.00, $2.50, $5.00, or $10.00 intervals, with price increments at both above and below the current market price of the underlying. The strike value designations and the month of expiry are set by the exchange that has listed them. If the price of the underlying security moves above or below existing strikes before expiration, new option strikes are created. The older contracts stay in quotation, even if there are no remaining option contracts in the series.

Expiry (When the Option Expires)

Life was simpler in the past: only monthly options existed, and these always expired on the Saturday following the third Friday of the expiration month. Today, many stock issues with high volume have *weekly* and even *quarterly* expiration options. Weekly expiration options expire on one-, two-, three-, and four-week cycles. Furthermore, some options now expire on Mondays, Wednesdays, and Fridays. Some exchange-traded funds (ETFs) also have quarterly expirations. In short, some of the more active stocks have an immense selection of expiration time frames.

The record number of active option expiries probably belongs to options of the SPDR S&P 500 ETF (SPY), which offer Monday-Wednesday-Friday weekly cycles for six consecutive weeks, an additional two weeks of Friday expiry options, 12 months of regular monthly options, and 1½ years of quarterly options while also carrying three-month expiration cycles an additional six months beyond the quarterlies. All told, at any given week, SPY has 38 different expiries covering 2½ years!

Option Exercise

- Option Exercise: Exercise means that: *a call holder will have purchased the underlying at the strike price* before the next business day following expiry; *a put holder will have sold the underlying at the strike price* before the next business day following expiry.

If an option is in-the-money (ITM) at expiry, the holder of the option *exercises the option*. Remember: options are contracts, and the holder has the right of asset transfer at the prearranged price (the strike). When an option is exercised, the holder is merely doing what the contract says the holder can do.

In the past, options required oral or written notice of exercise, which needed to occur prior to 4 p.m. Eastern time on the Friday before expiration (or the last trading day before the third Friday if the market is closed on the Friday before expiration). Today, *the exercise process is automatic—no notice is required* if the underlying closes at- or in-the-money. This means that a call holder will receive the underlying so that on the next business day following expiry, instead of having a call option at a given strike, the investor will have 100 shares of the underlying with a cost basis at the strike and no call option. A put holder will have sold the underlying at the strike so that on the next business day following expiration, instead of having 100 shares of the underlying issue as well as a put option, the account will show an increase in the cash balance equal to the strike price times 100, but 100 shares less of the underlying and no put option.

For the party that relinquishes stock pursuant to terms of the option contract, shares previously held by that party are *assigned* to the new owner.

Adjusted Options

Each standardized equity option contract involves the potential transfer of shares in round lots (100 shares = a round lot). If the shares of a company split, standard option contracts will be adjusted pursuant to the terms of the split, altering the *contract multiplier* (number of shares per contract of the underlying involved), as well as the strike price. For instance, consider a stock priced at $112 that announces a two-for-one split. The 100-strike option contract series for both puts and calls will be adjusted contemporaneously with the split announcement date. Thus, the holder of one 100-strike call option will be issued two new options with a $50 strike and will trade on a "when issued" basis. Adjustments are made for stock splits, reverse stock splits, **stock dividends** or distributions, **rights offerings**, reorganizations, recapitalizations, or reclassification of the underlying. However, for cash distributions of 10% or less, no adjustments are made.

Simple splits are easy, but what happens for a three-for-two split? Or a five-for-four split? The adjusted number of shares is simple to calculate, as follows:

Number of Shares *x* Ratio = New Share Amount

And the new strike price is also a simple arithmetic calculation:

Number of Shares × Strike Price = New Number of Shares × New Strike Price

Based on our previous example, the 100-strike would be adjusted to $\frac{100 \times 100}{150} = 66.67$ strike, for 150 shares, calculated by $(100 \times \frac{3}{2})$. For truly strange and unusual distributions, such as a rights offering or special dividend, an adjustment panel from the OCC meets to determine contract adjustments. When the adjustment panel issues its determination, all adjustments, simple and complex, are then published by the Options Clearing Corporation. The adjustments are listed in reverse chronological order, oldest first. The effective date is the ex-date[1] established by the primary market in the underlying.

Special Risks of Options

Options are not risk free for either the buyer or the seller. For the buyer of an option, the break-even point (initial cost of the option) may not be achieved, resulting in capital loss. Or more likely, the price of the underlying can move away from the strike price so that it is illogical to exercise. When this happens (the option expires "out-of-the-money"), the option buyer loses its entire investment since the option expires valueless. Here are some examples that demonstrate financial risks to the option holder:

a. *Long Call: out-of-the-money expiry*. You buy 5 SPY 440 Calls for $222 each because you are confident the market will rise. It doesn't, and in fact it closes at 439.87 the day of expiry. You lose your entire investment of $1,110 because the options have no value.

b. *Long Call: partial recovery*. You buy 5 SPY 440 Calls for $222 each because you are confident the market will rise. It does, and in fact it closes "in-the-money" at

---

1 Ex-date: the date that a stock is ex-dividend; meaning, the last date necessary for a stock to be owned in order to be paid a dividend. If purchased after the ex-date, the new owner will not receive the dividend for that quarter.

441.25 the day of expiry. But you lose because the market didn't move enough to recoup your full investment. At expiry, your option is quoted at $1.20 bid, $1.25 ask. You sell at the bid and lose $500: **5 contracts × $120 each = $600 minus $1,100 initial cost = −$500**. These are, of course, frustrating trades. You guessed correctly—the market *did* rise—it just didn't rise *enough* to offset the cost of the option.

c. *Long Put: out-of-the-money expiry*. You buy 5 SPY 430 Puts for $254 each because you are confident the market will fall. It doesn't, and in fact it closes at 437.87 the day of expiry. You lose your entire investment of $1,270 because the options have no value.

d. *Long Put: partial recovery*. You buy 5 SPY 430 Puts for $254 each because you are confident the market will fall. It does, and in fact it closes "in-the-money" at 429.37 the day of expiry. But you lose because the market didn't move *enough* to recoup your full investment. At expiry, your option is quoted at $.60 bid, $.63 ask. You sell at the bid and lose $955: **5 contracts × $63 each = $315 minus $1,270 initial cost = −$955**. These are also very frustrating trades. You guessed correctly—the market *did* fall—it just didn't fall *enough* to offset the cost of the option.

Meanwhile, *the option seller* also carries risks, which are partially offset by the premium paid to them by the option buyer. Risks become particularly high if a ***call writer sells an uncovered, or "naked," call***. This means that the investor writes and sells a call, but does not own the stock that would be delivered if the option is exercised. The naked call writer has potentially unlimited risk because if a call is exercised, the seller of the call *must deliver the shares* to the option buyer, so the call option seller must buy the shares to fulfill the option's exercise terms (delivery of the shares to the call buyer). Here is an example:

a. **Short "naked" call: potential unlimited risk**. You are fully convinced that ChargePoint Systems will decline by at least 10%, so you sell five 30-strike calls for $2.02—even though you don't own the shares. You figure that you will collect the premium of $1,010 and the options will expire worthless. Instead, trading is halted pending news. Later that day, an announcement is made that the company has agreed to be purchased for an all-cash offer of $75 per share. The options are now worth $4,500 each. Because you do not have the shares to deliver, you can do two things; neither is good. You can close out the call position by buying them back for $45, or you can buy the stock at the market, $75 per share, and deliver them for $30 when the options are exercised—which will happen with 100% certainty. You lose $21,490: **–5 contracts × $202 each = $1,010 inflow minus $22,500 outflow from "bought-to-close" options = –$21,940**. Ouch!

For the short seller of a put, the situation is very different. Recall that the buyer of a put may, at its discretion, elect to exercise a put. When a put is exercised, it is *sold at the strike price to the writer* of that put. Therefore, **the writer of a naked put receives premium from the sale, but also may receive the stock**. If the writer wants the stock, she or he is better off writing a put and selling it and then being assigned the stock than placing a limit order. But if the stock continues to drop, losses are incurred. Here are examples:

a. **Short "naked" put: option position closed.** You think Plug Energy will rise because renewable energy is all the rage. You sell five $20 naked puts, but expect the shares to rise in value with your put position expiring worthless. You are excited to learn that someone out there paid you $180 each for them! Your enthusiasm wavers when you see that the stock had a weaker-than-expected earnings report and has opened at $15.82 per share. The options are now quoted at $4.27 bid, $4.45 ask. You elect to close the position or risk assignment. You close out the position by buying the contracts back for $445 each. You lose $1,345: **initial cash-flow from option sale of 5 contracts at $180 each = $900 minus 5 contracts × $445 each = (–$2,225 + $900) = –$1,345.**

b. **Short "naked" put: stock is assigned.** You are really enthused by Plug Energy and you want to own it. You sell five $20 naked put, which means you are obligated to buy the stock at $20 per share, and you are excited to learn that someone out there paid you $180 for them! Your enthusiasm wavers when you see that the stock had a weaker-than-expected earnings report and has opened at $15.82 per share. The options are now quoted at $4.27 bid, $4.45 ask. You elect to keep the puts and take assignment, buying them at $20, even though the stock is now at $15.87 a share on the ask. In your mind, you have a paper loss only because you are holding for the long term, and you still think the company has a bright future. As far as you are concerned, you didn't "buy" at $20 a share; **you really bought the shares for $20 per share—$1.80 in premium = $18.20 a share, and that becomes your cost basis**. You have a losing position, down $1,190, but now there is time for you to perhaps recoup your losses, and you wanted the stock at $20 anyway.

Option Order Types

These examples bring us to the last detail, which is the language used when orders are placed. As you can probably infer from the examples, there are two different buy order types and two different sell order types:

Orders When Opening a Position:

- **Buy-to-Open (BTO)**—you are purchasing a long option. You spend cash from your account.

- **Sell-to-Open (STO)**—you have written an option and are selling it to someone. You receive premium (income), and the cash is credited to your account.

Orders When Closing a Position:

- **Sell-to-Close (STC)**—you are selling an option you own. Cash is credited to your account.

- **Buy-to-Close (BTC)**—you are "canceling" your short option position by buying an offsetting position.

Summary and Conclusion

This chapter explores the specifics of put and call option contracts. We explained that options are a form of derivative offering contingent benefits and risks, depending on which side of the contract is taken—buyer or seller—and allows the transfer of ownership (and the risk of ownership) of the underlying only if certain price levels are achieved. We also discussed how options represent a leveraged instrument for those who wish to speculate or hedge.

The remainder of the chapter discusses specific attributes of the standardized option contract, including a definition of types, styles, classes, and series; as well as a discussion of the nature of expiry, strike prices, adjustments to options from stock splits, and what happens when an option is exercised. We concluded with an analysis of the risks of holding or selling-to-open option positions.

We can conclude from this discussion that options do possess an elevated level of risk because of the rights they contain. Their price moves with the direction of the underlying, so call options can be a "cheap" way to own a stock. Similarly, puts can be a safer and cheaper way to short a stock. But because they have a limited lifespan (very short term compared to the lifespan of a business), options can either deteriorate in value if the stock moves against your expectations or, as we will see shortly, options have a time premium that deteriorate as expiry approaches.

Going Forward

In the next chapter, we will get specific about how trades are made and who is involved in the trade. In Chapter 7, we will explore the Black-Scholes model, which will enable us to go into further depth concerning the factors that facilitate option values.

Chapter 6

The Options Micro-Market

The Purpose of the Options Market

> • The Purpose of Option Markets: There are two basic reasons why option markets exist today: one is to establish *trust and confidence* in each transaction, and the other is to *create adequate liquidity* so that investors can obtain options at reasonable prices.

In the introduction, we learned that options have been in existence for about half a millennium, but organized markets are only 50 years old. Now we acquire a sense of their current function and structure. Option exchanges are central to the trading of options for two basic reasons: to establish trust and to provide liquidity.

The continuous functioning of a market relies on **the trust of its customers** in the product and the process. The overall concept—established by both FINRA and the SEC, who are jointly responsible for oversight of all option exchanges—is to promote the "fair and orderly doctrine" by

- establishing terms of the standardized contracts
- establishing trading rules and procedures
- providing the physical plant, the hardware, and the software to facilitate trading

We have seen these concepts in the futures market and once again, the rationale is the same. By creating standardized contracts, these derivative instruments can be freely exchanged in any options exchange. Meanwhile, contracts are standardized to explicitly define the number of shares each option covers, their contingent value (the strike), and date of expiry. Furthermore, esoteric contract terms, such as procedures for stock ownership transfers and procedures in the (unlikely) event of third-party defaults, enables the investor to know exactly what each option represents: investors understand what they are buying and selling. Any concerns about operational unknowns are removed. Standardization also streamlines exchange recordkeeping and diminishes the chance of error on behalf of the exchanges themselves. Imagine the chaos that would ensue if each trader was able to change the terms of their option contracts. Each seller (buyer) would need to find that individual willing to buy (sell) that particular quantity of the underlying at the specific terms stipulated in each contract. Pricing would be near impossible, and trade volume would likely collapse. Usually, option rules and regulations are set by FINRA under guidance from the SEC. The SEC also regulates option trading by promoting contract guidelines, but mostly by overseeing activities of brokers and dealers, market-makers, and exchanges, as well as individual investors. All of this oversight activity is intended to maintain confidence in the trading system without impinging on operational efficiency. In the overwhelming number of cases, the existing oversight and regulatory system has worked remarkably well despite its complexity.

This leads us to the second reason markets exist, which is to **create sufficient liquidity** to the marketplace. Active trade volume creates a better environment for price discovery. We usually see wide spreads between bid and ask prices only in illiquid markets. If transactions are hours or days apart, confidence in the posted price is diminished. Thus, markets must be able to *fulfill all market orders* or they will lose customers to competitors. (How this is done is explained below.) This enlightened self-interest allows for a smooth and orderly transaction flow and promotes an accurate and robust quotation system. To assure smooth and liquid markets, markets

- link investors, brokers, and dealers on a centralized system, so that traders can establish firm and accurate bid and ask prices;
- guarantee trades by *taking the opposite side* of each transaction.

Trade orders for non-market orders such as limit, stop limit, stop, OCO, FOK, GTC, or all-or-none will not necessarily execute immediately. These will be entered into a dealer's order book and ranked. (The order book is not an actual "book," but is an electronic inventory ledger that lists all orders.) Order flow—which exchange, which dealer, or which market-maker—is managed by order routers that either seek out the highest bid, lowest ask, or an order match from a counterparty who has already placed a limit order.

The CBOE

All major option markets in the United States operate on *price-time priority schedules*. Order execution conformity is a function of exchange competition and enables seamless integration of trading platforms across markets. The CBOE remains the largest options exchange in the United States, but NASDAQ OMX and NYSE Euronext (including Arca and AMEX) follow closely behind. Approximately 80% of all option trades are now executed between these three exchanges.

The Chicago Board Options Exchange (CBOE) is the oldest and largest options exchange in the United States. The exchange has set the standard for other markets in many ways and continues its market share lead in United States option trading, as indicated in Table 6.1. The CBOE traditionally handles almost twice the volume of its nearest competitor, the Philadelphia Options Exchange, and more than its nearest two competitors combined. We will now look at the current technologies and processes regarding the execution of orders, who handles them, and their settlement. We will use the CBOE as the model, since it is the market leader and also the model for all other options exchanges.

TABLE 6.1 Monthly option contract volume by exchange, Oct. 2016–Sep. 2017.

EXCHANGE	2017									2016		
	SEP	AUG	JUL	JUN	MAY	APR	MAR	FEB	JAN	DEC	NOV	OCT
CBOE	92,559	109,887	84,573	95,696	96,180	87,693	102,469	87,846	82,728	82,585	100,696	77,764
PHLX	48,646	55,349	46,810	57,394	56,256	44,014	54,309	48,758	52,197	49,987	52,570	41,825
BATS	27,307	34,474	29,677	39,012	41,405	33,834	39,592	33,994	33,764	31,535	40,128	32,948
ISE	25,451	28,177	24,266	29,295	30,983	24,258	30,433	27,103	28,657	31,137	38,183	32,451
NASDAQ	25,016	30,044	26,248	31,595	31,104	28,713	31,887	25,339	28,534	24,065	28,897	25,375
ARCA	24,867	28,593	24,289	29,125	24,717	18,219	25,999	19,587	20,703	26,057	41,375	29,469
AMEX	23,066	25,809	21,320	26,978	24,195	20,797	25,552	20,573	22,267	25,529	27,862	22,626
ALL OTHERS	58,197	68,649	55,883	65,300	60,941	52,143	64,234	60,198	59,827	57,587	53,485	47,150

Source: CBOE

Order Routing

All option markets today are currently an order-driven electronic auction and also a quote-driven screen-based continuous market. But progress toward complete automation is ongoing. To demonstrate the process, we will examine the mechanics at the CBOE, which is still the largest options market in the United States.

Currently at the CBOE, the selection of a platform to fill an order depends on the complexity and size of the order. "Complexity" refers to the structure of the options order—how many different options are extant in the order—whereas "size" refers to the number of single contracts or the number of multi-leg spreads. CBOE is constantly updating its routing and platform technologies. Their intent is to provide greater order efficiencies, thereby further reducing exchange fees and transaction costs. Most orders today are electronically routed to the CBOE ORS (Order Routing System) platform, which directs the order to the electronic order book of the specific TPH who clears that particular class of option. ORS thus functions as the main order hub, and it processes over 90% of all CBOE orders and automatically directs orders based on CBOE-proprietary algorithms and conditions. Market orders are then sent to the Retail Automatic Execution System (RAES), which executes retail market orders automatically and almost instantaneously. RAES bid-ask quotes are constantly updated by the market. Any order not fillable via RAES enters the CBOE eBOOK on a first-in first-out basis. CBOE eBOOK processes approximately 30% of ORS orders, with an average turnaround of 21 seconds based on 2019 data:

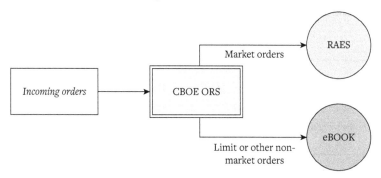

FIGURE 6.1 Electronic order flow to TPH holders. Market orders fill immediately; average fill for eBOOK orders is 21 seconds.

Market-makers are able to assess risk, process trades, and monitor market conditions in real time. Upon execution, trade information is immediately and simultaneously sent to both the broker and the Options Price Reporting Authority (OPRA), which is the central authority for all listed options. OPRA is responsible for immediately sending all the options exchanges' data to vendors and brokerage firms. CBOE also developed its own, proprietary screen-based trading system in 2013 called CBOE*direct*. This screen-based trading system is intended to provide traders and investors with expanded trading hours as well as greater informational efficiencies.

"Fair and Orderly" Rationale for CBOE Trade Rules

The purpose of exchange by-laws, procedures, and rules are to enable both the governance of the exchange and to assure that markets operate in a "fair and orderly" manner. Indeed, it is the job of regulators to eliminate or limit both "unfairness" and "disorderliness." As the market structure exists today, the arbiters of the meaning of "fair and orderly markets" are the administrators of the exchanges and secondarily, federal regulatory boards, commissions, and offices. These rules and regulations are, in turn, necessitated by the exchanges to engender trust in the exchanges themselves, obviously necessary to assure the markets' continued financial viability.

On the federal level, the Securities and Exchange Commission encourages exchanges to police exchange clearing and trading members. Accordingly, exchanges enable rule-making authority by the exchange board, subject to SEC approval. To the extent that the SEC embraces exchange regulations, SEC rules tend to mirror extant rules put in force by the exchanges and their respective clearing corporations.

Option Trade Mechanics

The NBBO

- <u>Price-Time Priority Schedule</u>: A sequence of order execution whereby orders are *first ranked according to their price; then ranked on time of day entered.* Contrast with the pro-rata model, in which orders go to specialists who act as dealers.

As you may recall, in the past, options were traded OTC by dealers who posted prices in booklets. The creation of CBOE (and later, its competitors) linked these diverse broker/

dealers in a computer network which posted all bid-ask prices. Only the highest bid and lowest ask is posted as "the quote," and is the point of transaction known as the **National Best Bid and Offer** (**NBBO**). (The terms "bid" and "ask" are often confusing for a neophyte trader. For those who are new to all this, look at it this way: the terms "bid" and "ask" are from the perspective of the dealer or market-maker. If you want to buy, you want to know the cost, and the dealer would say, "I am ASKING x." Similarly, if you want to sell, the dealer says, "I BID x for the option." If you like the price, you transact.) A typical Level II quotation would look like this:

TABLE 6.2 Hypothetical sample of Level II market depth quotation for a single option issue of SPDR Dow Jones Industrial Average ETF Trust (DIA).

DEALER	BID	SIZE	SIZE	ASK	DEALER
AA	1.30	25	17	1.37	DD
BB	1.29	15	9	1.39	AA
CC	1.28	7	3	1.40	EE

In this example, the NBBO would be 1.30 Bid, 1.37 Ask. This means that a market order to buy would immediately fill at $1.37 ($137.00 for the option, plus commission and exchange fees), and a market order to sell would immediately fill at $1.30 ($130.00 for the option, plus commission and exchange fees). If two orders are entered simultaneously (a near impossibility), sequence is based on type of order and the time received. From this we see that option trades are filled similar to stocks—the buyer *at the market* buys at the NBBO ask price and the seller sells at the bid price. Market orders enable investors to transact within nanoseconds. In exchange for rapid trade access (called "immediacy" in academic jargon), dealers are rewarded the NBBO, a *maximum* bid-ask spread at the market.

The exchange facilitates trades by allowing intermediaries called *market-makers* to buy and hold inventory of options for their own account. These entities are **only obligated to buy or sell inventory when market orders are received**. Market-makers are free to transact orders "inside the spread" (i.e., prices that are more advantageous to the buyer or seller), but they aren't obligated to do so. When the transaction is completed, the account identities and security description is immediately transferred electronically to the clearing agent (the OCC for the CBOE), who is responsible for matching buyer and seller and for the proper crediting and debiting of each account.

Option Market Participants

All markets are built to serve individual investors' needs, so it is the individual investor who retains the most important role in price discovery. However, because options are derivatives, with a pricing regimen derived from underlying assets but also with pricing driven by the peculiarities of options, *market-makers* are critical participants in the options market.

Market-Makers

> • Market-Makers: Option dealers who provide liquidity when there is no immediate market-priced inventory. *Market-makers provide immediacy* by guaranteeing trades at market and can be in the form of a corporation, SEC-registered broker-dealers, partnerships, and even sole proprietorships.

Considering the size of the CBOE, when literally billions of options are traded each year, there are relatively few market-makers. In 2018, there were only 104 market-makers registered with the CBOE. All of these entities now use algorithms in some capacity; either to manage inventory, control risk by hedging, or in the process of setting optimal pricing for market orders. This last function—*setting optimal pricing for market orders*—is adjunct to price-setting forces of supply and demand. Market-makers are therefore key participants in the price discovery process.

Types of Market-Makers; Trading Privilege Holders (TPH)

> • Trading Privilege Holder (TPH): A certificate held by a market-maker, either as an individual or as an organization that *enables the holder to be registered with the Exchange for the purpose of making transactions* as a dealer-specialist on the Exchange.

The CBOE has different classifications of market-makers. The differences between the types of market-makers do not so much constitute a hierarchy as much as it assigns distinct roles. However, some options may become more favored than others, with greater potential for market-maker profits. The tendency is that an exchange "rewards" the most efficient market-makers by providing them with authority to make markets in the most liquid issues, such as options on the SPDR S&P 500 Index.

To be a CBOE member market-maker, the candidate must become designated as a Trading Privilege Holder (TPH), which entails submittal of a detailed application to the CBOE. *CBOE rules require that all market-makers be TPH holders.* The CBOE has authorized 2,500 TPH certificates and has sole authority to issue more or reduce that number. Despite the potential value of a TPH designation, less than half of authorized TPH certificates have been issued. In fact, the number of TPH members has been in decline in recent years, despite their potential value. Any existing market-maker is incentivized to adhere strictly to exchange rules and behaviors or risk losing their TPH status. The intent is to encourage risk-averse market-making behaviors.

The CBOE naturally retains the right to terminate the registration of a market-maker if it deems the market-maker unqualified or "has failed to properly perform as a Market-maker" (Rule 8.2 of the Exchange). The privilege granted to make markets in certain options is governed by the Exchange, which "appoints" registered market-makers to certain classes. Appointment criteria are stipulated in Rule 8.3 and give deference to the market-maker's financial capability, the need for competition because of the popularity of a given class, and the abilities of the market-maker to handle expected volume.

Regulators and Regulations

> - <u>Regulators and Regulations</u>: The mandate to regulate trading has been *relegated to the exchanges*, subject to oversight by regulatory authorities. Therefore, any entity that has membership privileges at any option exchange *must comply with exchange rules.*

The CBOE and other exchanges are under the jurisdiction of the SEC for equity, equity index options, and ETF product options. Options on commodities, also traded through the CBOE, are regulated through the CFTC. However, the overarching *modus operandi* is that the exchanges regulate themselves, coordinating their regulatory activities with the SEC and CFTC as well as other options exchanges so that regulatory goals are uniform and complete.

Regulation of Market-Makers

CBOE rules affect the behavior of market-makers by: (1) instituting *capital balance requirements*; (2) adopting rules that address *administrative and structural issues*; (3) creating stringent *margin rules*; (4) adopting rules to regulate *short-selling and risk management*; and (5) rules that govern *bid-ask behavior*. The CBOE also conducts a thorough vetting of market-maker candidates who apply for registration with the Exchange. Rules are vigorously enforced: any undisciplined, disorderly, or unfair market behaviors would likely inspire federal regulatory intervention, a condition exchanges generally don't want to see.

The first two categories set organizational standards, generally unique to the needs of the options market. The third category is intended to assure the smooth ("orderly") operation of markets by encouraging market-maker liquidity. The fourth category is intended to assure reasonable ("fair") option pricing practices.

TPH Capital Requirements

Capital requirements of TPH market-makers are closely monitored. All details of market-maker financial sources must be disclosed to the Exchange. Furthermore, market-makers cannot transact any business unless there is an "effective Letter of Guarantee" that has been issued by a clearing Trading Permit Holder and filed with the Exchange. A market-maker is also required to file a separate letter of guarantee to *each clearing Trading Permit Holder with whom the market-maker transacts business*. The importance of these guarantees is obvious, given the implications which could occur if counterparty failures were permitted without recourse.

To underscore the necessity of avoiding counterparty defaults, to maintain their TPH, all market-makers must maintain a balance of at least $2.5 million in cash or cash equivalents by the close of business each day. This amount must be free and clear of any claim or margin. Further, a member must notify the OCC in writing by close of business the following day if net capital falls below *either* $2,500,000 *or* below an amount equal to 10% of total member indebtedness, *whichever is greater* [emphasis mine].

Market-makers are disallowed to be as leveraged as banks. The initial aggregate principal amount of a member's "satisfactory subordination agreements" cannot be more than 70% of a member's initial total indebtedness.[1] Also, any member faces involuntary liquidation of

---

1   As it relates to equity options, **satisfactory subordination agreements** are counterparty obligations created through naked or spread option positions by and between the TPH and the OCC or other members (Code of Federal Regulations §240.15c3-1d).

assets to cover subordination agreements if, after marking to market, net capital falls below $2,500,000 at the time of market close. A member cannot enable an opening position—long or short—if the capital minimum is breached. In other words, a TPH can utilize margin, but they are also subject to the possibility of margin call and forced liquidation. Thus, even very large firms can face forced liquidation if they become too highly leveraged.

Liquidity of clearing members is always the primary goal. TPH firms cannot withdraw funds from subordinated loan accounts without the direct written consent of the OCC, *even if the loan accounts have matured,* if there is a danger that by withdrawal capital minima will be breached. The intention of the restriction is to prevent member capital withdrawal in the event the member is unable to cover counterparty default. The consequence to these member firms is that member capital becomes nonfungible: firms become unable to seek higher returns outside market making. Members may prefer to take larger risks but cannot do so without endangering their member standing.

Trading Privilege Assignment by CBOE

In addition to the TPH, which all market-makers must maintain, the CBOE awards a *tiered preferential system to those who maintain continuous bid-ask quotes for their assigned issues.* In exchange for this, the CBOE can designate a market-maker as: *Preferred Market-Makers* (PMM), *Lead Market-Makers* (LMM), or *Designated Primary Market-Makers* (DPM). A DPM has an obligation to provide "continuous" bid and ask prices *in all option series in the DPM's appointed option classes.* In return, the DPM is guaranteed certain rights to participate in each trade and has first rights to order flow to and from the exchange, subject to certain limitations. Such participation can be lucrative, as it may mean per-option order flow fees, credits, or profit sharing, if any. If no DPM is active in a certain class of options, independent market-makers provide bid-ask prices electronically.

Similarly, an LMM must risk some of its own capital to buy and sell ETFs (and their options) to maintain their sponsored ETF liquidity. In exchange for providing continuous bid-ask quotes in their assigned securities and option classes, firms acting as LMMs receive rebates on exchange fees. Some also provide start-up financing for an ETF from exchanges, provided that the LMM then exclusively list the ETF and its derivatives with the exchange. In these instances, the LMM is given proprietary market making rights to that ETF and its respective option types.

Privileges afforded a PMM stipulate that, in exchange for providing continuous quotes on appointed option classes, transactions involving the trade of those appointed classes by the PMM (including legs of complex orders) provide exchange fee discounts of 40% to 50%, depending on the number of market-makers in the same class, type, and strike. However, no additional exchange discounts can overlay these transactions.

TPH Option Position Regulation

CBOE regulations determine market-maker limits for both options and their underlying securities, including size of issue and average daily volume. The CBOE requires registered, NMS-listed shares characterized by a minimum of 7 million shares, widely held by a minimum of 2,000 holders, and with at least 2,400,000 shares of volume over the preceding year. Other regulations concern option listing criteria for shares of restructured companies, partnership units, ETFs, and ADRs.

TABLE 6.3 CBOE option contract position limits.

6-month Underlying Volume:	<20 million	20 million	40 million	80 million	100 million
Total Float:	<40 million	40 million	120 million	24 million	300 million
Contract Limits:	**25,000**	**50,000**	**75,000**	**200,000**	**250,000**

The CBOE has set limitations on the number of contracts held, or escrow accounts affecting the number of shares held, tied to overall volume levels, as illustrated in Table 6.3 (above). By today's standards, virtually no listed issues will be subject to CBOE position limits, but could matter if enough market-making firms withdraw from that business. For example, at present, ETF limitations range from 300,000 contracts for the DIAMONDS Trust (DIA), to 900,000 contracts for the PowerShares QQQ Trust (QQQ). In the instance of DIA, with open interest of slightly more than 900,000 contracts, fewer than four market-makers would violate position limit rules, and the same is true for QQQ. The justification for these position limits is based on the concern that concentrated positions could exacerbate volatility (even triggering market circuit breakers). But even these larger position limits could see all market-maker activity concentrated among a handful of market-makers.

TPH Bid-Ask Quote Spread Regulations

The CBOE has authority to establish bid-ask differentials temporarily or permanently for various classes and/or types of options traded on the Exchange. These modifications are almost always coordinated with actions taken by other options exchanges such as NYSE Archipelago and PHLX. The intent of these rules is to balance exchange commitment to fairness and its need for orderly trade execution.

Based on precedent, it became clear that sometimes an underlying price at auction became unruly and volatile, which can cause the bid-ask regimen to become either too wide or too narrow. Usually, these regulations are imposed on securities with small float and light volume. For example, any orders that lie outside the National Best Bid and Offer (NBBO) are subject to possible rejection at the open.[2] (Orders outside the bid-ask spread are referred to as "too executable" because, from the perspective of market-makers, more profitable, being higher than the reported ask and lower than the reported bid.) The CBOE uses the NBBO as reference prices immediately prior to conducting a trading auction. If an option series has buy and sell interest at locked or crossed prices[3] before the open, an opening auction is required to commence to ensure a fair and orderly market in the series. More importantly, certain "legal widths" for a market-maker's quotes are required. A "legal width" is defined per the schedule on Table 6.4 below. Any series requiring an opening auction will not open until a legal width market has been established. This functionality is available during pre-open for single-leg as well as multi-leg orders.

TABLE 6.4 Exchange-defined bid-ask spread limits.

LEGAL WIDTH, MAX:	$0.25	$0.40	$0.50	$0.80	$1.00
WHEN NBBO IS:	<$2.00	$2.00–$5.00	$5.00–$10.00	$10.00–$20.00	>$20.00
PERCENT SPREAD:	12.5%–100%+	12.5%–19.9%	5%–10%	4%–8%	<2%

As can be seen in Table 6.4, the percentage spread trends down as options become more expensive, even as the allowed spread width in absolute terms is permitted to widen. Higher-priced options are typical for both deep in-the-money options and for near-the-money options of high-per-share value equities and ETFs. The former poses a particular illiquidity risk for market-makers, while the latter form inventory holding risk, since the spread may be inadequate to accommodate small changes in price. Meanwhile, deep out-of-the money options typically carry small prices so that the prescribed 12.5% maxima for cheap options may also be inadequate. Meanwhile, the most active options (near-the-money; nearest expiry) are

---

2   This is known as an NBBO reject. The NBBO reject process is intended as a fail-safe procedure to avoid orders erroneously placed.
3   "Locked" prices occur when the underlying moves up or down, daily limit (in particular, a commodity). Prices remain at that price level until auction moves the price away from the locked price. "Cross" prices (also "opening cross") refer to the process required to accommodate price jumps between close of the previous day and the open of the next day's opening. These jumps may occur as a consequence of either favorable or unfavorable news.

limited to spreads of up to about 20%. This is plenty of room for market-makers to adjust spreads to induce or discourage buyers and sellers (which market-makers regularly do as a means of controlling inventory risk). However, the market rarely exceeds a percent bid-ask spread of 12% of the option value.

The CBOE has developed algorithms (HALO-O, among others) to discourage large price jumps either at the open or during trade hours. Most equities can be subject to news-driven overnight price jumps. Inventory holding risk, if unhedged, is very real indeed, especially for short, uncovered option positions.

Market-Makers and Price Dynamics

It is simplistic and wrong to assume that market-makers have no impact on option pricing, but it would be very wrong to assume that market-makers conspire to earn undue profits. Market-makers carry considerable inventory risk, which makes them particularly risk-averse. Market-makers, being tightly regulated by exchange rules, place their own *non-immediate (limit) orders* in good faith, usually to clear inventory at favorable prices. For example, suppose market-maker *y* provided immediacy by selling 100 call option contracts at $2.18 to various buyers. Market-maker *y* now holds an inventory position of 100 *short call options* with attendant contingency risk. The market-maker places a day limit sell order at $2.17, despite the current ask at $2.19. This order will fill if the ask price retreats to the favorable $2.17 level and would clear unwanted inventory and eliminate contingent risk. Algorithms run by market-makers perform these order entries automatically when inventory levels change, setting a favorable *passive market-maker order* at a price level with high probability of fill, per calculations performed by the algorithm, with market data dynamically stored continuously. As the business day moves closer to 4 p.m. Eastern time, the urgency to cover short positions becomes much more intense. No market-maker wants to receive a noncompliance order from the OCC. The market-maker then has choices to make: lower the ask of their inventory, or hedge the short calls by purchasing shares in the underlying. This activity can be seen almost every day during closing moments when prices gyrate noisily. The price moves are never enough to cause a sensation; they are more like a wobble, but it does indicate actions to clear risk imbalance before market close.

Order Splitting by Traders

Order splitting is a process whereby large accumulation of trader liquidation orders are broken into smaller orders and distributed over time and venue. The intent is to reduce overall transaction costs by reducing supply pressure at a given exchange and time. Instead, a series of smaller orders are scattered to prevent sudden and substantial changes in bid or ask prices. Consider trader x, who is short 500 contracts of a particular call. The trader will break the block into several smaller parcels, whose size would be determined by previous trade sizes, level of open interest, and daily volume. If the average volume of this particular option is 300 contracts per day, this trader would probably require several days to close the position. Trader x would use an algorithm to model the best approach from a cost-benefit standpoint, given past history of supply-demand dynamics of this and similar options. If, for example, the size in question is determined to be 50 contracts, the algorithm could model the approximate effect ten 50-contract blocks would have on option ask prices. However, trader x could also legally "hide" some or all of these trades by entering the order electronically via eBOOK at CBOE, NYSE Arca, and NASD Precise, as well as through the traditional market-maker. Because no central limit order book exists in the United States at present, trader x could place limit orders for all trades so that the actual size of the position would remain unknown.

Trade Clearing Mechanics

> - <u>Trade Clearing</u>: The process of *matching the buyers and sellers* of option contracts, or matching option assignments between short and long option holders, as well as all buy-to-close orders from option writers.

The Options Clearing Corporation (OCC)

The Options Clearing Corporation (OCC) was originally a wholly owned subsidiary of the CBOE but is now jointly owned by its option exchange member firms. The OCC issues all listed options and controls and affects all exercises and assignments, acts as the counterparty to clear all option trades involving its member firms, and ensures that sales are transacted according to the current rules. The OCC *guarantees all trades by acting as the other party* to all purchases and sales of options. Because the OCC is *always a party to an option transaction*, an option writer can close out his position by buying the same contract back ("buy to close"), even while the contract buyer retains his position, because the OCC draws from a pool of contracts with no connection to the original contract writer and buyer.

The OCC itself is subject to oversight by both the Securities and Exchange Commission (SEC) and the Commodities Futures Trading Commission (CFTC). Under its SEC oversight, OCC clears transactions for put and call options on common stocks and other equity issues, stock indexes, foreign currencies, interest rate composites, and **single-stock futures**. In regard to options on futures, the OCC is a registered Derivatives Clearing Organization (DCO) and is authorized by the CFTC to clear and settle transactions in both **futures and options on futures**.

Mechanics of Option Exercise and Assignment

> - <u>Assignment</u>: The *transfer of underlying assets* from the owner of an option to the writer of an option. Stock assigned due to the *exercise of a short put* means the writer of that put (the party that "sold-to-open") buys the stock at the strike from the counterparty who owns the put option. Stock assigned due to the *exercise of a short call* means the writer of that call (the party that "sold-to-open") sells the stock at the strike to the counterparty who owns the call option.

Upon notification, exercise instructions are sent to the OCC, which then *assigns* the exercise to the Clearing Member who is short the same option. The Clearing Member will then assign the exercise to that client who is short that option. The customer is selected either on a first-in, first-out basis or other random procedure approved by the exchanges, such as a lottery. *There is no direct connection between an option writer and a buyer—each is unknown to the other.*

If an option holder wants to exercise her option before expiry, a so-called "early exercise," she must notify her broker of her intent. It is the legal duty of the option holder to notify her broker to exercise the option before the cut-off time. If the option holder does not desire to exercise in advance of cut-off, if the option is ITM, it is general practice by brokerages to automatically exercise American-style options. However, for European-style options, the option holder must notify intent to exercise. If not, a European option *will expire worthless*. Because options have a time value in addition to intrinsic value, most options are not exercised early. However, there is nothing to prevent someone from exercising an option, even if it is not profitable to do so, and sometimes it does occur, which is why anyone who is short an option should expect the possibility of being assigned early. In practice, any option ITM by even $.01 will automatically exercise.

Frequency of Option Exercise

The most current data suggests that almost half of ITM short put and call options were closed out by investors executing buy-to-close orders. Approximately one-third of short put and call options expired worthless, and only one in five were exercised.

Summary and Conclusions

We covered the basic mechanics of orders sent to the option markets in the United States. Our model was the CBOE, the largest options market in the world. The CBOE has been modernizing since its inception and today is completely electronic and automatic for market orders. Non-market orders, however, are routed to a specific market-maker for execution. These orders include all limit orders and most complex orders such as multi-leg spreads. We learned that market-makers have an important role in price discovery and have flexibility in setting the bid-ask spread, provided they do not violate exchange rules. Market-makers may widen or contract these bid-ask spreads to accommodate inventory management objectives.

The OCC is the clearing agent for all option transactions, both at CBOE and other exchanges. Clearing is a vital function that assures smooth transfer of assets when exchanged. The OCC also facilitates all options that exercise and assignments resultant from exercise.

Chapter 7

The Pricing of Options

Background

Prior to the early-to-mid 1970s, option pricing was wrought through over-the-counter trading and was therefore the province of only the most sophisticated and esoteric clients. At the time, there was no options market *per se*, but there were many stock warrants[1] traded at that time, which were structured similarly to call options. Only a few dealers existed who negotiated prices between party and counterparty. This condition was, of course, suboptimal and consequently became the focus of vigorous academic pursuit. By applying the principles of Treynor's capital asset pricing model (CAPM), advancements in stochastic calculus, and the relevant probability applications of Edward Thorpe, the development of the Black-Scholes model emerged. Its development revolutionized options trading globally and earned Robert Merton, Myron Scholes, and Fischer Black (posthumously) the Nobel Prize in Economics in 1997. Today, the Black-Scholes model is widely accepted as the theoretical cornerstone of option price theory.

The Black-Scholes Model

> - <u>Black-Scholes Model</u>: The Black-Scholes model is a descriptive *mathematical model that prescribes the price dynamics of European-style options*. It was later revised by Robert Merton at MIT to include the effects of dividends on option pricing.

---

1   Stock warrants are securities that entitle the holder to buy the underlying stock of the issuing company at a fixed price called exercise price until the expiration date, just like a call option. However, warrants are issued by the underlying corporate body and usually have a multiple-year life. They are frequently attached to, and separable from, either a preferred share or bond offering as an investor incentive to purchase the underlying security. Once very common, they have been mostly supplanted by options not originated by the underlying entity.

What Is the Black-Scholes Model?

The Black-Scholes model (BSM) is a mathematical model, published in 1973, which describes the dynamics of a financial market containing derivative instruments. The famous Black-Scholes formula was constructed from the model's principal equation (the so-called Black-Scholes equation), providing a robust calculator which can provide *a theoretical estimate of the price of European-style* options. The formula led to a boom in options trading and provided mathematical legitimacy to the activities of the Chicago Board Options Exchange and other options markets around the world. It is widely used, although often with some adjustments, by options market participants.

BSM Model Assumptions

In the absence of actual data involving option markets, BSM embarked *tabula rasa*. For practical purposes, therefore, the builders of the model made several assumptions, all of which simplified reality to make the model more accessible. These original assumptions have been grouped in various ways over the years, but my personal preference is to categorize them as (1) assumptions about market behavior; (2) economic theory assumptions; and (3) practical assumptions instituted to make the model more generalized.

Assumptions Regarding Market Behavior

Random Walk. Consistent with the efficient market hypothesis, CAPM, and portfolio theory, price movement in risky asset markets such as equities were assumed to follow a random walk.[2] This is a broad assumption and necessary so that the model would not carry a directional bias.

Prices Are Normally (and Lognormally) Distributed. In other words, very large moves are rare; smaller moves predominate. Further, up/down price action, if plotted as a percent of price, would reveal a bell-shaped curve. This assumption has been challenged repeatedly over the years and remains a significant thorn in the side of efficient market theorists.[3] The rationale for using lognormal distribution is clear: negative asset prices are an impossibility; lognormal distributions are always positive.

---

2   *Random walk is not the same as random*, but is rather a Markovian process whereby each successive price is dependent *only* on the immediately previous price point, and predictability as to direction is unknowable. History is an irrelevancy in random walks.

3   See, for example, Benoit Mandelbrot, *The (Mis)Behaviour of Markets*, Basic Books (2004) and Andrew Lo & A. C. MacKinlay, *A Non-Random Walk Down Wall Street*, Princeton University Press (1999).

Economic Theory Assumptions

Markets are Efficient. It is necessary to assume that information is immediately absorbed in the market and information is free flowing in a "semi-strong" context.

Standard Deviation as the Metric for Risk. Throughout all of finance theory, including equity price theory and CAPM, lay the belief that risk is *defined and measured as the standard deviation of price distribution* over time. The greater the range (dispersion) of prices, the greater the risk. However, BSM goes farther: volatility (another word for risk) in the BSM world is *constant and known in advance.* Therefore, an investor may not know the direction of a stock price tomorrow, but they can predict the stock's volatility and *probability* of price. (Careful thought reveals that price and risk are not the same thing.)

Borrowing and Lending. Investors have the ability to borrow and lend any amount of cash at the risk-free rate. This assumption is consistent with CAPM.

Short Selling and Long Buying. Investors can short or buy any stock at any quantity, even fractional shares. This assumption is also consistent with CAPM.

There Is No Arbitrage. This assumption is an offshoot of the efficient market hypothesis: riskless profits are assumed to be impossible.

Practical Assumptions

The Market Is Frictionless. A frictionless market has no transaction costs. This is, of course, patently false, but that is not the point of the assumption. Making this assumption makes the model easier to build and less cumbersome to use. This assumption is easy to rectify in specific application.

Interest Rates Are Constant and Risk Free. History shows us that interest rates are rarely constant, even risk-free rates. Usually, "risk-free rates" means the one-year treasury rate.

No Early Exercise. The model assumes that only European-style options are being priced. To date, attempts to modify the model assuming early exercise have proven elusive.

Equities Pay No Dividends. This assumption is easy to rectify in specific application and was indeed rectified eventually by Merton Miller in 1978.

The BSM Equation and the BSM Formula

- <u>Black-Scholes Equation</u>: The Black-Scholes equation is the summary findings of the original academic paper wherein it was *determined that it was possible to create* a *risk-free trade*, without arbitrage, given certain assumptions about markets and option pricing.

- Black-Scholes Formulas: The Black-Scholes formulas are *the models used widely today to determine the theoretically correct value of European puts and calls.*

Given the assumptions and limitations listed above, Black and Scholes derived the famous Black-Scholes formula from the broader Black-Scholes equation, which is at the heart of the option pricing model. The Black-Scholes formula is an expression of the current value of a European call option on a stock that pays no dividend. This is the Black-Scholes *equation,* a fairly straightforward partial derivative equation (PDE):

$$\frac{\partial V}{\partial t} + \frac{1}{2}\sigma^2 S^2 \frac{\partial^2 V}{\partial S^2} + rS\frac{\partial V}{\partial S} - rV = 0 \qquad \text{[Eq. 7.1]}$$

It holds for all $S > 0$ and $t \in [0,T)$. The equation is frequently reformulated by finance academicians and practitioners:

$$\frac{\partial V}{\partial t} + \frac{1}{2}\sigma^2 S^2 \frac{\partial^2 V}{\partial S^2} = rV - rS\frac{\partial V}{\partial S} \qquad \text{[Eq. 7.1a]}$$

where V is the option price, S is the stock price, r is the risk-free rate, t is time, and σ is the stock's historic volatility. In brief, the equation stipulates that an option and a stock can, in combination, create a condition of zero price differences—regardless of stock price conditions, volatility, or time, since these factors affect the option price as well. The key takeaway is that the *Black-Scholes equation demonstrated that it is possible to perfectly hedge an underlying position by employing options* and by doing so sharply reduce risk.[4]

Let's analyze Equation 7.1: (a) the first term, $\frac{\partial V}{\partial t}$, describes the relationship of the option value over time (this subject will be discussed more fully in Chapters 9 and 10); (b) the second term, $\frac{1}{2}\sigma^2 S^2 \frac{\partial^2 V}{\partial S^2}$, is the set of lognormally distributed random values that stocks undertake over time, affected by of the stock's volatility times the partial derivative, representing the value of the given option as a function of stock price, $\frac{\partial^2 V}{\partial S^2}$. Added to these terms is (c) the third term, $rS\frac{\partial V}{\partial S}$, which is *the future value* of the stock times the first derivative of option price as a function of the stock price. The sum of terms a, b, and c is equal to the expected future

---

4 Fischer Black & Myron Scholes. (1973). The pricing of options and corporate liabilities. *Journal of Political Economy* 81 (3): p. 637. https//doi.org/10.1086/260062

value of the option itself, rV, so that, if subtracted from the sum of the other three, equals zero. This is, therefore, the "perfect hedge."

- <u>Theory: There Is Only One Correct Option Value</u>: The value would be the proper hedge *leading to a zero change in value* after the hedge is instituted.

The all-important implication of this revelation was that there exists *one and only one "correct" value for an option*. Further, the *Black-Scholes formulas* identified the generalized factors that affect the value of options. The formulas are:

$$\text{For Calls:} \quad V_c = S_0 N(d_1) - Ke^{-r\tau} N(d_2) \qquad \text{[Eq. 7.2]}$$

$$\text{For Puts:} \quad V_p = Ke^{-r\tau} N(-d_2) - S_0 N(-d_1) \qquad \text{[Eq. 7.3]}$$

These formulas express the call value as the current stock price times a probability factor $N(d_1)$, minus the discounted exercise payment (i.e., the strike value K) times a different probability factor $N(d_2)$. The put value is expressed as the discounted exercise payment times $N(d_2)$, minus the current stock price times $N(d_1)$. (Puts and calls are reciprocal to each other: one rises as the other falls in price). In shorter language: an option's value is the difference between a risk-adjusted stock price and the strike price, modified by a risk-adjusted discount rate: *option values are the arithmetic difference between the expected future value of a stock at time τ and the risk-adjusted strike price of the option.*

- <u>The Theoretical Value of an Option</u>: The value of an option, based on the BSM, is *the arithmetic difference between the stock price and the option strike*, subject to probabilistic considerations (i.e., speculative expectation).

This is all well and good, but what about the scary-looking variables in the formulas? What do they mean? The simplified answer is that call value (Equation 7.2) is equal to its expected future value minus its strike price, modified by the effects of probabilities over time. The same is true for a put option (Equation 7.3) but in reverse, *since its value rises as stock prices decline*: its value is equal to its strike price modified by the effects of probabilities over time, *minus* expected future value of the stock.

BSM Variables

Despite the seemingly esoteric nature of the Black-Scholes model, the beauty of BSM is its relative simplicity of form. Only a few variables populate the model. We saw these listed above as **V** (option price), **S** (stock price), **r** (risk-free rate), **t** (time), and **σ** (asset volatility).

Euler's Constant e

The number **e** (Euler's number, a constant, not a variable), which is evident in both formulas, is an irrational number that we see expressed in all kinds of phenomena—and most importantly in this instance, exponential functions such as compounding and discounting. Here, we see it expressed as the term $e^{-q\tau}$ affecting the probability function $N(d_1)$ and $N(d_2)$. These notations express option values as the *likelihood of the option being exercisable* at expiry. These values change over time, with a long-term maturity having less impact on K than a short-term maturity.[5] However, at maturity, $e^{-q\tau} = 1$, and the option value is equal only to the difference of the risk-adjusted value of S minus the value of K, the strike price.

This notation solved the potential Black-Scholes problem of the calculation of possible negative option prices. Consider Equation 7.2 again. Notice that the strike price is discounted such that if time goes to zero, $e^{-r\tau} = 1$, when the second term becomes $K \times N(d_2)$. But if the option is OTM, the probability of exercise is zero, and the second term becomes zero. This holds true for the first term as well: if that probability is equal to zero, then the first term is also zero. Therefore, the option carries no value if it is OTM at expiry.

However, although we know that the probability of an option being exercised is either zero (OTM) or one (ATM) at expiry, there are infinitely more points of time before expiry. The role of the significant and mysterious variables $N(d_1)$ and $N(d_2)$ that underlay the entire option valuation effort are discussed next.

The Variable N(d$_x$)

- N(d$_x$): *N(d1) is the risk-adjusted probability that an option will be exercised. N(d2) is the likelihood that the value of the underlying will be greater than the strike.*

---

5   Remember that a negative exponent such as $e^{-q\tau} = \frac{1}{e^{q\tau}}$ means that as $-q\tau$ gets larger, the quotient gets smaller.

The nature of $N(d_x)$ was not developed by Black and Scholes at the time their paper was published; nor was it a subject by early theoreticians until the late 1980s. Ultimately, the accepted definition of $N(d_1)$ and $N(d_2)$ follows: $N(d_1)$ is the risk-adjusted probability that the option will be exercised, and $N(d_2)$ is the factor by which the present value of a contingent receipt of the stock exceeds the current stock price. (It is important to realize that option exercise is not completely random but is closely correlated to the stock price; or for early exercise, an ex-dividend date.) Since modern market theory stipulates that stock prices are Markov processes, $N(d_1)$ and $N(d_2)$ are therefore *standard normal probability density functions* for a set of prices with a mean of μ and standard deviation σ. Details follow.

The exact meaning of $N(d_1)$ and $N(d_2)$ is of great import today due to the widespread use of option pricing models and algorithmic trading through the use of AI among other techniques. Simply throwing in a variable such as d_1 and d_2 is algorithmically inadequate. Therefore, since the late 1980s, the exact nature of these variables has been a motherlode for finance and financial engineering research. Before reaching its most recent iteration, the inspirational sources employed to describe stock movements were from physics. Specifically, d_1 is constructed to assume that stock prices follow a specific Markov process known as a *geometric Brownian motion*, defined in BSM terms as $S_O e^{-r\tau}$, where $\tau \geq 0$. So, the discounting factor has as its root a stochastic variable with values generated via a geometric Brownian motion. In its currently accepted iteration, the actual equation for modeling $\boldsymbol{d_1}$ is as follows (Equation 7.4):

$$d_1 = \log(S/K) + \frac{(r - q + \sigma^2)\tau}{\sigma\sqrt{\tau}} \qquad \text{[Eq. 7.4]}$$

As intimidating as this equation seems, it is mostly repurposed. Note that the variable $\boldsymbol{d_1}$ is composed of two terms. First, the term $log(S/K)$ is a standardized ratio of the stock price to the strike.[6] This means that the d_1 *increases in value as the stock price increases* and is the primary driver of the likelihood that the option will be exercisable at expiry. This number is further increased by a smaller factor composed of the risk-free rate modified by *subtracting the dividend rate* while *adding an amount representing the degree of stock risk* (measured by the variance of stock prices, σ^2).[7] The denominator is the standard deviation of the stock

---

6   The number would become too small to be of consequence if a stock was deep OTM and too large if it was deep ITM. Taking the log of the ratio solves this problem. (In some sources, the natural log is taken.)
7   Academic controversy (minor compared to real-life controversy) has centered on the measure of risk. There is no longer a consensus that equity risk is measured by price distribution.

price movement times the square root of the amount of time left until expiry: an increase in the denominator decreases the total value of d_1. An increase can occur (1) if either volatility increases, or (2) time to expiry lengthens. Thus, the denominator acts as a *risk-weighted* discount factor. However, since volatility (σ^2) and time (τ) are expressed in the numerator as well, the denominator has some, but not an overwhelming, effect on option value. The meaning of $N(d_2)$ is easy by comparison, since it is based on $N(d_1)$:

$$d_2 = d_1 - \sigma\sqrt{\tau}$$ [Eq. 7.5]

By modifying d_1, it is transformed into simply being a factor that describes how much the expected value of exercise proceeds exceed the value of the stock at expiry. The influence of volatility over time is excised out of the strike, leaving it subject to the effects of opportunity costs only.

It is important to note that, consistent with finance theory, the probability distributions used in $N(d_x)$ are *risk adjusted*. Stock prices are still lognormally distributed, but now they have a mean of $log S + \left(r - \frac{\sigma^2}{2}\right)\tau$ and a variance of $\sigma^2 \tau$: the property that the current value of any stock-price contingent claim equals the *risk-less discounted value* of the expected future payoff.[8]

Option Payoff Values

- Option Payoff Values: Option payoff values refer to *how much is received* from an option in the event of exercise.

The payoff to the call option at maturity is defined as the amount received if a contingent claim is received. For a call, the payoff is defined mathematically as:

$$C_\tau = max\{0, S_\tau - K\} = \{S_\tau - K \,|\, S_\tau \geq K, 0 \text{ } otherwise\}$$

Technically, payoff at expiry consists of two parts, both assuming an ITM expiry. The first part is the *payment* of the exercise price. This amount is a contingent claim equal to $C_\tau^1 = \{-K \,|\, S_\tau \geq K, 0 \text{ } otherwise\}$. The second part is the receipt of the stock, whose payoff is $C_\tau^2 = \{S_\tau \,|\, S_\tau \geq K, 0 \text{ } otherwise\}$. Let's consider this in graphic form (Figure 7.1):

---

8   Lars Nielsen, op. cit., p. 12.

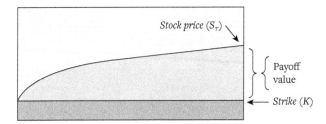

FIGURE 7.1 The call payoff equals the distance in value between the stock price (St) and the strike price (K) at expiry: $S_\tau - K$.

For a put, the payoff is defined mathematically as:

$$P_\tau = max\{0, K - S_\tau\} = \{K - S_\tau \mid S_\tau \leq K, 0 \; otherwise\}$$

For clarity, we graphically represent this as follows (Figure 7.2):

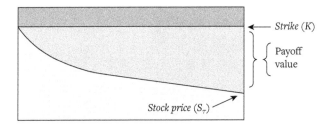

FIGURE 7.2 The payoff is similar to calls and equals the distance in value between the stock price (St) and the strike price (K) at expiry: $K - S_\tau$.

For both calls and puts, their value is equal to the difference between the two parts. The current value of both the contingent payment of the exercise price and the contingent receipt of the stock is the expected future payment, computed on the basis of the risk-adjusted probability distribution, discounted at the risk-free rate. Based on this notion, if an option is OTM at expiry, it has zero payoff. However, if an investor has zero payoff, the investor undoubtedly has incurred a capital loss equal to the cost of the option, which would be the option's market value at the time it was purchased.

Market Values

The payoff value is the net difference between the risk-adjusted strike and stock price. What, then, is the risk-adjusted value of an option? In theory, the risk-adjusted price is the market price. The price of an option is, however, a composite of values. BSM assists in the total valuation of an option—the sum of extrinsic value and the simple arithmetic value of intrinsic value.

Value Components

All option values are composed of two components: *intrinsic value* and *extrinsic value*. However, whereas it is *possible for an option to have no intrinsic value*, almost all options carry some extrinsic value until expiry.[9] The process to determine extrinsic value is the central *raison d'être* of the Black-Scholes model, discussed above. Here, we describe the basic descriptive components of option values.

Intrinsic and Extrinsic Value

- Intrinsic Value (IV): This term refers to the *amount of dollars per share that an option is in-the-money.*
- Extrinsic Value (EV): This term refers to any *option value that is in excess of intrinsic value.* Extrinsic value is also known as "TIME PREMIUM."

Intrinsic Value (IV)

Intrinsic value represents the base value of an option, calculated as the difference between the strike of the option and the market price of the underlying. Mathematically, intrinsic value is defined as:

$$\text{IV for a call:} \quad IV_c = S_o - K \backslash IV_c \geq 0 \qquad\qquad \text{[Eq. 7.6]}$$

$$\text{IV for a put:} \quad IV_p = K - S_o \backslash IV_c \geq 0 \qquad\qquad \text{[Eq. 7.6a]}$$

where K is the strike and S_o is the stock price today. Some examples are indicated in this table:

---

9   Options with zero extrinsic value are options that are very deep out-of-the-money and very close to expiry. Even these options carry zero extrinsic value at the bid, yet small but positive extrinsic value at the ask. OTM options have zero intrinsic value.

TABLE 7.1 Intrinsic value is defined as the arithmetic difference between the strike price and the underlying price, given that their difference is not less than zero.

CALLS			PUTS		
S_o	K	IV_c	K	S_o	IV_p
$26.58	26	$0.58	26	$26.58	$0.00
$84.77	90	$0.00	90	$84.77	$5.23
$55.22	55	$0.22	55	$55.22	$0.00
$7.50	7.50	$0.00	7.50	$7.50	$0.00

As indicated in the equation, intrinsic value cannot be negative. (This also conforms to the Black-Scholes valuation equations and schema.) These equations (Equations 7.6 and 7.6a) simply state that intrinsic value is the arithmetic amount of moneyness—the difference between the market price and the strike, assuming the option is ITM.

Extrinsic Value (EV) or Time Premium

Extrinsic value is the premium added to option value due to time remaining, volatility of the underlying, and the moneyness of the option. Its value is often, but not always, correlated with price changes to the underlying. EV exists even if an option is out-of-the-money. As indicated above, unless an option is very deeply out-of-the-money, it will always carry some time premium. Options on actively traded underlying issues, such as options on SPY, QQQ, or DIA, will even carry time premium with only minutes until expiry. There are indeed some traders who deliberately sell-to-open naked positions on these options with 15 minutes left in the trading session, just to capture what they consider to be excess time premium. (Don't try this at home: it is a potentially risky strategy best left with those who have financial capacity and trade algorithms. Relatively large moves are possible during the closing minutes of a trading day, when market-makers and funds try to hedge inventory or otherwise "square" their positions.)

Volatility

Now we consider the impact of underlying asset price volatility on extrinsic value. The greater the volatility, the higher the amount of time premium. Let's consider two individual stocks which are trading at exactly the same price of $50.75 per share. One is a mature, giant company with growth about the same as overall growth in the economy, and the other is a small-cap biotech company with huge growth prospects. You are considering the purchase of a nine-month 55-strike call option for either one, but aren't sure which company's options get the nod. You see that one option is much more expensive than the other. Intuitively, which company's options do you think would have the highest time premium (calculated as a percent of the total option price)? If you thought it is the small-cap biotech, you are correct and get a gold star for the day. As usual, we consider why. The answer reflects human judgment. If I know there is a greater chance that the biotech will jump 25% over the same time period as the large-cap's meager 5% move, *I would be inclined to spend more on that option because it has a greater chance of making a substantial price move than the other*. This is extremely important: we now realize that *future price expectations can fuel expansion of option premium*. And what happens when an option has a lot of time premium? *Ceteris paribus*, it should have a delta that responds more slowly to price change.

Table 7.2 illustrates the effect of volatility (often referred simply as *vol*). These stocks were all close to the 25-strike when this table was assembled (except ALKS, near 24; and VIRT, near 26). The table has listed the option quotes in ascending order by volatility, and both bid and ask option quotes have been adjusted to approximate their value as though the underlying was priced exactly at the value of the option strike.[10] The option prices gradually rise as volatility rises. Also note that the bid-ask spreads are not equal, which one would not intuitively expect. (The reason for this is complex and is more related to market-maker risks than investor activity. Contributing factors include the size of the underlying outstanding stock issue, liquidity of the market-maker, pending news such as an expected earnings report, and option open interest.)

Historic Volatility

- <u>Historic Volatility</u>: Historic volatility is a *measure of stock risk measured as the standard deviation* of daily stock returns.

Historic volatility is a measure of price dispersion of the underlying over a specific period, usually a year. It is comparatively easy to calculate historic vol on Excel and historic prices are relatively easy to get. The primary issue regarding these calculations is in the determination of the time frame. Is historic vol calculated with daily numbers, weekly numbers,

---

10 A rudimentary adjustment: [(the strike price – stock quote) × Delta] + option bid or ask.

TABLE 7.2 Option prices rise as volatility of the underlying rises, ceteris paribus.

NAME	SYMBOL	PRICE	EXPIRY (DAYS)	STRIKE	TYPE	PRICE BID	PRICE ASK	B/A SPREAD	ADJ PRICE BID	ADJ PRICE ASK	VOL
NISOURCE INC	NL	$24.88	57	25	CALL	$0.55	$0.70	$0.15	$0.61	$0.76	21.20%
CENTERPOINT ENERGY	CNP	$25.09	57	25	CALL	$0.85	$1.00	$0.15	$0.80	$0.95	24.80%
NORTON LIFELOCK	NLOK	$25.67	57	25	CALL	$1.55	$1.70	$0.15	$1.15	$1.30	31.75%
SPROUTS FARMERS MKT	SFM	$24.68	57	25	CALL	$1.10	$1.20	$0.10	$1.26	$1.36	34.10%
INVESCO LTD	INV	$25.23	57	25	CALL	$1.40	$1.50	$0.10	$1.28	$1.38	36.83%
VIRTU FINL INC	VIRT	$25.81	57	25	CALL	$1.25	$1.40	$0.15	$1.34	$1.49	37.15%
ALKERMES	ALKS	$24.08	57	25	CALL	$1.50	$1.65	$0.15	$1.46	$1.61	42.62%
COGNYTE SOFTWARE	CGNT	$24.99	57	25	CALL	$1.55	$1.80	$0.25	$1.56	$1.81	47.57%
IHEART MEDIA	IHRT	$25.09	57	25	CALL	$1.75	$1.95	$0.20	$1.70	$1.90	50.70%
AVAYA	AVYA	$24.89	57	25	CALL	$1.90	$2.05	$0.15	$1.96	$2.11	55.14%
CALERES INC	CAL	$24.10	57	25	CALL	$1.80	$2.20	$0.40	$2.24	$2.64	65.99%
CHARGEPOINT	CHPT	$24.57	57	25	CALL	$2.56	$2.71	$0.15	$2.79	$2.94	74.64%
CEREVEL THERA	CERE	$24.76	57	25	CALL	$2.90	$3.20	$0.30	$3.03	$3.33	81.02%

or even monthly numbers? Accordingly, is the database one year, two years, or five years? This is a problem similarly facing another measure of volatility, beta.

The Calculation of Historic Volatility

Mathematically, historic volatility refers to the annualized *standard deviation of return*. Typically, the data set is comprised of one calendar year of day-to-day continuously compounded returns (i.e., percent change of value from close of previous day to close of current day).

The procedure is a standard approach to determination of a population standard deviation: (1) calculate the natural log of daily returns: $R_n = ln(C_n/C_{n-1})$; (2) calculate the average of these returns, $R_{avg} = \frac{\sum_{i=1}^{n} R_n}{n}$; (3) calculate the squared deviation from the average for each of the returns: $(R_n - R_{avg})$; (4) and calculate the sample variance of $\sigma^2 = \frac{\sum_{i=1}^{n}(R_n - R_{avg})}{n-1}$; and then

the standard deviation $\sigma = \sqrt{\frac{\sum_{i=1}^{n}(R_n - R_{avg})}{n-1}}$, which is the historic volatility.[11]

Implied Volatility (IV)

> • Implied Volatility: Implied volatility is a measure of *how much volatility a stock should theoretically have*, given the amount of extrinsic value the option actually has.

The concept of implied volatility (IV) is of significance to the option investor, even if it is not widely understood. Granted, the concept is hard to explain, and formal definitions require well-above-average linguistic skills to navigate. A simpler approach is this: the IV of an option **implies** a certain volatility *of the underlying, given how much extrinsic value an option actually has.* Since an option value reflects the impact of historic volatility, an option with value that is *greater than what it should be* theoretically, given the underlying historic volatility, is "overvalued" and *implies* a certain higher volatility of the underlying than it actually has. In other words, a given option may carry an extrinsic value that should only occur if the underlying has a historic volatility of, say, *y*, even though the underlying has historic vol of *x*.

Most practitioners regard implied volatility as a metric to estimate future volatility of a security's price based solely on the price of the underlying options. Thus, implied volatility,

---

11   For Excel users: perform step 1; use =AVERAGE function in step 2, and then use =STDEV function instead of steps 3 and 4.

often denoted by σ^{12}, is frequently considered to be a proxy of market risk. The mind-twisting implication for nonpractitioners, or non-investors, for that matter, is that option prices always correctly assess risk because markets are "efficient" and that, therefore, all prices are "correct." It is not necessarily a good idea to be so sanguine in that assessment. Options can be "overvalued" because they have been driven higher by either hedgers, market-makers, speculators, or Reddit readers.

Table 7.3 below provides some examples of what it means to be "overvalued" or "undervalued"; that is, when IV is greater or lesser than historic volatility of the underlying. The traditional reaction to those who find these options to "sell the premium" or selling-to-open the option. But be careful if you decide to do so. Please keep in mind the oft-quoted admonition of John Maynard Keynes: "Markets can remain irrational longer than you can remain solvent."

TABLE 7.3 The price of an option is a function of the underlying historic volatility. In this table, option values do not do so. Instead, the price of the option "implies" a certain volatility for the underlying; option prices that are higher than theoretical values imply a higher volatility than the stock actually has.

UNDERLYING			OPTION					
SYMBOL	PR	H VOL	EXPIRY	TYPE	STRIKE	THEO PR	IV	ACTUAL PR
CHPT	$21.91	79.0%	15-Oct	Call	21	$3.57	73.4%	$3.35
AAPL	$154.34	25.2%	19-Nov	Put	150	$5.33	30.1%	$5.40
UNH	$423.14	28.3%	21-Jan	Call	420	$29.42	23.6%	$24.90
PFE	$423.14	28.3%	21-Jan	Put	420	$28.93	23.6%	$22.95
OSS	$5.95	89.0%	19-Nov	Call	5	$1.44	95.7%	$1.50
KZIA	$10.30	83.8%	17-Dec	Call	10	$1.97	119.3%	$2.70

Also, IV is not static. It tends to rise as time-to-expiry lengthens. An example follows in Table 7.4, which tabulates actual quotes for ATM call options on the S&P 500 SPIDER ETF, one of the most liquid of all option chains.

12　The use of sigma is problematic because it can be confused with stock price standard deviation, which carries other connotations. To avoid confusion, going forward, we will use "IV" when discussing implied volatility and will use "intrinsic value" without initials.

TABLE 7.4 IV rises as time to expiry lengthens; time premium decay slows down.

| | SPY 450 STRIKE CALLS | | | SPY PRICE: $450.25 | | |
EXPIRY	DAYS LEFT TO EXPIRY	CALL PRICE	INTRINSIC VAL	EXTRINSIC VAL	AVG DECAY/ DAY	IMPLIED VOL
9/3/2021	5	$2.13	$0.25	$1.88	$0.38	9.95%
9/8/2021	10	$2.74	$0.25	$2.49	$0.25	9.13%
9/17/2021	19	$4.12	$0.25	$3.87	$0.20	10.15%
10/15/2021	47	$7.60	$0.25	$7.35	$0.16	12.15%
11/19/2021	82	$11.76	$0.25	$11.51	$0.14	14.39%
12/17/2021	110	$14.41	$0.25	$14.16	$0.13	15.31%
1/21/2022	145	$17.11	$0.25	$16.86	$0.12	15.96%
1/20/2023	509	$35.60	$0.25	$35.35	$0.07	18.45%

The Effect of Time

The increase in IV over time increases exponentially. This fact has ramifications regarding the choice of option strategy, as we shall see later in this book. However, this fact is a consequence of an equally exponential decline in time premium as time-to-expiry nears. Both phenomena are illustrated in Figures 7.3a and 7.3b (below) using the data from Table 7.4. The important consideration here is that IV is not static but can and will change over time.

It should be no surprise that the longer an option has until expiry, the more extrinsic value an option carries. Common sense would suggest that longer-term options have more

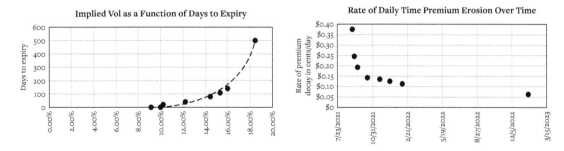

FIGURE 7.3A (L) IV increases exponentially as a function of time. **Figure 7.3B (R):** Exponential decline in IV translates to exponential rate of premium erosion as expiry approaches.

premium because the underlying has more time for price action to perform in accordance with the option buyer's preferred direction. What is interesting, however, is that if a near-month option has positive implied vol (greater then theoretical vol), it does not necessarily mean that *all* options of the same class of the underlying will also carry high implied vol. Implied vol is chimerical, fluid, and dynamic. Theory on this point is unclear. Possibly, implied volatility, being a deviation from "theoretical value," is driven by the "animal spirits" of the markets, a notion widely dismissed as rubbish by believers in the efficient market hypothesis (of which, alas, the author is not an adherent). Nonetheless, as we have seen in Table 7.4 above, option extrinsic value increases as time left to expiry increases and decreases as options approach expiry. This holds, regardless of the level of implied volatility.

An example will illustrate this point. Suppose a certain company, popular in the blogosphere, is about to report earnings. Speculators decide to rush in and buy near-the-money options with relatively little time until expiry. This rush of demand affects only certain options and certain strikes, and these options exhibit excessive premium; other strikes and expiries remain reasonably priced.

Critiques of the Black-Scholes Model

Investor Expectations

> • <u>Investor Expectations</u>: The *composite belief* of all market participants *as to the future performance* of an asset's price.

This discussion begs the question, what is (are) the driving force(s) behind the degree of implied volatility in option valuation? The forces behind changes in option intrinsic value is simple to understand; it is a direct function of change in the price of the underlying. However, extrinsic value is another matter altogether because it can change dramatically over time even if an underlying asset does not change in price. When all is said and done, *it is the investor who determines at what price an option is bought or sold, but it is the market-maker who posts the bid and ask on option price quotes*. This push-pull dynamic is entirely human (so far) and has been widely discussed since the early 1960s.[13] Most of the theorists

---

13   The subject has a name: micro-market theory, or micro-market economics.

feel that market-makers may adjust their bid and ask away from theoretical quotes because they *also* have physical constraints, not the least of which is *inventory risk*. Sometimes a market-maker may want additional options to hedge against other long or short positions in their inventory. If so, they have the authority to raise their bid. At other times, a market-maker may want to discourage any further option purchases for similar reasons. If so, they are entitled to drop their bid. Therefore, market-makers are important participants in the price game. However, at most, bid-ask spreads are *distortions* of price and are statutorily limited by exchange rules. The predominant pricing factor remains investor sentiment and expectation.

The option supply/demand function is contingent upon individual investors making a judgment by weighing risk and return and then deciding to buy to open or close, or to sell to open or close. Unlike stock itself, options do not have static supply. The supply moves up or down depending on demand. Therefore, if IV becomes truly extreme (from the market's viewpoint), more options *should* be written in response, and in theory, option prices *should* return to theoretical levels. Although this is what happens frequently, it doesn't always happen. Even if all market participants reference the Black-Scholes model (or derivative models thereof) as an assist in assessing the "true" value of an option, departure from theoretical price is remarkably common and therefore implies a certain suspension of belief in any price-setting laws among market participants—and to a certain extent, a belief suspension of the supply/demand dynamic.

One logical explanation is to redefine what we mean by "the market." The market is not composed of every individual in the marketplace. *The market only consists of those entities who are interested in a particular asset.* If someone simply doesn't like a particular asset—for any reason—that entity is not "in the market" for that asset. This clearly should bear ramifications on how we view price discovery. For instance, if markets are composed only of those individuals interested in a given asset, then there exists a risk of *adverse selection*[14]—and a possible directional bias. In other words, if enough entities believe an asset should have a higher price, then it will, even if there is no justification for it. This is a controversial statement because the efficient market hypothesis holds that information is freely available to all and that, on the aggregate, the market has all available information, good and bad. (It also holds that all investors are rational actors.)

In aggregate, all information is surely available, but to paraphrase George Orwell, all information is equal, but some information is *more equal* than other information; not all

---

14   Adverse selection refers to a situation where a buyer has information or thinks it has, that a seller does not have about a product or asset and acts to exploit it (or vice versa).

information is attended to with the same level of analysis and inspection. Furthermore, many beliefs are widely held but factually suspect. Finally, it is impossible to truly grasp the rationale for an asset purchase (assuming there is one) unless we can read the mind of every entity that commits to buy or sell. Example: a fund manager decides to buy a hot issue because all of its peers are doing so. The primary takeaway of this thought-thread is that *no one truly understands price discovery, which can be capricious and arbitrary at times.* However, in general, markets are *reasonable* discoverers of value.

Behavioral Finance

> - <u>Behavioral Finance</u>: The study of the *influence of psychology on the behavior of investors or financial analysts*, including effects on the markets.

Since the 1970s, a school of thought has arisen that has studied the psychological motivations in investment decision-making. It focuses on the fact that investors are not always rational, have limits to self-control, and are influenced by their own biases.

Even today, many theoreticians conjecture that retail investors are the ones who bring about "irrational" prices and the "rational actors," namely, professional dealers and fund managers, gain (excess) profits from these poor souls by acting as arbitrageurs to bring these prices in line. If this were true, of course, then there would be no irrational prices and no implied volatility. (Yet, traders exist because they believe the market is "wrong.") Behavioral finance holds that all participants in the market—investment professionals and retail investors—carry their own non-financial motivations to the market that influence their financial decision-making. Markets are populated by *normal* people, not necessarily *rational* ones; prices can be arbitrary.

Consider the narrow definition of "rational" and "irrational" market players. Theorists define "rational" in the context of profit maximization. Perhaps each actor in the marketplace acts "rationally" relative to its own peculiar risks and limitations they face. It is not necessarily "irrational" for a market-maker to post "irrational" quotes to engender a reduction (or increase) of inventory, if existing conditions are unhedged and pose an existential threat to the firm itself. Fund managers face similar pressures if and when they rely on options to hedge long or short positions. It would seem unlikely that only the retail investor would be more inclined to be "irrational" and succumb to fear and greed. Behavioral finance emphasizes that humans employ heuristics to assist in decision-making, and these "shortcuts" can be influenced by emotion or attitude.

Moreover, finally, as described above, social scientists have commented on the idea of market rationality for the past 30 years, and the discussion has finally entered the academic mainstream of finance in the 21st century.[15] Its impact is gradually being felt in finance theory today and has been cited as a significant factor in the rise of financial engineering and the use of computer algorithms and AI in trading.

Mathematic Critique

Some critics of BSM point to mathematical syllogisms as a source of criticism. Benoit Mandelbrot[16] found that markets are not necessarily normally distributed but instead feature "fatter tails" than a Gaussian distribution would possess. Mandelbrot did not specifically criticize BSM, but this critique of a singular assumption of the model clearly upended confidence in it. Other academicians take issue with some of the other statistical assumptions made by the model.

For example, lognormality in price distribution and price volatility is assumed, yet calculation methodology remained undefined. The exact method of calculation was left undefined. This matters because parameters result in different volatility numbers; different volatility numbers lead to a wide discrepancy of IV.[17]

Furthermore, BSM adopts the traditional line that markets are efficient. The efficient market hypothesis has been questioned by science professionals outside finance for many years. For example, John Allen Paulos has demonstrated that markets are not "efficient" in the manner described by finance theory.[18]

Summary and Conclusions

We have delved into a detailed discussion of the meaning and function of the Black-Scholes model and were able to examine some of the more important details thereof. We were able to see that the valuation of options is, to a remarkable degree, an assessment of the probability that a stock will be worth something at expiry. However, that only tells part of the

---

15   Cf. Daniel Kahneman & Amos Twersky (1979). Prospect Theory: An Analysis of Decision Under Risk" *Econometrica*, 47(2), 263–292.; Robert Schiller (1993). *Advances in Behavioral Finance*. Russell Sage Foundation; D. Hirshleifer (2001). Investor Psychology and Asset Pricing. *The Journal of Finance*, 56(4), 1533–1597.
16   Benoit Mandelbrot was a Polish American mathematician best known for fractal theory. However, he also determined that market prices were not necessarily distributed normally, thus upending an important pillar of finance theory (see Benoit Mandelbrot, *The (Mis)Behavior of Markets*).
17   A similar problem faces the calculation of stock beta.
18   John Allen Paulos (2003). *A Mathematician Plays the Stock Market*. Basic Books, p. 202.

story because, as we have seen, markets were created, used, and modified by human action. Being a construct of a human culture, it is subject to the cultural biases and attributes of its authors. Thus, even though BSM has been revolutionary in creating a method for evaluating the discovery of option prices, it has shortcomings.

Academicians and some mathematically inclined investors have recognized the limitations of the Black-Scholes model over the years, leading to a multitude of revisions and modifications. Most of these address the more obvious assumptions made by Black and Scholes. Indeed, the very existence of implied volatility should be a direct reminder that BSM is, first and foremost, a *model. Models are not reality; they mimic reality and try to explain reality.* By doing so, models engender profound insights. Yet it needs to be understood that BSM is *not religious dogma* and should not be slavishly observed. No one should burn at the stake because of a failure to adhere to the dicta of BSM. The model performs more than adequately and consistent with its mission: to provide a method to estimate *approximate theoretical option values manifest by forces of time, volatility, and moneyness.* The option practitioner is well advised to retain a good understanding of insights of BSM without getting lost in the details.

Looking Forward

All being said, option practitioners *do* concentrate their brain power on the option Greeks, for reasons that will become clear both in the next few chapters and when we begin to concentrate on option strategies. Chapter 8 will introduce concepts that build upon and enhance our understanding of implied volatility, volatility smiles, smirks, and skews. We will then be prepared to move in to get a close look at the all-important Greek functions in Chapters 9 and 10.

Chapter 8

Put Call Parity and Volatility Smiles

Introduction

We have now learned about the price dynamics of options as defined by the Black-Scholes model. We also now know that options carry *intrinsic value* as well as *extrinsic value,* or as it is commonly called, *time premium*. And finally, we know that time premium can vary from what should be expected given the historic volatilities of the underlying, a phenomenon measured by what is called implied volatility, or simply IV. If we graph the IV of the time premium across strikes and/or expiries, patterns emerge that add depth to our understanding of time premium, and—to an important extent—the behavior of option investors. These patterns are called volatility smiles, and sometimes also volatility smirks or volatility skews, whose names offer obvious clues as to their shape. Accordingly, in general and in circumstances when IV is present, IV is lowest for ATM options and rise as strikes go further **out of the money** (OTM) or **in the money** (ITM).

Remember that the Black-Scholes model *does not infer the existence of IV*: BSM defines the theoretical value of an option as a *monotonic increasing function*[1] of the volatility of the underlying asset, which is why one computes IV from the market price of an option instead of from its theoretical value. As discussed in the previous chapter, the Black-Scholes model expresses the value of options in terms of several constants, and volatility is considered one of them. However, research has found that volatility itself is a function of time-to-expiry, moneyness, and an abstract species of "magic sauce" called the marketplace. In this chapter, we are going to define and examine IV further by first discussing a phenomenon called put-call parity, and then by examining the simpler graphic form of implied volatility—volatility smiles and skews—and their implications for the option user.

---

1   Monotonic increasing function is non-exponential: its rate of change is constant.

Put-Call Parity

> • Put-Call Parity: Put-call parity is the name given to a *theoretical price relationship between puts and calls* whereby each represents fair value of the other, in combination with various long and short underlying positions.

Put-call parity refers to a theoretical relationship between the extrinsic value of puts and calls of the same series and strike. Put-call parity focuses on extrinsic value, since option intrinsic value is clear-cut and incontrovertible. Accordingly, in theory, *a call option price implies a "fair price" for the corresponding put option*, and vice versa. Put-call parity was first proposed in the late 1970s and 1980s as a logical consequence of the Black-Scholes model. Put-call parity therefore carries with it the same limitations and assumptions that burden BSM: investors are rational wealth maximizers, markets are efficient with perfect information, it is assumed that no dividends are paid on the underlying, arbitrage is impossible, and—most importantly—the model only applies to European-style options. Considering these limitations, it is a marvel that put-call parity was formulated at all. However, we need to understand that, prior to the advent of standardized (and tradable) options contracts, the problem of how to value contingent claims such as option contracts was palpable and complex, vexing economists as well as finance professionals for decades. Recall, also, that even after the establishment of the CBOE in 1973, only a handful of stocks were approved for option trading, and these were limited to call options. Puts would not be tradable until 1977. The pricing of puts was therefore still mysterious, and at the time, put-call parity was cutting-edge research with real-world option pricing application.

The logic behind put-call parity is rather straightforward and firmly grounded in the efficient market hypothesis. The thinking can be summarized as follows. Consider the existence of an investor seeking to buy an asset with a hedge. That investor could either purchase an asset outright and then buy a put to hedge against price risk, or similarly, the investor could short the asset and buy a call. Or the investor could simply purchase a call. With efficient markets,[2] the price of the hedge should be the same and be equal to the price of the call. We call this put and call price relationship put-call parity.[3] The advantage of such a near-equality

---

2 Efficient markets also assume unlimited capacity to borrow and lend at the risk-free rate, arbitrage is ever-present and vigorous (or would be, thus eliminating any mispricing), and that the securities pay no dividends during the hedge period.

3 See Stoll (1969), Merton (1977), and Klemkosky, R., and Resnick, B., Put-Call Parity and Market Efficiency, *The Journal of Finance* (1979), Vol. 34:5, pp.1141–1157.

is that the average investor need only examine the volatility structure of either calls or puts, interchangeably, to develop a sense of IV of the other option type. We see this demonstrated in Table 8.1; it is a primary rationale for put-call parity.

For our purposes, it is not necessary to run all of the theory details. However, a mathematical explanation illustrates the concept well. Suppose the positions enumerated in the previous paragraph are expressed, given these symbols: K = strike price; S_o = current price of a stock; S^* = the market price of the stock at expiration of the option; C = price of a (European) call option; P = price of a (European) put; i = a constant risk-free rate for the duration of the option life.

The following (Table 8.1) expresses these relationships as follows[4]:

TABLE 8.1 Illustration of prospective cash flows from certain strategies as demonstration of put-call parity.

STRATEGY	CASH FLOW $T = 0$	CASH FLOW AT EXPIRY	
		IF $S^* \leq K$	IF $S^* > K$
A BUY CALL	$-C$	0	$S^* - K$
A' BUY STOCK	$-S$	S^*	S^*
BUY PUT	$-P$	$K - S^*$	0
BORROW	$K/(1 + i)$	$-K$	$-K$
TOTAL	$-P - S + K/(1 + i)$	0	$S^* - K$
B BUY PUT	$-P$	$K - S^*$	0
B' SHORT STOCK	S	$-S^*$	$-S^*$
BUY CALL	$-C$	0	$S^* - K$
LEND	$-K/(1 + i)$	K	K
TOTAL	$S - C - K/(1 + i)$	$K - S^*$	0

This table (Table 8.1, above) demonstrates the primary thesis of put-call parity. Given that markets are complete and efficient, that these options are European-style, and that borrowing and lending at the risk-free rate is unlimited, then: (1) the purchase of a call results in identical cash flows as buying a put and buying stock on margin; and (2) the purchase of a put results in identical cash flows as buying a call and shorting stock.[5] The explanation for these

---

4   Table from Klemkosky, op. cit.

5   A call and an artificial long position (Strategy A' Table 8.1) are interchangeable. The change from one to the other is sometimes referred to as *conversion*.

equalities is that *arbitrage forces them to occur.* The result is clear: there is a specific linked relationship in the price of corresponding puts and calls, and neither will deviate from theoretical (economic) values because market efficiency will assure price "correctness."

Despite such early confidence in the efficiency of option markets, empirical results indicate something else. Instead, violations of put-call parity exist since at least the time of the 1987 crash. Some explanations of these apparent violations involve: (1) inclusion of the effects of dividend payments; (2) restrictions on short sales; (3) transaction costs; (4) margin requirements; (5) taxes; and (6) early exercise risks borne by American options.[6] All of these elements—singly and in tandem—may explain these deviations, but the size and scope of many deviations suggest behavioral reasons as well, including directional bias, anchoring, and other heuristic behavior-related realities. Indeed, some researchers have noted a small "predictive" attribute to unusually high IV values, as much as 50 bp per week for the S&P index.[7] Furthermore, an absence of parity was not determined to be a consequence of short position constraints.

Nonetheless, for a given strike price and maturity, the *correct volatility* to use in conjunction with the Black-Scholes-Merton model to price a European call should always be the same as that used to price a European put. This means that the volatility smile (i.e., the relationship between implied volatility and strike price for a particular maturity; see below) is the same for European calls and European puts. It also means that the volatility term structure (i.e., the relationship between implied volatility and maturity for a particular strike) is also the same for European calls and European puts.

Volatility Smiles

- <u>Volatility Smiles</u>: Volatility smiles *represent that shape of the function* that shows the *relationship between the option strike and IV* when graphed. When options with the same expiration date and the same underlying asset, but with different strike prices, are graphed as a function of implied volatility, the tendency is for that graph to appear like a smile.

---

6   Cremers and Weinbaum (2010).
7   Cremers and Weinbaum, ibid.

For a decade starting in the late 1980s, finance research focused on the findings of famous papers that "discovered" the volatility smile for equity options.[8] Since then, the volatility smile—used by traders to price equity options (both on individual stocks and on stock indexes)—has had the general form shown in Figure 8.1. The smile shows that those options that are either furthest in the money (ITM) or out of the money (OTM) have the highest implied volatility. Implied volatility tends to be lowest among at-the-money and near-the-money options. With moneyness charted as a function of volatility, the relationship has a smile-like appearance (Figure 8.1): the more an option is ITM or OTM, the greater its implied volatility.

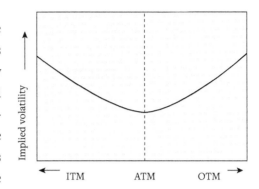

FIGURE 8.1 Generalized schematic of the volatility smile. Actual smiles are not as symmetric.

Interestingly, implied volatilities only became a widespread phenomenon after the historic stock market crash of late September 1987, when major stock indexes in the United States fell a record 22.5% in a single day. Prior to the crash, there is no evidence that time premiums swayed too far from values predicted by the BSM.

There is no consensus as to why this has happened. Some have suggested that after 1987, traders developed a sanguine sense of risk and built new models to account for black swan events such as what happened in 1987. This new reality was factored into options pricing, and the net result is the volatility smile evident today. Others suggest that higher ATM options suggest greater demand for those options. This would make sense, since ATM options have a 50% chance of either being ITM or OTM at expiry and are more actively traded and usually have higher open interest than either in-the-money or out-of-the-money options. However, as mentioned before, option supply is not fixed; if ATM vol is higher than elsewhere on the chain, wouldn't more ATM options be sold? Do the dynamics of supply and demand not apply?

Another explanation for this pricing anomaly has its origins in the relatively high volume and open interest of at-the-money equity options. To explain, consider two options: one has very little extrinsic value and the other has a considerable amount. The one with less time premium is more volatile because it does not possess the time premium. Consider the math: if an ITM option has $1.00 of intrinsic value and only $.10 of extrinsic value, a $.50 move in the underlying moves the option up $.50/$1.10 or 45.5%. Another option, also with $1.00 of

---

8 See Rubinstein (1985; 1994); Jackwerth and Rubinstein (1996).

intrinsic value but with $1.00 of extrinsic value, will only appreciate $.50/$2.00 or 25%. Thus, in the very short run, the additional extrinsic value "dilutes" the volatility. ATM options carry the highest amount of time premium of any option in the chain—presumably because that is where most option activity is located. Because ATM options carry more extrinsic value than any other option in the chain, they also have the lowest implied volatility.

Irrespective of these mysteries, ATM options are less volatile than options farther ITM or OTM. The basic reason for this harkens to the behavior of extrinsic value itself.

Using the Volatility Smile

In its essence, the volatility smile is an IV "map" that can graphically show option users which options in a class have *relatively more or less IV*. Therefore, examination of the smile provides option investors with some idea which options are "too expensive" or "too inexpensive." For those who sell-to-open option positions for income, overpriced options permit an opportunity for greater returns. Similarly, for those who buy-to-open option positions for speculation, undervaluation allows the investor to achieve lower cost and therefore lower risk. (In Chapter 9, we will learn the importance of this relative value attribute relative to Greek functions. No spoiler alert, but keep this in mind: higher-than-theoretical premium brings lower delta but higher theta.)

Some use IV dissonances as a means of ascertaining overall market sentiment. In theory, thanks to put-call parity, IV should be the same for puts and calls that share the same strike and expiry. If calls show higher IV than their put counterparts, some suggest this implies greater bullish sentiment in the market because investors are willing to pay more for them than they should, based on BSM valuations. Similarly, more expensive puts imply bearish sentiment.

However, investors must maintain some perspective. The market incorporates a random assortment of events into the term structure of volatility. For instance, the impact of the upcoming results of a drug trial can cause implied volatility swings for pharmaceutical stocks. Since many events are time sensitive, expectations tend to drive up short-term volatilities, while volatility barely changes for longer term. The differences in effects of time-sensitive news on the volatilities of options of different expiries is referred to as *IV term structure*. Volatility term structure illustrates the relationship between implied volatilities and time to expiration. The term structures provide another method for traders to gauge relatively cheap or expensive options, but generally, longer-term options have much flatter smiles than shorter-term options. As we shall see, this knowledge can be beneficial when structuring calendar spreads.

Real conditions show a more complex smile configuration than is evident in theory, for a host of reasons; all of which, in combination, provide an element of apparent randomness. Consider the following charts adapted from option price data for Cohu, Inc. of September 2021 (Figure 8.2):

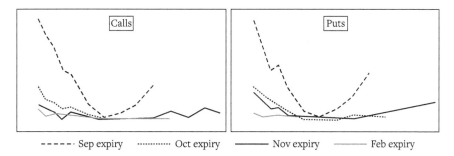

FIGURE 8.2 Volatility charts for Cohu, Inc. (COHU). Smiles and smirks are rarely smooth. Note how volatility flattens out as expiry lengthens, and the similarity between puts and calls is a demonstration of put-call parity. Data source: TD Ameritrade.

First, we observe that there is adherence to expected form for both puts and calls in regard to volatility: put-call parity seems to hold. Second, in general and across all expiries, ATM options have the lowest volatility, and the smile is evident. This has ramifications for the options investor. Most naive investors buy ATM options, believing they will move more generously when the stock moves and because they are inherently less expensive since they lack intrinsic value. The volatility smile suggests this approach is incorrect. Because vol is low, the option will not move as aggressively than one that is ITM. Therefore, there is an inherent tradeoff: cost of option versus volatility.

Third, *volatility declines as expiries lengthen*. This has ramifications for the spread writer and justifies the use of calendar spreads (discussed in Chapter 12). Lower volatility of lengthier expiries provides the necessary buffer to profit if the investor sells-to-open the short-term option and buys-to-open a long-term option.

Fourth, the irregularity of the smile points to the noise that characterizes all markets. Analysis of the actual data is done by some to determine the level of volatility of the smile itself. (Financial engineers have developed statistical measures of the volatility of volatility, including oddities such as *vega convexity*, *vomma*, *zomma*, and *gammas decay*. These more esoteric measures are beyond the scope of this text.) There may be many reasons why some issues are inherently more volatile than others (which would be evident in a comparative analysis). The most common causes would be: (1) option liquidity—low open interest induces market-makers to widen spreads; (2) date-specific expected news, as mentioned earlier; and (3) popularity of the underlying—some names are more popular in the investing community for reasons not fully understood.

Volatility Smirks and Skews

> • Volatility Smirks: Volatility smirks *represent that shape of the function that shows when the IV for options at the lower strikes are higher than the IV at higher strikes.* Reverse skew suggests that ITM calls and OTM puts are more expensive compared to OTM calls and ITM puts. The pattern is also called "forward skew."

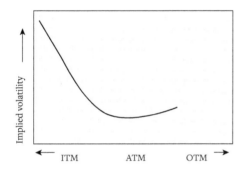

FIGURE 8.3 Example of a volatility smirk with standard left-hand skew.

Volatility smirks are so named because the relationship resembles a smirk when graphed. An example is seen below in Figure 8.3. Empirical results suggest that near-expiry equity options tend toward a volatility smile, while index options and long-term equity options tend to align more with a volatility smirk with **forward skews**. In the reverse skew pattern, the IV for options at the lower strikes are higher than the IV at higher strikes.

Empirical stock return distributions, however, tend to exhibit fat-tails (**kurtosis**) and skew. For options of different maturities, we also see characteristic differences in implied volatility. However, in this case, the dominant effect is related to the market's implied impact of upcoming events, such as earnings announcements. Indeed, IV tends to rise as much as three weeks prior to an earnings announcement. Unfortunately for the naive investor, this artificially built up IV rapidly dissipates when the news is released, leaving this naive investor with losses of extrinsic value. It is also important to note that options with earlier expiries exhibit more aggressive swings in implied volatility (sometimes called "vol of vol") than options with longer maturities.

The other variant of the volatility smirk is the forward skew. In the forward skew pattern, the IV for options at the lower strikes are lower than the IV at higher strikes. This suggests that out-of-the-money calls and in-the-money puts are in greater demand compared to in-the-money calls and out-of-the-money puts. The forward skew pattern is common for options in the commodities market. When supply is tight, businesses would rather pay more to secure supply than to risk supply disruption. For example, if weather reports indicate a heightened possibility of an impending frost, fear of supply disruption will cause businesses to drive up demand for out-of-the-money calls for the affected crops.

Another possible explanation is that in-the-money calls have become popular alternatives to outright stock purchases as they offer leverage and hence increased return on investment (ROI). This leads to greater demands for in-the-money calls and therefore increased IV at the lower strikes.

Volatility skew is the name given to the IV phenomenon extant with volatility smirks. It measures the amount that implied volatility diverges from theoretical values. Similarly, skew is present if *either* OTM or ITM options of the same expiry demonstrate different slopes on a same standard, two-dimensional chart. In the example above (Figure 8.3), the left-hand slope of the curve, representing the various IVs of ITM options, is steeper than the right-hand side, representing OTM option IV. Skewness is very common, particularly among near-expiry options, where strike price–inspired changes on option IV is more dramatic.

Volatility Surfaces

As seen in the illustration above, implied volatility has a *term structure*, meaning, the behavior of the smile—its rate of change and its angle—is known to vary, depending on option maturities. To better visualize the term structure of an option series' IV, a composite three-dimensional surface can be generated, whereby implied volatility (z-axis) for all options on the underlying is plotted against the strike (y-axis) and time to maturity (x-axis). The result is a two-dimensional curved surface plotted in three dimensions (see Figure 8.4) called an *implied volatility surface*.

An implied volatility surface visually describes how (implied) volatility

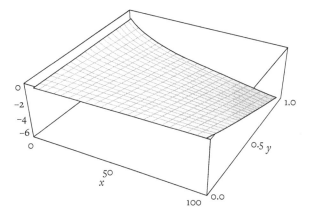

FIGURE 8.4 Example of a 3-D implied volatility surface.

differs for related options with different strikes and maturities. An implied volatility surface is also *static*: it describes the implied volatilities only at a given moment in time. How the surface changes as the spot changes is called the *evolution of the implied volatility surface*. In theory, option traders use an implied volatility surface to identify particular strikes and maturities that appear anomalous to the overall surface, and therefore, mispriced.

Limitations of Using the Volatility Smiles, Smirks, and Skews

As implied above, when IV was first noted, it was believed that options with "high" IV (i.e., time premium higher than predicted by BSM) should be sold short, and options with "low" IV (i.e., time premium lower than predicted by BSM) should be bought long. The idea was to exploit the mispricing of these options with the expectation that market efficiency would rapidly adjust their value back toward the theoretical ones. However, the persistence of IV up to this day has rendered that strategy obsolete.

The very notion of "relatively high" and "relatively low" option premiums brings about its own problems and issues. If the efficient market hypothesis is accepted, then these prices are not in excess; the market has logical explanation(s) for these price structures. But unfortunately, we have no way of knowing whether the market is "right" or "wrong" until hindsight provides the answer.

Summary and Conclusions

We have seen that implied volatility is not static or constant because IV is investor driven and is therefore naturally chimeric and variable. Nonetheless, we observe certain typical relationships among option prices that generally hold regardless of strike and expiry. First is so-called put-call parity, which describes an inherent relationship between corresponding puts and calls of the same expiry. It has been shown that these corresponding options often share approximately equal IV. This phenomenon is graphically represented as a "smile." However, for various reasons, many option chains also exhibit prices that have skewed IV smile patterns that are conveniently referred to as volatility smirks and/or volatility skews.

For the options practitioner, the variability of IV presents a set of challenges that can only be assuaged by electing to neutralize excessive IV by means of selling-to-open other options on the chain. This will be an important topic in chapters to follow.

Looking Forward

We now turn our attention exclusively to the use of options. The next few chapters are designed to show present and future practitioners how to exploit the robust flexibility that options offer. It is possible to create long and short option combinations to suit any risk/reward scenario desired. Indeed, in some instances, the use of a given option strategy clearly outperforms other non-option alternatives if properly structured. The chapters to follow are designed to help.

Chapter 9

The Option Greeks: Delta, Gamma, and Vega

Introduction

The "Greeks" are statistical measures that describe anticipated price performance of an option. All of them were made possible by the theoretical groundwork set up by the Black-Scholes model, and they have become an essential tool to use when building option positions. The Greeks include delta, gamma, theta, vega, and rho. This chapter and the one that follows are arguably among the most important chapters in this text. Mastery of Greek mechanics often is the difference between a profitable and unprofitable option trade. Delta and theta are the key statistics of the group, and a chapter will be devoted to each. Gamma and vega relate closely to delta and will be discussed in this chapter. Chapter 10 will discuss theta and rho, which are time-related functions.

Delta

> • <u>Delta</u>: Measures the *rate of change of the price of the option with respect to a move in the underlying* asset.

Delta is the best known of the option Greeks, and measures the rate of change of the price of the option *with respect to a move in the underlying asset.* Delta was so named because it is calculated as the partial first derivative[1] of the change in the option price as a function

---

[1] Recall from your calculus that a derivative measures the rate of change of two variables with respect to each other and a partial derivative measures the rate of change of variable with respect to another.

of the change in the underlying stock price, and rates of change frequently use delta as a symbol representing rates of change. The formal definition is:

$$\text{Option Delta} = \Delta = \frac{(Vo_{t+1} - Vo_t)}{(Vs_{t+1} - Vs_t)} = \frac{\partial Vo}{\partial Vs}$$

Accordingly, it is used most frequently to determine approximately how much an option price will change given a certain price change in the underlying. It is displayed as a percent which, when multiplied by the amount of price change in the underlying, provides a *theoretical estimate* of how much the value of the option should change. Specifically, the delta tells us how much the price of a given option change will be for each underlying price change of $1.00. However, we would not say the delta is $.50; we would say the delta is .50 (or more commonly, just "50").

Let's consider an example. Suppose you have purchased a call option for XYZ Corporation 50 strike for $1.35. You observe that the stock is currently trading at $44.72, which means the option is OTM and its delta is less than 50 (that is, less than .50). In fact, when you check the statistics for the option, the delta is .38. The next day, you see that the shares of XYZ Corporation have risen by $2.86 per share. You are excited, of course, and recalling that the option has a delta of .38, you should expect that the option will increase in price by $2.86 x .38, or about $1.09. (Of course, had the stock declined by an equal amount, the option would have decreased by about $1.09 as well.)

You confirm that your option is priced at $2.44,[2] but you also note that as of the close, your option has a delta of .43. Now, for every dollar increase in the underlying, your option will increase $0.43. Congratulations: you have just learned the important fact that *delta is not a constant factor but will rise or fall depending on the option's level of moneyness.*

Delta and Option Price Behavior

On a per-dollar-price-move basis of an underlying asset, an option with a relatively high delta will move more in price compared to one with a relatively low delta. The delta value itself is a function of three variables: ***moneyness, time to expiry, and the historic volatility of the underlying***. In regard to the delta option's moneyness, we find that for all options, delta rises as it moves deeper into the money and falls as the option moves further

---

2   Previous close for option: $1.35. With an increase of $2.86 of the common stock times a delta of .38, your option increased in value by $1.09 (because $2.86 x .38 = $1.09). Your option value at the open today is $2.44.

out-of-the-money. Delta approaches zero for deep OTM options and approaches one for deep ITM options, as illustrated on this schematic graph[3] (Figure 9.1).

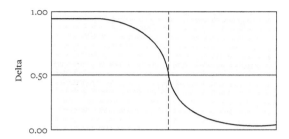

FIGURE 9.1 Option delta is approximately .50 when at-the-money, limit to zero as strikes move out-of-the-money, limit to 1.0 as strikes move deeper in-the-money.

Furthermore, options that are exactly at the money will have a delta at or near .50. However, for a put, it will move toward –1 when the stock is falling and toward 0 when the stock is rising. (ATM puts will have values of about –.50.) A second important consideration is that time left until option expiry is also a factor in delta, as noted in this schematic graph (Figure 9.2).

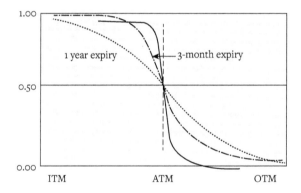

FIGURE 9.2 The shape of the delta function changes, depending on time left until expiry.

Now consider Table 9.1. The delta of an option with less time before expiry is generally more responsive to price change of the underlying than those options expiring later—the delta function becomes more linear for more distant expiries. The reason for this relates to the behavior of time premium, which we will cover when we discuss **theta** in more detail in

---

3 Because delta is a mathematical function based on the mechanics of a derivative, the delta value is asymptotically bound by 0 and 1 for long calls and short puts and by 0 and -1 for puts and short calls.

Chapter 10. First, the rate of time premium decay accelerates as an option nears expiration, as you will soon see. If time premium does not decay much—such as when an option has lots of time before expiry—then its time decay does not significantly affect the option price. But as expiry nears, the value of the option will decline regardless of changes to the price of the underlying as time premium erodes.

TABLE 9.1 Nearer expiries have more volatile deltas.

| | DAYS TO EXPIRATION | | | DAYS TO EXPIRATION | |
| | 37 | 9 | | 37 | 9 |
OPTION	DELTA	DELTA	OPTION	DELTA	DELTA
70 Call	100	100	70 Put	−1	0
75 Call	97	100	75 Put	−3	0
80 Call	91	100	80 Put	−9	0
85 Call	85	99	85 Put	−15	−1
90 Call	78	95	90 Put	−21	−5
95 Call	68	87	95 Put	−32	−13
100 Call	59	71	100 Put	−40	−29
105 Call	48	48	105 Put	−52	−52
110 Call	37	26	110 Put	−63	−74
115 Call	27	10	115 Put	−73	−89
120 Call	18	3	120 Put	−82	−97
125 Call	10	1	125 Put	−90	−99
130 Call	6	0	130 Put	−93	−100
135 Call	2	0	135 Put	−99	−100

Think of it this way: suppose you are on a rowboat and are moving against the river flow. You find that rowing upstream is arduous because the force offsets your rowing efforts. In this rather poetic maritime analogy, the river current represents time decay, which occurs whether the price of the underlying changes or not, and the upstream rowing would be a positive change in the underlying price. Thus, time decay slows the amount of price change that would otherwise occur if there was little time decay. This analogy explains why delta values nearer to expiry are more volatile delta: there is less time premium erosion to influence the option price.

The Role of Historic Volatility

How does volatility affect delta? As we have seen, the greater the volatility, the higher the amount of time premium. It should hold therefore that options with more time premium, *ceteris paribus*, will have a less volatile delta than other option series with less volatility. Generally speaking, this holds, but other factors can also increase premiums, such as liquidity of the underlying or micro-market considerations. To determine the specific role of changes in the underlying volatility, an investor would look at *vega*, described below.

Negative Deltas

For *long calls and short puts*, the delta is always positive. The reason is that both positions benefit the holder if the underlying moves higher in price. However, *for short calls and long puts*—which benefit the owner when prices decline—deltas are always negative.

Delta and Probability

- Delta Probabilities: Delta provides *an approximate probability* that an option will be in-the-money at expiry.

We often hear that delta is a measure of the likelihood that an option will expire ITM. For instance, an ATM option with a delta of about .50 would have about a 50% probability of expiring in-the-money, while an OTM option with a delta of .01 would only have a 1% chance of the same outcome. This belief follows from the Black-Scholes definition of delta, which is as follows:

Delta for calls: $\Delta_{call} = e^{-q\tau} \phi(d_1)$

Delta for puts: $\Delta_{put} = e^{-q\tau} \{\phi(-d_1) - 1\}$

where: $d_1 = \dfrac{\ln(S/K) + (r - q + \sigma^2)\tau}{\sigma\sqrt{\tau}}$

and where: $\phi(d_1) = \dfrac{1}{\sqrt{2\pi}} \int_{-\infty}^{x} e^{r(y^2/2)}$

where S is the stock price; K the strike price; r the risk-free rate; q the annual dividend yield[4]; τ time until expiration; and σ volatility of the underlying. This math may look intimidating, but if we analyze it piece by piece, it becomes understandable and provides important insights into the function and uses of delta.

Since these probabilities can range from 0% to 100%, as the underlying value S_0 moves out-of-the-money (by moving below the strike K for a call and above the strike K for a put), the variables d_1 and d_2 approach zero, and the value of delta also declines toward zero. Similar to N(d1) and N(d2), the variables fd_1 and fd_2 represent the likelihood of the option expiring ITM and therefore exercisable. Because recent work by Mandelbrot, among others, challenges the assumption that stock prices are normally distributed, the notion of delta as a probability measure should be questioned. However, that detail should not deter the investor from using delta to assess risk-reward attributes of a position and/or potential position profitability.

First, we see right away that the formal definition of delta is different between puts and calls, The component terms are the same, except that (a) the order of the terms are switched; and (b) the sign in front of e and in front of the variable d_1 are changed between put and call. This change in sign addresses the effects of negative price changes (i.e., asset price declines) and results in negative deltas for those derivatives that benefit from declining prices, such as long puts and short calls. Despite these changes, the formal definition of puts and calls is straightforward and the same for each: the value of delta is the *risk-adjusted probability of the occurrence of a specific stock price level* (as indicated in the variable ϕ) times the variable d_1 (which was discussed in detail in Chapter 7). And then all of this is modified by multiplying by an expression of e (Euler's number), which we discussed before, in Chapter 7; there is no need to pursue it further here. It is sufficient to stipulate here that delta is affected by time value erosion. Delta remains close to .50 for ATM options, but delta changes dramatically both for ITM and OTM as time left to expiry winds down. Probability of being ITM and probability of being profitable are two different things, indeed.

Delta for Puts and Calls

There is an interesting mathematical phenomenon regarding delta, whereby the sum of *the absolute value of the deltas of each call and put pair of the same series will always equal* 1. This truism harkens back to the probability attributes of delta. Underlying prices in the future will either be up, down, or the same from where they are now. Therefore,

---

4   Merton Miller demonstrated the role of dividend payments on option premiums, and this factor was added to the BSM equation in 1978.

the probabilities of *either the call or the put* being ITM at expiry will always be 100%, or 1. Note these examples:

TABLE 9.2 The absolute values of the put and call options of the same strike and expiry add up to 1.00.

ISSUE	SYMBOL	EXPIRY	STRIKE	CALL DELTA D_c	PUT DELTA D_p	$D_c + |D_p|$
IBM	IBM	20-Aug	155	0.18	−0.82	1.00
APPLE	AAPL	20-Aug	145	0.57	−0.43	1.00
GENERAL ELECTRIC	GE	20-Aug	12.5	0.70	−0.30	1.00
ABBVIE INC.	ABBV	20-Aug	117	0.55	−0.45	1.00

Gamma

- <u>Gamma</u>: Gamma measures *the rate at which the value of delta changes* in relation to how the price of the underlying security is moving and is *the same for puts and calls.*

The Precise Meaning of Gamma

Gamma measures the **change in delta** of an option **as the underlying price changes**. In other words, gamma measures the sensitivity of delta to changes in the price of the underlying. Formally, the gamma of an option is the *second derivative of the option premium with respect to the price of the underlying* or as the *first derivative of the delta of the option with respect to the price of the underlying* asset, defined as:

$$\text{Option Gamma for calls and puts:} \quad \gamma = \frac{\partial^2 \Delta}{\partial S^2} = \frac{\partial \Delta_c}{\partial S} = \frac{e^{-q\tau}\phi(d_1)}{S\sigma\sqrt{\tau}}$$

The key difference between delta and gamma is the denominator $S\sigma\sqrt{\tau}$. The denominator shows that gamma is the delta discounted by the volatility of the underlying as well as by the square root of time left until expiry. **Gamma is, in essence, the "delta of the delta."**

However, unlike delta, *gamma is always positive for long puts and long calls.* (For short calls and short puts, the gamma is always negative.) Let's consider this closely. We have seen that put deltas are negative and cal-l deltas are positive. Also, we know that the sum of the absolute values of call and put deltas equals one. Thus, any change in price—up or down—will have a reciprocal effect on the delta of each, and the gamma must be the same for both puts and calls. For example, consider an at-the-money put and call with delta of –.50 and .50, respectively. If gamma is .10, then if the stock rises, the call is now in-the-money, with a delta of .50 +.10 or .60. The put, however, is now out-of-the-money, and has a delta of –.50 +.10 or .40. If the stock falls an equal amount instead, the reciprocal delta falls to .40 (i.e., .50 –.10 =.40)—the call is now out-of-the-money. Meanwhile, the put delta "rises" to –.60 (i.e., –.50 –.10 = –.60)—the put is now in-the-money.

The discussion above leads us to this conclusion: as a stock price increases, the call deltas increase and approach 1.00 at a rate prescribed by gamma. Meanwhile, due to the reciprocal nature of the put/call relationship, the deltas of the puts also "increase" by approaching zero as the stock price increases. Because puts have a negative delta, the more "positive" the gamma, the closer delta will be to zero—puts are OTM if their call counterparts are ITM.

The Black-Scholes Gamma

This reciprocal relationship holds for call/put deltas, and a same-sign gamma preserves this reciprocity. (This also relates to the reciprocal BSM equations for put and call valuation.) However, as discussed above, the math is clear: gamma *must be the same for calls and puts.* The Black-Scholes model defines gamma as follows:

$$\text{Black-Scholes Gamma:} \quad \gamma = \frac{e^{-q\tau}\phi(d_1)}{S\sigma\sqrt{\tau}} = \left(\frac{e^{-qt}}{S_o\sigma\sqrt{\tau}}\right) \times \left(\frac{1}{\sqrt{2\pi}}\right) \times e^{-\frac{d_1^2}{2}}$$

where d_1 is equivalent to that defined in BSM's delta, and the other symbols also conform to the BSM's delta. The first equality is the Black-Scholes gamma. The second equality is a deconstructed version of the first one, factoring out the probability measure $\phi(d_1)$ and further factoring it to equal $\left(\frac{1}{\sqrt{2\pi}}\right) \times e^{-\frac{d_1^2}{2}}$, which is a transformation of the delta $\boldsymbol{d_1}$ and represents the specific probability for achievement of a given underlying price, given a specific initial price. This points to the extremely close mathematical relationship between delta and gamma.

Probability and Gamma

The discussion above allows us to examine probabilities in more detail. Recall that delta provides an approximate measure of the probability that the particular option will be in-the-money at expiry. Accordingly, consider the following example. Assume an underlying stock is valued at $55.22 per share, and its nearest expiry 55 call has a delta of .56 and a gamma is 0.12:

- If the underlying falls by $1.00 per share, the delta of the call will fall from .56 to **(.56 – .12) = .44 and there is now only ~44% chance of the option expiring ITM**.
- If the underlying rises by $1.00, the delta will rise from .56 to **(.56 + .12) = .68 and there is now ~68% chance of the option expiring ITM.**

Now, let's assume that all else holds true, except that we consider the nearest expiry 55 put, with a delta of –.44 and a gamma of 0.12:

- If the underlying falls by $1.00 per share, the delta of the put will rise from –.44 to **(–.44 – .12) = –.56, and there is now a ~56% chance of the option expiring OTM.**
- If the underlying rises by $1.00, the delta will fall from .44 to **(–.44 + .12) = – .36 and there is now a ~36% chance of the option expiring OTM.**

It is extremely important to know that gamma is a continuous and dynamic function, as is delta, since both delta and gamma change as the price of the underlying changes. Both delta and gamma will change from day to day due to time premium erosion (*theta*) and the dynamics of price change. The only inference that can be drawn is that the delta *today* will change at a rate equal to the gamma for each dollar change in the underlying. As for the day after tomorrow, one must recalculate the value of gamma, given the new value of delta. The good news is that it is possible to get a sense of future gammas by studying the behavior of gamma across several different strikes along the chain.

Consider another example (Table 9.3). The chart shows the put and call option chain on an underlying stock trading at $104.91, with 10 days to expiration. Consider the at-the-money 105 strike: the call delta is .53 and the put delta is –.48. A gamma of .04 for these options suggests that the delta is going to **change by +4% for every point increase in the underlying**. Thus, if the stock moves from $104.91 to $105.91, the 105 call and put will have .57 (.53 + .04) and –.44 (–.48 + .04) delta, respectively. But if the stock moves to 110, the call delta would not be .53 + (5 × .04) = .73, but only .69 per the chart. The *change in delta from gamma is not linear* but is explained by *e*.

TABLE 9.3 Hypothetical option chain; gamma and delta.

CALL		STRIKE	PUT	
DELTA	GAMMA		DELTA	GAMMA
.96	.01	85	−.16	.01
.91	.01	90	−.19	.01
.81	.02	95	−.23	.02
.69	.03	100	−.31	.03
.53	.04	105	−.48	.04
.35	.03	110	−.71	.04
.28	.02	115	−.82	.03
.25	.02	120	−.91	.02
.22	.01	125	−.94	.01

The even better news is that almost all trading platforms today have applications that provide the investor with valuation estimates for options assuming various price levels reached by the underlying.

Gamma and Time

The equation also implies that gamma behavior changes as a function of time. As time to expiry increases, the value of the denominator also increases, which, *ceteris paribus*, should lower the value of gamma. Similarly, as time to expiry approaches zero, the value of the denominator also approaches zero, which again, *ceteris paribus*, should increase the value of gamma. However, time premium is higher for longer-term options and the probability of an option expiring in-the-money, $f(d_1)$, increases. The increase or decrease in time to expiry has a neutralizing effect on the mathematical impact of the denominator. All said, the effect of time to expiry has a similar effect on gamma as it does on delta (see Figure 9.2), as illustrated here:

BSM assumes that stock prices move in the manner of a Wiener process (i.e., random walk), as described above. Accordingly, the term $\left(\frac{1}{\sqrt{2\pi}}\right) * e^{-\frac{d_1^2}{2}}$ is the standard normal probability function corresponding to the delta f, carried to a negative power of the standardized square of d_1. And finally, the first term, $\left(\frac{e^{-qt}}{S_o\sigma\sqrt{\tau}}\right)$, is the function $\frac{1}{S_o\sigma\sqrt{\tau}}$, times the familiar e^{-qt}.

How Gamma Behaves Closer to Expiration

Using the example above, let us fast-forward from 37 to 9 days before expiration and compare the deltas and gammas for each strike (for the sake of comparison, we'll assume that the stock price didn't move during the 28 days). As demonstrated in Table 9.4 (below), the closer the options get to expiration, the range of the deltas is more concentrated. Gamma ranges are also more concentrated, but gamma never shows a steady progression from zero to 100 like delta; gamma *values are symmetric*, with the at-the-money option showing the highest values, and with values trailing down for both in-the-money and out-of-the-money strikes (as seen in Figure 9.3).

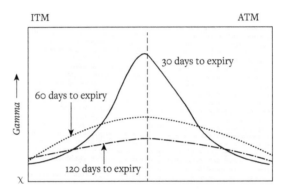

FIGURE 9.3 Effect of time to expiry on gamma.

Gamma and Moneyness

- <u>Gamma Risk</u>: This term refers to *the risk of dramatic changes in the option delta* manifested by underlying price moves contrary to the intended direction of a trade.

From what has been presented up to this point, we can deduce that the most volatile gammas are for close-to-expiry at- or near-the-money puts or calls. Because gamma (and consequently delta) is most volatile for these options, any purchase (or sale) of them subjects the investor to potentially disproportionate swings in option value. This risk is known as *gamma risk*. As we venture forth into a discussion of option strategies, awareness of this factoid will assist in an understanding of the structural logic of the strategies presented (and their follow-up).

TABLE 9.4 Gamma changes over time and volatility.

CALL				STRIKE	PUT			
37 DAYS TO EXPIRY		9 DAYS TO EXPIRY			37 DAYS TO EXPIRY		9 DAYS TO EXPIRY	
DELTA	GAMMA	DELTA	GAMMA		DELTA	GAMMA	DELTA	GAMMA
1.00	.00	100	0	65	0	.02	0	0
1.00	.06	100	0	70	−1	.04	0	0
.97	.12	100	0	75	−3	.12	0	0
.91	.12	100	.02	80	−9	.12	0	.02
.85	.14	99	.08	85	−15	.12	−1	.08
.78	.20	95	.16	90	−21	.22	−5	.16
.68	.18	87	.32	95	−32	.24	−13	.32
.59	.22	71	.46	100	−40	.24	−29	.46
.48	.22	48	.44	105	−52	.22	−52	.44
.37	.20	26	.32	110	−63	.20	−74	.30
.27	.18	10	.14	115	−73	.18	−89	.16
.18	.16	3	.04	120	−82	.16	−97	.04
.10	.08	1	.02	125	−90	.14	−99	.02
.06	.08	0	0	130	−93	.12	−100	0
.02	.04	0	0	135	−99	.02	−100	0
.00	.00	0	0	140	−100	0	−100	0

Graphically, we can see in Figure 9.4 that the largest percent changes in gamma values occur for the near- or at-the-money strikes (correspondingly true for option delta). While at-the-money options disproportionately gain gamma, ITM and OTM options lose gamma disproportionately.

Gamma Behavior to Changes in Underlying Volatility

In general, as *volatility decreases, gamma flattens across all strikes*. This intuitively correct pattern is familiar, and once again relates to the corresponding effects of volatility on delta. However, when volatility is high, gamma *stabilizes across all strike prices*. This unexpected

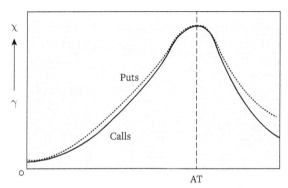

FIGURE 9.4 Highest gamma volatility is for at- or near-the-money option strikes.

result is *due to the increased time premiums generated by greater volatility* and is not the consequence of increased volatility *per se*. Accordingly, as the underlying price approaches a strike, the option will show some additional increase in time value, but the increase adds to an already distorted value; the change in gamma will therefore feature more stability than usual.

This counterintuitive result can also be mathematically explained. If delta represents the probability that the option will expire ITM, then it holds that the sum of all deltas for any given underlying price equals 1. Since $\gamma = \frac{\partial^2 \Delta}{\partial S^2} = \frac{\partial \Delta}{\partial S}$ and $\int_0^\infty \phi(d_1)\, dS = 1$, it follows that $\int_0^\infty \gamma(S)\, dS = 1$ also. Since the change in gamma function is "diluted" by the amount of time premium (similarly to delta), high-volatility options with correspondingly high premiums have lower gamma ATM. Therefore, all other near-the-money gammas are also lower, so that the entire spectrum of gammas is wider (as a function of the underlying price) in order to sum to 1. Low volatility does not generate extra premiums, so that gamma retains a "typical" high value near-the-money and ATM options. Accordingly, gamma ranges are much narrower.

The bottom line is this: as we see in Figure 9.5, when volatility is low, gamma is more volatile, with gamma for an ATM option high and with gamma for deep OTM and ITM options rapidly approaching zero. If volatility is high, gamma values experience less volatility (they change more gradually across strikes). The use of gamma to anticipate the change in delta is what makes it such a valuable measure of risk. Looking at the overall gamma, traders can see that it proves the worth of gamma. It assists in evaluating how time-sensitive your option position is, as well as assess how the option will respond to short-term changes to underlying prices.

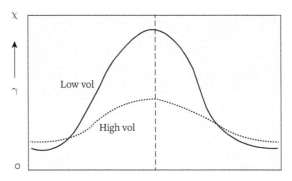

FIGURE 9.5 Impact of implied volatility on option gamma.

Vega

> • <u>Vega</u>: Vega measures the *effect of volatility on option* prices. Vega is used as a factor that *changes the price of an option* assuming a 1% change in implied volatility.

Yes, I know: *vega* is not a Greek letter.[5] But it is still a *Greek function*. **Vega** is a measure of how **sensitive an option is to changes in volatility** of the underlying. In other words, the option's vega is a measure of the impact of changes in the underlying volatility on **the option price**. Specifically, the vega of an option expresses the percent change in the price of the option *for every 1% change* in underlying volatility.

Formally, vega is defined as the partial first derivative of the change in the option price with respect to change in underlying volatility. This dynamic is summed up in the formal definition of vega:

$$\text{Option vega for calls and puts: } v = \frac{\partial V_O}{\partial \sigma_S}$$

As discussed previously, options tend to be more expensive when volatility is higher. Thus, whenever volatility goes up, *ceteris paribus*, the price of the option goes up, and vice versa. Vega measures this relationship as *the price change*. An analysis of the vega

---

5 How vega was named is rumored to be a result of *V* as in *volatility*. The symbol v is a version of the uncapitalized Greek letter *nu*, which looks like a "vee." It is also rumored that the name *vega* is also derived from that Latin letter, then altered to sound Greek.

Black-Scholes formula helps us understand this relationship more deeply. The Black-Scholes equation for vega is:

$$\text{Vega for puts and calls:} \quad v_O = S_O \phi(d_1)\sqrt{\tau}$$

$$\text{where:} \quad \phi(d_1) = e^{-\frac{d_1^2}{2}} 2\pi\sqrt{\tau}$$

$$\text{and where:} \quad d_1 = \frac{\ln(S/K) + (r - q + \sigma^2)\tau}{\sigma\sqrt{\tau}}; d_2 = d_1 - \sigma\sqrt{\tau}$$

The equation is very simple when compared to other Greeks: the usual probability adjuster functions as a coefficient to the stock option price. Hence, the result is an additive dollar-denominated value, pure and simple.

As you see from these examples in Table 9.5, option prices are modified upward (downward) if volatility increases (decreases) by the vega amount times the percent change in volatility.

TABLE 9.5 Examples of option price change by vega.

CALLS					PUTS		
PRICE	VEGA (v_O)	NEW PRICE	VOL	D VOL	PRICE	VEGA (v_O)	NEW PRICE
$1.25	.03	$1.205	26.5%	−1.5%	$3.55	.03	$3.505
$3.57	.04	$3.674	85.6%	2.6%	$7.80	.05	$7.93
$.95	.01	$.938	10.7%	−1.2%	$1.30	.02	$1.286

Effect of Time Value of Vega

> • Vega Is Additive to Option Price: Vega, by definition, directly increases or decreases the option premium depending on increases or decreases in implied volatility. Thus, *the degree of price change depends on the size of extrinsic option value.*

Because vega is a function of the Black-Scholes standard normal probability distribution of the option price, vega has an immediate effect on the price of the option, dependent upon the size of extrinsic value. Thus, anything that affects the amount of time premium also affects vega. The most basic influence on extrinsic value is, of course, time remaining until expiry. Therefore, the greater the time to expiry, the greater the vega.

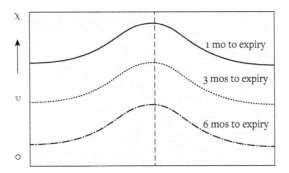

FIGURE 9.6 Impact of time to expiry on vega.

Moneyness and Vega

For the same reason, at-the-money options have the highest vega because these options have the highest time premium. Furthermore, vega decreases for both out-of-the-money and in-the-money options. However, out-of-the-money vegas fall at a sharper rate than ITM ones. Figure 9.7 shows this relationship:

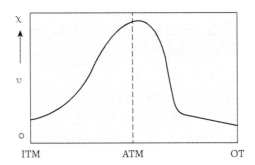

FIGURE 9.7 Impact of moneyness on vega.

Implied Volatility and Vega

If an option has a small amount of implied volatility—usually because the underlying has low historic volatility—it would stand to reason that any upward shift in IV would have a large impact on vega because a percent change from a low number has more impact than a percent change in a higher number.[6] Consequently, vega has the fastest impact in low vol issues:

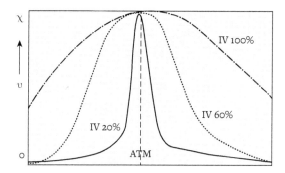

FIGURE 9.8 Impact of IV on vega.

Summary and Conclusions

This chapter discusses the meaning and function of three closely related Greek functions: delta, gamma, and vega. All three of these functions respond to changes in the underlying price, regardless of time left until expiry of the option.

The single most important (and most closely observed) is the delta, which we saw is the sensitivity of the option price to changes in the price of the underlying. We found that delta also carries a certain probabilistic flavor whereby the delta provides a sense of the likelihood that it will expire ITM. The primary use of delta is to give you an idea of how much your options will change in value if the underlying stock moves as expected (or contrary to your expectations).

Gamma is the partial second derivative of the price of the option with respect to the price of the underlying. It measures how delta changes as the price of the underlying changes. As the second derivative, its value behavior is remarkably like delta and is affected by similar factors, including moneyness and time to expiry.

Vega measures how much the price of an option changes for each percent change in the implied volatility of the option. Vega is typically relatively small and consequently isn't often considered important. However, a comparatively low vega shows that its option could be subject to substantive changes if the underlying undergoes a rapid change in implied volatility, such as the emergence of an FDA approval or pending earnings report.

---

6 The change from an IV of 1% to 2% is 100%, while the change from 99% to 100% is only 1%.

Taken together, these functions help the option buyer and seller anticipate possible option price changes based on various underlying price change scenarios. They are of major importance to the option investor, regardless of strategy employed.

Looking Ahead

The next chapter continues our discussion of the Greeks, beginning with the all-important theta and concluding with the rho. Theta particularly underscores the importance of the most significant attribute of options: that whatever their value, all extrinsic value erodes to zero. How quickly it does so is what theta is all about.

Practice Problems

Problems on Delta

1. Two call options on the same stock are expiring on the same day. Option A has a delta of .67, while Option B has a delta of .45. Which one has a strike closer to the current market price of the underlying?

   a. Option A. Explain.

   b. Option B. Explain.

2. One option has a negative delta, while another has a positive delta. What two reasons could there be to explain this phenomenon?

3. A stock with a higher IV will have a lower delta, *ceteris paribus*, than an option with no or little IV. Explain your answer.

   a. True.

   b. False.

4. The call option on the $15 strike is currently worth $1.02 and has a delta of 0.43. How much would the call option be worth if the underlying increases by $0.50? (Ignore the effects of theta and gamma.)

   a. $1.20

   b. $0.80

   c. $1.24

   d. $0.85

5. Two call options on two different stocks are expiring on the same day and have the same strike. Option A is priced at $3.25 ask, while Option B is priced at $4.38. Assume the two stocks are only priced $.25 apart. Which underlying is likely to have a higher historic volatility?

6. An option has a delta of .10 with 15 days before expiry. What is the approximate likelihood that the option will expire in-the-money? Explain.

7. An option has a delta of .10 with 15 days before expiry. What is the approximate likelihood that the option will be profitable? Explain your answer.

8. Two call options with the same strike on the two different stocks are expiring on the same day. Option A has a delta of .67, while Option B has a delta of .45. What reasons could explain the difference in delta?

    a. The two stocks could have different volatilities.

    b. The two options could vary in their degree of moneyness.

    c. The two options have different vegas.

    d. Choices a and b only.

    e. Choices b and c only.

    f. None of these.

9. You have been watching a particular call option. At close yesterday, it was quoted at $3.47 bid, $3.50 ask. Today you were too busy studying for finals to buy it, and to your amazement the underlying rose $6.54 on good earnings. The option is now $5.15 bid, $5.22 ask. Aside from rage and frustration, what is the delta of the option? (Ignore theta and gamma effects and assume vol hasn't changed.)

10. Is the option in Problem 9 in-the-money, at-the-money, or out-of-the-money? Why?

Problems on Gamma

1. At the close yesterday, IBM was down $2.64 per share from the day before. Also at the close, an IBM 138 call was priced yesterday at $ .98 bid, $1.01 ask, with a delta of .36. This morning, IBM was up $ .50 per share and the option is priced at $1.15 bid, $1.18 ask with a delta of .51. What was the option's gamma?

2. The gamma of Option A is .17. Option B, for the same underlying and strike but different expiry, has a gamma of .05. Which one has fewer days left?

    a. Option A. Why?

    b. Option B. Why?

3. A call has a gamma of .15 and a put—same stock, strike, and expiry—has a gamma of .06. Which one is OTM? Explain your answer.

    a. The call.

    b. The put.

4. A put has a gamma of .13 and a call—same stock, same expiry, different strike—has a gamma of .05. Which one has a strike closest to the stock price? Explain.

    a. The put.

    b. The call.

5. A put has a gamma of .11 and a delta of –.30 today. It is priced at $.55 bid, $.60 ask. If the delta was –.41 yesterday, what is the put's gamma?

6. A call has a gamma of .11 and a delta of .30 today. It is priced at $.55 bid, $.60 ask. If the delta was –.41 yesterday, what is the call's gamma?

7. When Stock X was trading at $115, the put option on the $113 strike with 30 days to expiry was worth $1.34. It had a delta of –0.3357 and a gamma of 0.062. How much would the put option be worth if the underlying increases to $117?

    a. $ .55

    b. $ .79

    c. $ .67

    d. $ .92

8. A stock is trading around $16.40. The call option on the $16 strike has a gamma of 0.617. What is the gamma of the put on the $16 strike?

    a. –.617

    b. .383

    c. .617

    d. –.383

9. Look at the following table of quotes. If they have the same strike, which one has the most time left before expiry? Explain your answer.

    a. Option A.

    b. Option B.

    c. Option C.

    d. Option D.

CALLS			PUTS	
LAST PRICE	GAMMA		GAMMA	LAST PRICE
$5.65	.15	OPTION A	–	–
$1.67	.20	OPTION B	–	–
–	–	OPTION C	.08	$1.95
–	–	OPTION D	.18	$.75

10. Look at the table for Problem 9. If these did not have the same strike but expired on the same day, which one would be closest to being at-the-money? Explain your answer.

    a. Option A.

    b. Option B.

    c. Option C.

    d. Option D.

Problems on Vega

1. A stock trading at $65.45 shows an increase in its historic volatility of 3.5% as the date approaches for an FDA approval letter. The price of the 65-strike call was $3.16. If the stock price is the same, what would the new price of the option be?

2. Which of the following options (on the same expiry) have the largest vega when the stock is trading at 100?

    a. 100-strike put.

    b. 120-strike call.

    c. 120-strike put.

    d. 80-strike call.

3. What can we say about the vega of an ATM option?

    a. The vega is (greatly) increasing as volatility increases.

    b. The vega is (greatly) decreasing as volatility increases.

    c. The vega is (mostly) constant as volatility increases.

Chapter 10

The Greeks: Theta and Rho

Introduction

We are continuing our discussion of the Greeks, the statistical measures that describe anticipated price performance of an option. Whereas Chapter 9 discussed those functions which the Black-Scholes Model used to define the relative speed of changes to option premiums, this chapter will discuss theta and rho. These Greek functions are grouped together because they both measure time-related decay of time premium.

Theta

> - <u>Theta</u>: Theta measures how quickly extrinsic value, or *time premium, decays over time*. Theta tends to accelerate as options approach expiry and is negative for all long puts and calls.

Theta represents how quickly extrinsic value erodes per day and is measured in cents per option (per share). For example, an option with a theta of –.13 today will have 13 cents shaved off its time premium by tomorrow, *ceteris paribus*. Theta is expressed as a negative number (except if the position is short, then theta is positive) to represent the loss of value as time passes. Since the time remaining on an option can never increase, time decay is a one-way street. Thus, theta is a critically important consideration, not only in the purchase of long calls and puts, but as we will see in later chapters, also for various spreads and other strategies.

Since all options—puts and calls—ultimately expire, *time premium gradually decays to zero over time*. This reality, one of the very few absolutes in finance, makes theta as important as delta in the assessment of whether to invest in a particular option or not.

Delta and theta share this in common: both are _not natural phenomena, but are created, nurtured, and destroyed by human greed and fear._ Their existence carries a certain internal logic, as discussed in Chapter 7, but their ebb and flow depend on human estimates of trade profitability. Theta is directly a function of how much time remains until expiry, relative to the amount of premium extant. Since theta depends upon the amount of existing time premium, theta is dependent on the major factors that affect the size of time premium, including moneyness, time until expiry, and volatility of the underlying. (Dividend payments also affect time premium, as we have seen, but its calculation is arithmetic by subtracting the payment directly from time premium.) There is also some interest rate influence on time premium, which will be discussed below, when we cover _rho._

The Black-Scholes Theta

The equation for theta is straightforward: it is the equation for call and put valuation, as discussed in Chapter 7, divided by the number of days remaining until expiry. Merton Black and Byron Scholes were not specific as to whether time premium decay was based on calendar days or trading days, but experience demonstrates that calendar days are preferred. This fact has an effect on those who transact an option trade on a Friday or before a long weekend.

The Black-Scholes formula for call theta:

$$\theta = \frac{1}{T}\left[-\left(\frac{S_O \sigma e^{-q\tau}}{2\sqrt{\tau}} \times \frac{1}{\sqrt{2\pi}} \times e^{-d_1^2/2}\right) - rKe^{-r\tau}N(d_2) + qS_O e^{-q\tau}N(d_1)\right]$$

The Black-Scholes formula for put theta:

$$\theta = \frac{1}{T}\left[-\left(\frac{S_O \sigma e^{-q\tau}}{2\sqrt{\tau}} \times \frac{1}{\sqrt{2\pi}} \times e^{-d_1^2/2}\right) + rKe^{-r\tau}N(d_2) - qS_O e^{-q\tau}N(d_1)\right]$$

where T = calendar days until expiry.

As esoteric as the equation appears, most of it should look very familiar: the entire set of terms after the quotient $1/T$ is the Black-Scholes equation for the valuation of calls and puts. The equation suggests that theta is nothing more than the pro rata dispersion of time premium over the remaining life of the option, but do the arithmetic and you will find that the function is actually a Taylor series, and so the actual amount per day gradually increases until about one month remains until expiry, after which theta becomes increasingly large.

The Time Premium Erosion Function

- <u>Theta Increases as Expiry Nears</u>: The amount of *time premium erosion increases* as a percent of time value remaining (and in absolute terms) *as expiry nears.*

The erosion of time premium increases geometrically as expiry nears, and this is perfectly logical. It doesn't require an understanding of calculus to consider the idea that investors are generally willing to pay more for an option that has more time to perform, compared to one with less time until expiry. Furthermore, it is important to be reminded that *only extrinsic value is subject to time decay*; ITM options will carry intrinsic value until the day of expiry. OTM options only carry extrinsic value and will gradually diminish in value over time until it reaches zero, if the option remains OTM. In other words, if an underlying stock is trading at $42, the 40 call will always have $2 of intrinsic value, whether there are three or 300 days remaining until expiration.[1] Any value above $2 will be extrinsic value and therefore subject to time decay.

As suggested above, *the rate of time premium erosion is geometric*, governed by the number *e*, as follows (Figure 10.1):

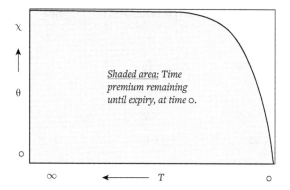

FIGURE 10.1 Value of time premium falls slowly initially but sharply as expiry nears.

---

1 Unless the underlying pays a dividend or other return of capital. Then, the intrinsic value declines an amount equal to the distribution.

If we graph the value of *theta* over time, the function looks like this:

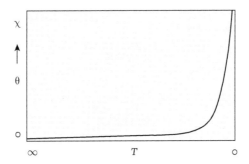

FIGURE 10.2 Theta increases geometrically as expiry nears.

Note that theta changes over time. Assuming the price of the stock doesn't change, an out-of-the-money $3.50 option with a theta of –.20 will be worth $3.30 tomorrow. At that point (the next day), the theta may then have a value of –.22. If so, the option will only be worth $3.08 the day after, assuming prices remain constant. Gradually, the value of the option will approach zero if the option remains out-of-the-money, and the theta will gradually increase. The following table illustrates this point (Table 10.1):

TABLE 10.1 Theta increases as expiry gets nearer. Stock price $30.53 per share, 30 strike.

CALL PRICE				PUT PRICE		
BID	ASK	THETA	DAYS TO EXPIRY	BID	ASK	THETA
.72	.74	–.07	10	.18	.19	–.02
1.13	1.15	–.03	45	.52	.53	–.01
1.63	1.66	–.01	136	1.29	1.33	–.01
1.98	2.05	–.01	255	2.13	2.19	–.01
2.75	2.92	.00	619	3.90	4.05	.00

Here, we see that the theta factor is less as more time exists before expiry, and this is true for both puts and calls. Parenthetically, one may see a zero theta, but it is never *actually* zero. Instead, it would be so small that it doesn't register with two decimal places. However, the key point is the approach to zero theta at the limit the further out in time.

The Relationship Between Theta and Strike Price

- <u>ATM Options Have the Highest Thetas</u>: This is the *consequence of more extrinsic value for at-the-money options*. Theta drops as options move deeper in-the-money or out-of-the-money.

You may have noted that both OTM and ITM options also carry less theta than ATM options. We have previously observed that at-the-money options have the highest extrinsic value. For this reason, these options also have the highest thetas, *ceteris paribus*. This is reflective of the fact that theta affects only extrinsic value, which we have seen is highest for ATM options, and which drops off for both ITM and OTM options. Similarly, deep in- and out-of-the-money options have lower thetas because they have less extrinsic value; the less value they have, they less they can lose through decay.

Consequently, as evident in Figure 10.3, the theta function has the same shape as the gamma function and for similar reasons: more time premium means more theta effect, just as more premium has more gamma effect.

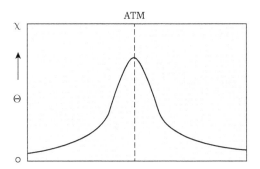

FIGURE 10.3 Effect of moneyness on theta, which is highest ATM.

For those who are selling to open an option position, at-the-money options represent the highest potential return, but they also present the most uncertain degree of risk. With a delta near .50, the odds are equal to a coin toss as to whether the option expires ITM. This phenomenon is further illustrated in Table 10.2:

TABLE 10.2 Call options for near month (9 days to expiry), underlying price $113.72 per share.

STRIKE	BID	ASK	B/A SPREAD	MID	DELTA	THETA	OI	IV
110	$3.95	$4.10	$0.15	$4.03	0.84	−0.05	536	22.41%
111	$2.93	$3.25	$0.32	$3.09	0.79	−0.05	33	19.69%
112	$2.23	$2.42	$0.19	$2.33	0.70	−0.06	13	19.19%
113	$1.62	$1.72	$0.10	$1.67	0.58	−0.07	26	18.82%
114	$1.07	$1.13	$0.06	$1.10	0.46	−0.07	304	18.01%
115	$0.64	$0.71	$0.07	$0.68	0.34	−0.06	7118	17.46%
116	$0.37	$0.42	$0.05	$0.40	0.23	−0.05	551	17.30%
117	$0.19	$0.23	$0.04	$0.21	0.14	−0.04	888	17.05%
118	$0.12	$0.14	$0.02	$0.13	0.09	−0.03	2474	17.86%
119	$0.05	$0.09	$0.04	$0.07	0.05	−0.02	518	18.12%
120	$0.05	$0.06	$0.01	$0.06	0.04	−0.02	12555	19.76%

Notice that the 114 call—just out-of-the-money and carrying no intrinsic value—has an extrinsic value (midpoint) of $1.10 per share with 9 days remaining until expiry. A theta of −.07 carried over 9 days only equals erosion of $.63. What about the remaining $.47? The answer is that tomorrow, theta will be a little higher, and the day after that, higher still. On the day of expiry, theta will be equal to the remaining amount of time premium. Meanwhile, the 113 call—just in-the-money—has a midpoint value of $1.67 and extrinsic value of only $.95, with 9 days remaining. Just like the 114 call, the 113 call will have a steadily increasing theta until the day of expiry, when the theta will equal the remaining extrinsic value.

The question sometimes arises as to the precise meaning of "at-the-money," since it is rare when an option closes *exactly* at a strike price. Is it the 113 call or the 114 call? The answer is **both the 113 and the 114**, and some would also include a few strikes on both sides of 113–114. If one is the type who requires exactitude, you are probably studying the wrong subject. However, consider the option that has the highest extrinsic value. In the instance of Table 10.2, the 114 call has the highest extrinsic value. Note also that it is "closest" to the nearest strike: with the underlying at 113.72, only $.28 separates the underlying from the 114 strike, but $.72 separates it from the 113 strike.

Also note that the 120 call has over 12,000 contracts of open interest. This is a large number compared to open interest of other strikes and is probably large because 120 is a round number and the expiry is a popular month. This suggests that it has been on the calendar far longer than the one-dollar increment strikes, which were added to the chain as August expiry became either the lead or next-to-lead month; there was less time for the one-dollar strikes to accumulate open interest. The lack of contracts leads to a possible lack of market liquidity, which can be problematic if the investor wishes to liquidate prior to expiry. Low open interest can result in disadvantageous order fill. The role of market-makers in price setting was discussed in Chapter 5, and here we see a possible example.

Rho

- <u>Rho</u>: Rho measures the *effect of interest rates on option values*. The higher the interest rate, the greater the impact on option prices.

And finally, rho. Rho measures the impact of the prevailing interest rate on an option's value. More specifically, the **rho measures the change in an option's value given a change in interest rates**. Rho is calibrated such that for every point that the interest ratio or dividend increases, the option premium will increase the value stated by this Greek. In other words, rho measures how sensitive option price is to changes in interest rates. An increase in interest rates raises the carrying costs associated with holding an option position, a situation very similar to that found in futures contracts, as we have seen. As such, it *increases the value of the option to compensate for this cost*. Conversely, a decrease in interest rates lowers the rate of increase to the value of options. In either event, rho *is always additive to option value*. From this we infer that put premiums increase negatively, and the rho equations for put options are adjusted to accommodate this dynamic.

However, the impact of interest rates on price is so small, relatively speaking, that it makes very little difference overall. Familiarity with delta, gamma, and theta is much more important because each has a significant measurable impact on option prices. The greatest impact by rho would be for LEAPS, but even here, a change of 1% in the annual interest rate will have only a minor impact on the price of the option. The Black-Scholes model defines rho as follows:

Equation for Call Rho: $\quad \rho_c = Ke^{-r_d^2/2}\tau N\left(d_1 - \sigma\sqrt{\tau}\right)$

Equation for Put Rho: $\quad \rho_p = -Ke^{-r_d^2/2}\tau N\left(d_1 + \sigma\sqrt{\tau}\right)$

The equations describe a compounding effect on the option value. We immediately recognize the compounding factor, with r being the one-year T-bill rate (usually) used instead of d_1. Also note that the signs for K have been inverted for puts, which adjusts the rho influence to be effective for puts. The same logic prevails for change of sign for the $N(d_1)$ factor.

Summary and Conclusions

This chapter examines the two Greeks that fundamentally affect the extrinsic value of options, theta and rho. Of the two, theta is significantly more important and as we shall see, the critical factor in the construction of diagonal spreads and calendar spreads. Theta measures the rate of time premium decay. In the discussion on theta and time decay, we noted that decay speeds up geometrically as expiry nears. Logically, theta also has more impact on larger premiums than on smaller premiums, but all *premiums erode geometrically*.

The point must now be made that an option position benefits either from the passage of time or from market movement but cannot benefit from both. This means that either a trade is made for purposes of harvesting premium as it erodes or by profiting from price movement. Choose carefully.

Rho measures the discounting effects of interest rates on option prices. Rho is routinely dismissed and usually forgotten. That may not be the case if interest rates rise to double digits, as they did in the late 1970s. But for now, rho is of low importance because discount factors are tiny today with interest rates near zero.

Going Forward

We have concluded the all-important discussion on the dynamics of option pricing. The next chapters turn to the even more critical subject of how to put this knowledge to work.

Problems on Theta

1. Look at the following quotes. Each of these are at-the-money options. Which option has the most time left until expiry? Explain your answer.

   a. Option A.

   b. Option B.

   c. Option C.

   d. Option D.

CALLS			PUTS	
TIME PREMIUM	THETA		THETA	TIME PREMIUM
$3.65	–.15	OPTION A	–	–
$1.07	–.20	OPTION B	–	–
–	–	OPTION C	–.11	$1.10
–	–	OPTION D	–.18	$.95

2. Look at the following quotes. If these options are for the same stock and same expiry, which one has a strike deepest in-the-money? Explain your answer.

    a. Option A.

    b. Option B.

    c. Option C.

    d. Option D.

CALLS			PUTS	
TIME PREMIUM	THETA		THETA	TIME PREMIUM
$3.15	–.15	OPTION A	–	–
$3.85	–.25	OPTION B	–	–
–	–	OPTION C	–.10	$1.50
–	–	OPTION D	–.063	$.95

3. Look at the table for Problem 1. If these options are for the same stock and same expiry, which one has a strike nearest the current market price? Explain your answer.

    a. Option A.

    b. Option B.

    c. Option C.

    d. Option D.

4. Each of these are at-the-money call options. Which option has an underlying with the most historic volatility? Explain your answer.

    a. Option A.

    b. Option B.

    c. Option C.

    d. Option D.

CALLS		
TIME PREMIUM	THETA	
$2.19	–.15	OPTION A
$2.35	–.25	OPTION B
$1.95	–.05	OPTION C
$1.90	–.10	OPTION D

5. An option has $0.35 of extrinsic value and a theta of –.05. Approximately how many days are left before expiry? Explain your answer.

6. A stock *increases* in price. What effect does this have on the stock's call option theta? Explain your answer.

   a. Increases it.

   b. Decreases it.

   c. Has no material effect.

7. A stock *increases* in price. What effect does this have on the stock's put option theta? Explain your answer.

   a. Increases it.

   b. Decreases it.

   c. Has no material effect.

8. A stock *decreases* in price. What effect does this have on the stock's call option theta? Explain your answer.

   a. Increases it.

   b. Decreases it.

   c. Has no material effect.

9. A stock *decreases* in price. What effect does this have on the stock's put option theta? Explain your answer.

   a. Increases it.

   b. Decreases it.

   c. Has no material effect.

Chapter 11

Vertical Option Spreads

Introduction

> - Vertical Spreads: A form of investment that exploits the differences in intrinsic, extrinsic, or both values of two options with different strikes—type, expiry, and underlying being the same. Its structure consists of a long and short option of the same type.

The general idea in most option spreads is to capitalize on the difference that exists between premiums of different options for the same stock or commodity. This is usually accomplished by a simultaneous sale and purchase of either all puts or all calls.[1] The simplest form of spreads are vertical spreads, so named because they are of the same type from the same underlying with the same expiry, differing only in their strikes. Depending on the spread, this is done either for income or for speculative purposes. If established for income, the strategy is to create spreads with the belief that time will prevail and time premium on both options will expire worthless, thereby realizing a profit. If the spread is established for speculative purposes, then the profit is determined by the arithmetic difference in the strikes, minus the cost of the spread.

The means by which these objectives are accomplished is varied but hints as to option spread construction are often found in the names given to their respective strategies. In this chapter, all of the following examples are vertical spreads. They are constructed so that all

---

1   Vertical spreads consist of two "legs," one long and one short. A leg of a spread refers to any one of the individual option strikes involved in the spread. It is possible to "leg into" a spread, which means the investor first buys the long option and then sells the short option (or vice versa).

of the options expire simultaneously. They are "vertical" because the strike prices differ, but expiries are the same.

Types of Vertical Option Spreads

There is a very wide variety of option spread opportunities. Spreads can be constructed to favor bullish sentiment or bearish sentiment. They can be constructed for an initial credit or debit.

Bull spreads are so named because they are constructed when one has a bullish opinion on a stock or commodity. They will be profitable if the underlying stock or commodity moves up in price. Bull spreads can be:

- Bull Call Spreads (always a debit spread)
- Bull Put Spreads (always a credit spread)

Similarly, bear spreads are so named because they are constructed when one has a bearish opinion on a stock or commodity. They will be profitable if the underlying stock or commodity moves down in price. Bear spreads can be:

- Bear Call Spreads (always a credit spread)
- Bear Put Spreads (always a debit spread)

In practice, most investors will ultimately favor and use some types of spreads more than others, but it is still incumbent upon the options investor to at least be familiar with the varieties of option spreads, when they are used, how they are used, and why they are used.

Credit Spreads Versus Debit Spreads

- Credit Spread: A credit spread is any spread that, upon consummation, adds cash to an account. These spreads can be of any configuration, provided they add cash to the account.
- Debit Spread: A debit spread is any spread that, upon consummation, diminishes cash balance of an account. These spreads can be of any configuration, provided they have a net cost against the account.

As the names imply, a credit spread results in the addition of capital to the account as soon as the spread is initiated, whereas a debit spread results in a net expenditure in the account. Credit spreads rely on erosion of time premium to be profitable, whereas debit spreads rely on price moves of the underlying in the direction of the spread itself to be profitable. Both can be constructed in expectation of either a bullish move or a bearish move.

A credit spread is accomplished by selling-to-open an option that has a higher price and buying-to-open an option that has a lower price. Any spread can be arranged as a credit spread, although the most common credit spreads are plain vanilla vertical spreads, either bull put spreads or bear call spreads. In both instances, the desired result is for both options in the spread to expire OTM and the maximum profit is attained if the underlying price at expiry leaves the options OTM.

In contrast, debit spreads involve the opposite strategy: the investor buys-to-open the more expensive option and sells-to-open the lower cost option. The maximum loss is the cost of the spread, and the maximum gain occurs if the underlying price exceeds the strike of the higher strike option. Details follow.

Debit Spreads

Bull Call Spreads

> • <u>Bull Call Spreads</u>: Bull call spreads are a debit spread formed when a call option is bought-to-open and another call of the same issue and expiry, but at a higher strike, is sold-to-open.

An example is shown as Table 11.1:

TABLE 11.1 Example—Bull call spread (Apple Inc., Underlying Price: $146.06/share).

SYMBOL	QTY	TYPE	EXPIRY	STRIKE	BID	ASK	DELTA	INT VAL	EXT VAL
AAPL	1	Call	11/19	140	$10.10	$10.20	.57	$6.06	$4.14
AAPL	−1	Call	11/19	145	$7.00	$7.10	.42	$1.06	$5.94

The investor buys-to-open the lower strike (the 140 call at the ask of $10.20) and sells-to-open the higher strike (the 145 call at the bid of $7.00). In this example, the investor pays $1,020 per option and receives back $700 from the sale of the 145 call. Thus, the maximum loss for the investor is –$1,020 + $700 = –$320 per spread. This occurs if the underlying falls below $140 per share. The maximum profit for the investor occurs if the underlying rises to or above $145 per share. (The break-even point is at the price of the underlying equal to the lower strike, plus the cost of the spread. In this example, $143.20.)

For a bull call spread, the maximum profit earned is equal to the difference between the size of the spread and the cost of the spread, as follows:

$$(K_u - K_d) - (V_u - V_d) = \max (R_{bcs})$$

where K_u is the upper option strike, K_d is the lower option strike, V_u is the price of the upper strike option, and V_d is the price of the lower strike option. In the example shown above, the spread is 5 points (145–140) and the net difference between the price of the options is $3.20. The maximum profit is therefore 5-3.20 = 1.80. Since an option contract is (usually) for 100 shares, the maximum profit is $180 per spread. The profit/loss structure of this bull call spread is illustrated in Figure 11.1. (Figure 11.1 is an example of what is frequently called a "hockey-stick chart," which graphically describes the profit-loss potential of a given option position.)

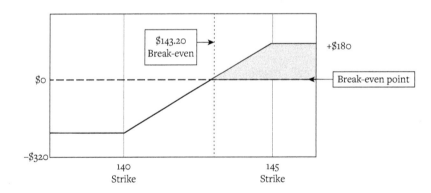

FIGURE 11.1 Profit/loss profile for sample bull call spread (debit).

With a maximum gain of $180 and a maximum loss of $320, this bull call spread example has a risk/reward ratio of 180/320 = .563. Further, based on the value of the delta and gamma, it is possible to estimate the probability of the spread reaching maximum profit (if AAPL reaches $145.00 or more by expiry). In this instance, the gamma has a value of approximately

.04. Therefore, we can estimate that the spread has an approximate probability of 64% of achieving full profitability.

Each individual investor has its own risk-return tolerance, so it is impossible to say that this is a great spread. However, the characteristics of this trade can be generalized as follows:

- A bull call spread works because the sale of the higher strike lowers the overall break-even point of the investment. In the example shown above, a purchase of the 140-strike option by itself cost $1,020, so that the break-even point for purchase of the straight call would be an underlying value of $150.20, or a 3.5% increase of the stock value. Compare the spread break-even point at $143.20, which is already below the current market price of the underlying. Therefore, the likelihood of success is much higher with the spread than the call option by itself.

- Probabilities of success can be used to provide an estimated risk-adjusted payoff. A reasonable estimate would use the delta of the profit-maximizing strike option, adjusted by gamma if necessary. If the probability of success is 64% as estimated, then the expected return would be $180 X .64, or $115.2. If the risk of success is 64%, then the risk of loss is 36%, and the expected loss would be $320 X .36, or $115.2. From this standpoint, the risk-adjusted risk/reward ratio is exactly one—the trade is a toss-up. Any risk/reward of less than one is not favorable. It implies a greater risk of loss than gain.

- The sale of the higher strike should be at-the-money or slightly out-of-the-money to "harvest" as much extrinsic value as possible. The purpose is to reimburse as much of the cost of the spread as possible, and ATM options have the highest extrinsic value as a percent of option value than any other options on the chain.

- The rate of return on invested capital is superior to the long call. As structured, the spread in the example returns a maximum of $180 on an investment of $320, a return on investment (ROI) of 56.3%. A comparable return on the long call would be $10.20 times 1.563, or a value of $16.94 at expiry. For this to happen, AAPL would need to be at $163—an 11.6% increase over current values. This would yield a profit of $674 but requires a considerably greater price move of the underlying. If the spread investor is looking at an equal return to the long call, it need only increase the number of spreads to two at a much lower total commitment of capital.

- If the probability of success for this example is too low, the investor can create a spread with lower strikes. The lower the strikes, the greater the chance of success. However, the amount of profit declines as the spread moves deeper in-the-money.

- Conversely, if the spread does not provide sufficient profit, the investor can create a spread with both legs OTM. However, the higher the strikes, the lower the chance of success, but the amount of profit increases as the spread moves further out-of-the-money.

- Based on these observations, buying-to-open a call rarely makes sense because the probabilities of success are much less than that for a spread, and the ROI is lower. The greatest enticement for a long call is the investor's sense of unlimited gain as opposed to a limited profit potential for a spread. Caution should be noted here: the probability of a very large gain is very small.

- A last point: *all bull call spreads are directional trades.* If the investor is not confident that the stock is rising short term, then this spread should not be initiated.

Because both calls would be ITM if the spread is successful, follow-up is necessary on the Friday of expiry. The spread writer must either (1) close out the spread; or (2) notify the broker/dealer of intention of exercising the long call. The choice depends on which alternative costs the least. Some firms do not charge commissions if an option is less than $5 in value (quoted as $.05), but the investor still must recognize the cost of the bid-ask spread. On the other hand, there are no fees to exercise an option, and assuming the owner of the short call exercises (almost always an automatic exercise if ITM), the asset purchased at the lower strike is sold at the higher strike, and your profit is realized. Many firms automatically exercise ITM options whether the client informs them of intent to exercise or not. Despite this, it is a better practice to inform the firm of intent to exercise.

If the lower strike is ITM but the higher strike is OTM, the best practice is to close out both legs of the spread on the last trading day before expiry. This avoids any problem of price risk on the long position held over the weekend if the lower strike is exercised but the upper leg is not.

Bear Put Spreads

> - <u>Bear Put Spreads</u>: Bear put spreads are a debit spread formed when a put option is bought-to-open and another call of the same issue and expiry, but at a lower strike, is sold-to-open.

In principle, the structure of a bear put spread is identical to the bull call spread. The bear put spread expects one option to accumulate intrinsic value as the stock declines in price and expects time premium to erode on the sold option. For a bear put spread, two put option positions, one long at a higher strike, one sold at a lower strike, are simultaneously opened. An example is shown as Table 11.2:

TABLE 11.2 Example—Bear put spread (AbbVie Inc., Underlying Price: $107.73/share).

SYMBOL	QTY	TYPE	EXPIRY	STRIKE	BID	ASK	DELTA	INT VAL	EXT VAL
ABBV	1	Put	11/19	110	$5.85	$6.30	–.64	$2.27	$4.03
ABBV	–1	Put	11/19	105	$3.40	$3.75	–.42	$0	$3.40

The investor buys-to-open the higher strike (the 110 put at the ask of $6.30) and sells-to-open the lower strike (the 105 put at the bid of $3.40). In this example, the investor pays $630 per 110 put and receives back $340 from the sale of the 105 put. Thus, the maximum loss for the investor is –$630 + $340 = –$290 per spread. This occurs if the underlying rises above $110 per share. The maximum profit for the investor occurs if the underlying price falls to or below $105 per share.

For a bear put spread, the maximum profit earned is equal to the difference between the size of the spread and the cost of the spread, as follows:

$$(K_u - K_d) - (V_d - V_u) = \max (R_{bps})$$

(The variables are defined as per bull call spreads.) In the example shown above, the spread is 5 points (110–105) and the net difference between the price of the options is $2.90. The maximum profit is therefore 5 – 2.90 = 2.10. Since an option contract is (usually) for 100 shares, the maximum profit is $210 per spread. The profit/loss structure of this bull call spread is illustrated in Figure 11.2.

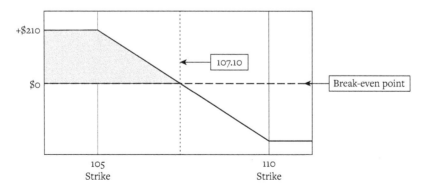

FIGURE 11.2 Profit/loss profile for sample bear put spread (debit).

With a maximum gain of $290 and a maximum loss of $210, this bear put spread example has a risk/reward ratio of 290/210 = 1.38. As in the bull call spread, we can estimate the probability of the spread reaching maximum profit (if ABBV drops to $105.00 or below by expiry). In this instance, the gamma has a value of approximately .04. Therefore, we can estimate that the spread has an approximate probability of 68% of achieving full profitability. Furthermore, based on similar calculations as in the bull call spread, with a 68% chance of success, there is a 32% chance of loss. Therefore, the estimated risk-adjusted profit is .68 × $290 = $197.20, with a risk-adjusted potential loss of $67.20. Since the expected profit is greater than the expected loss, the trade is favorable.

This example affords generalizations like those articulated in the discussion of bull call spreads. Spreads will always be better than a pure directional purchase of a put. The primary reason this is true is that all options have extrinsic value, and near-the-money options are always the most expensive. If an investor chooses to purchase OTM options to compensate for high cost, it assumes the greater risk of the underlying price being unfavorable at expiry. The further OTM, the less likely the option trade will succeed. If the investor wishes to increase the chance of success by buying an option deeper ITM, there is a trade-off: the investor faces increasing risk of loss in the event the underlying moves against the expected price trend because the spread will cost more.

All bear put spreads are directional trades. If the investor is not confident that the stock will fall in price short term, then this spread should not be initiated. Furthermore, as in the situation with bull call spreads, because both puts would be ITM if the spread is successful, follow-up is necessary on the Friday (or last trading day) before expiry. The spread writer must either (1) close out the spread; or (2) notify the broker/dealer of intention of exercising the long call. Similarly, if the higher strike is ITM but the lower strike is OTM, the best practice is to close out both legs of the spread on the last trading day before expiry. This avoids any problem of price risk on the short position held over the weekend if the higher leg is exercised but the lower leg is not.

Credit Spreads

Bear Call Spreads

- <u>Bear Call Spreads</u>: Bear call spreads are credit spreads formed when a call option is sold-to-open and another call of the same issue and expiry, but at a higher strike, is bought-to-open.

An example is shown as Table 11.3:

TABLE 11.3 Example—Bear call spread (SPDR S&P 500 ETF, underlying price: $441.40/share).

SYMBOL	QTY	TYPE	EXPIRY	STRIKE	BID	ASK	DELTA	INT VAL	EXT VAL
SPY	−1	Call	10/15	445	$5.07	$5.10	.40	$0.00	$5.10
SPY	1	Call	10/15	450	$2.62	$2.64	.27	$0.00	$2.64

This example typifies the structure of a bear call spread. The idea behind this strategy is that the underlying will fall in value to price levels at least as low as the lowest option strike in the spread. If this occurs, both calls expire OTM and worthless. The profit consists of the difference in the option values that were obtained when the spread was initiated, as defined by this simple equation:

$$\max(R_{bcs}) = (V_d - V_u).$$

(The variables are defined as per bull call spreads.) In the example above (Table 11.3), the maximum profit is $246 and occurs if SPY closes below the lower strike and both legs of the spread expire worthless. This is a credit spread: the maximum profit is achieved immediately upon the sale of the spread, and the amount is credited to the account as cash. The profit profile is indicated in Figure 11.3:

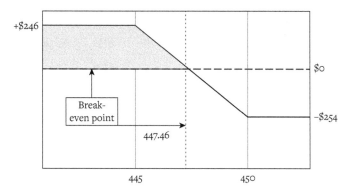

FIGURE 11.3 Profit/loss profile for sample bear call spread (credit).

With a maximum gain of $246 and a maximum loss of $254, this bear call spread example has a risk/reward ratio of less than one—246/254 = 0.97. But it is very close, and the trade appears better when risk adjusted. We can estimate the probability of the spread reaching maximum profit (if SPY stays below $445.00 by expiry). In this instance, the delta of the 445 call is .40, and its gamma has a value of approximately .02. Therefore, we can estimate that the spread has an approximate probability of 60% of achieving full profitability. Furthermore, with a 58% chance of success, there is a 42% chance of loss. Therefore, the estimated risk-adjusted profit is .58 × $246 = $142.68, with a risk-adjusted potential loss of $106.68. Since the expected profit is greater than the expected loss, the trade is favorable.

For credit vertical spreads, levels of aggressiveness depend on how far the spread is in-the-money. The least aggressive spreads would be those that are out of the money, such as the example above. What happens when both sides of the spread are in-the-money? When both legs of a bear call spread are in the money, the underlying price must drop below the lowest (short) strike to optimize profit. The probability of success depends on the likelihood that both calls expire worthless. The deeper the spread is ITM, the lower the chances the spread will be profitable. The odds of success, however, are smaller than more aggressive spreads. The following table compares various bull call spreads on SPY:

TABLE 11.5A Risk-return comparative, SPY selected bear call spreads.

	STRIKE		PRICE		SP SIZE	CREDIT SIZE	MAX LOSS	SUCCESS PROB	R/L RATIO (WTD)
SYMBOL	LOWER	UPPER	LOWER	UPPER					
SPY	455	460	$1.10	$0.42	5	$69	−$431	70%	.37
SPY	450	455	$2.62	$1.10	5	$152	−$348	65%	.81
SPY	445	450	$5.08	$2.64	5	$245	−$255	58%	1.33
SPY	440	445	$8.24	$5.10	5	$317	−$183	49%	1.66
SPY	435	440	$11.66	$8.27	5	$360	−$140	41%	1.79
SPY	430	435	$15.55	$12.05	5	$392	−$108	37%	2.13

The results demonstrate the trade-off between risk and return in bear call spreads. The deeper ITM the spread is, the greater the nominal return as well as the probability-weighted returns (last column on the right), and the probability of attaining the nominal return becomes smaller (second column on the right). ATM spreads are the middle ground, but for the risk averse, it may not be optimal. Many instead place the short call (the "lower" leg) above what is perceived to be a resistance price level. As usual, there is no free lunch in the marketplace. There is almost always a risk-return tradeoff.

Bull Put Spreads

> - Bull Put Spreads: Bull put spreads are credit spreads formed when a put option is sold-to-open and another put of the same issue and expiry, but at a lower strike, is bought-to-open.

An example is shown as Table 11.4:

TABLE 11.4 Example—Bull put spread (SPDR S&P 500 ETF, underlying price: $441.40/share).

SYMBOL	QTY	TYPE	EXPIRY	STRIKE	BID	ASK	DELTA	INT VAL	EXT VAL
ENPH	−1	Put	10/15	160	$8.10	$8.45	−.47	$0.00	$8.10
ENPH	1	Put	10/15	155	$6.00	$6.20	−.38	$0.00	$6.20

This example typifies the structure of a bull put spread. The idea behind this strategy is that the underlying will rise in value to price levels at least as high as the highest option strike in the spread. If this occurs, both puts expire OTM and worthless. The profit consists of the difference in the option values that were obtained when the spread was initiated, as defined by this simple equation (the same as the payout of a bear call spread):

$$\max(R_{bcs}) = (V_d - V_u).$$

(The variables are defined as per bull call spreads.) Maximum profit mirrors that of the bear call spread. We emphasize that bull put spreads and bear call spreads are always credit spreads and as such attain maximum profit—the initial credit—when both legs expire OTM. In the example above (Table 11.4), the maximum profit is the arithmetic difference between the short put and the long put and is equal to $190. It occurs if ENPH closes above the upper strike and both legs of the spread expire worthless. An investor creates this spread if it is bullish on the underlying—in this case, modestly so, since both legs of this spread are already OTM. As is typical of credit spreads, the maximum profit is achieved immediately upon the sale of the spread, and the amount is credited to the account as cash. The profit profile is indicated in Figure 11.4:

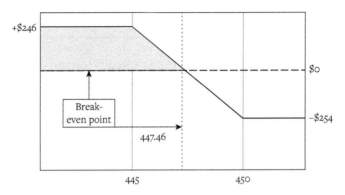

FIGURE 11.4 Profit/loss profile for sample bear call spread (credit).

This spread is another example of a near-the-money credit spread. As with the previous example, this spread example has a risk/reward ratio of less than one: 190/310 = 0.61. Similar to all other option positions, the probability of the spread reaching maximum profit (i.e., ENPH > $160.00 by expiry) can also be approximated. In this instance, the delta of the 160 call is –.47, and its gamma has a value of approximately .02. Therefore, we can estimate that the spread has an approximate probability of 56% of achieving full profitability. Furthermore, with a 56% chance of success, there is a 35% chance of loss. Therefore, the estimated risk-adjusted profit is .56 × $190 = $106.40, with a risk-adjusted potential loss of $108.50. Since the expected profit is less than the expected loss, the trade is NOT favorable.

Risk/Return Ratio

One would think that the choice of what spread to construct depends on its risk/return ratio. In this case, it is clear that the most favorable spreads are those whose returns outweigh the risk of loss. It is easy to calculate this by dividing the maximum potential profit by the maximum potential loss. The four examples in Table 11.5 are therefore calculated as follows:

TABLE 11.5 Ranking of vertical spread examples based on nominal risk/return ratio.

EXAMPLE	MAX. POT'L GAIN	MAX. POT'L LOSS	RISK/RETURN RATIO
1	$180	$320	0.56
2	$210	$290	0.72
3	$246	$254	0.97
4	$190	$310	0.61

Based on these simple calculations, the best choice is Example 3, but indeed, none would be optimal since they all have a risk/return ratio of less than 1.0. (In all cases, total costs—including commissions—should be included.)

However, this is not necessarily the case, because out-of-the-money debit spreads are likely to show the best risk/return ratios, yet their probability of success is considerably lower. Therefore, one must further weigh these returns with a probability factor (measured as a percent likelihood of success using delta as an approximate estimate) to determine which is most favorable:

TABLE 11.6 Ranking of vertical spread examples based on risk-adjusted risk/return ratio.

EXAMPLE	MAX POT'L GAIN	MAX POT'L LOSS	PROB. FACTORS	RISK-WTD RETURN RATIO
1	$180	$320	64%	1.00
2	$210	$290	68%	2.93
3	$246	$254	58%	1.34
4	$190	$310	56%	0.98

Now the choice is Example 2 by a very wide margin. Thus, the most important factor in assessing risk is the volatility of the underlying stock or commodity. In this instance, the best trade of the group is the SPY 445/450 bear call spread.

Moneyness and Spreads

The spread writer has a tremendous flexibility in selection, enough to satisfy any risk-return tolerance level. For example, consider the following quotes for SPY:

TABLE 11.7 Price and OI for SPY options, October 15 expiry (25 days left).

CALLS			MKT: $434.04	PUTS		
BID	**ASK**	**OPEN INTEREST**	**STRIKE:**	**BID**	**ASK**	**OPEN INTEREST**
$12.50	$12.56	5,083	429	$7.98	$8.02	10,076
$11.79	$11.85	7,534	430	$8.27	$8.31	116,612
$11.10	$11.15	3,194	431	$8.57	$8.61	6,177
$10.42	$10.46	4,876	432	$8.88	$8.92	14,747
$9.75	$9.78	5,629	433	$9.21	$9.25	14,677
$9.09	$9.12	4,478	434	$9.55	$9.59	15,346
$8.44	$8.48	7,020	435	$9.90	$9.95	57,211
$7.81	$7.85	3,360	436	$10.27	$10.31	11,396
$7.20	$7.25	4,514	437	$10.59	$10.79	7,198
$6.60	$6.64	7,683	438	$10.78	$10.96	19,398

These quotes represent a single expiry among many and a slice of the chain that ranges 400 points (although not all options have strikes in increments of $1). All of these represent relatively similar risk profiles: the 429/430 bull put spread has a 58% probability of success, while the 438/439 bear put spread has roughly the same (59%) probability. Further, the 438/439 bear put spread has a $29 return for each $100 committed (29% ROI), whereas the 429/430 bull put spread only brings in $25 for each $100 committed (25% ROI); one is a credit spread, the other a debit spread. One could write a 455/454 bear put spread with a 90% chance of success and yield approximately the same, or a 395/394 bull put spread with roughly the same probability of success but receiving only 7% ROI.

The difference is explained by the volatility smirk for these options (see Figure 11.5) and reinforces the need to understand the specifics of an option spread before venturing into one. OTM puts have more IV than ITM puts.

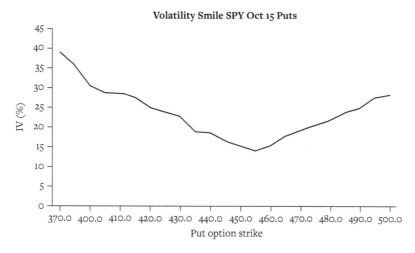

FIGURE 11.5 Volatility smirk for sample SPY puts.

Margin and Vertical Spreads

All credit spreads require margin, but debit spreads do not. The reason is simple; credit spreads, by their nature, have a portion of the spread uncovered, and that portion must be collateralized with cash or other equity in the account. Recall that credit spreads feature a more expensive short option and a cheaper long option. In theory (and in practice), if the underlying price is ITM relative to the short option, the underlying could be exercised, leaving exposure unless adequate equity is reserved to consummate the transaction. The minimum amount of margin required is set by the OCC, but each broker/dealer has the right to set more stringent margin requirements.

In contrast, debit spreads have the long option as the first to be ITM. Therefore, a short option beyond the long option is covered by the long option, and there is no risk of customer default.

Summary and Conclusion

We have completed an important step in understanding and using options. This chapter introduced you to the world of vertical spreads. You should now be familiar with the "twos": two different strikes in a vertical spread; two strategies—credit or debit spreads; two types of options—put spreads and call spreads; and two types of markets—bull spreads and bear spreads. Regardless of the type or strategy, vertical spreads are almost always better than a comparable single long option position, both in terms of commitment of capital and ROI. To equal the ROI equivalent of a spread requires an exceptional and low-probability outcome.

Risk-return attributes put to use our knowledge of IV and the Greek functions delta, theta, and gamma. We learned that the risk profile is influenced by the IV of the specific option. A word about risk-adjusted returns: ALL risk is assessed on the basis of the past. If markets were universally consistent to their reaction to news, if all investors and traders maintained the same risk aversion as traders and investors in the past, if global trading technologies were the same as always, and if human behavior was as predictable as subatomic particles, then past behavior is a reasonably close approximation of future results. Unfortunately for option users, none of these things are attributes of investor and trader reactions and behavior. Therefore, treat any statistic with some caution. Wade into turbulent waters conservatively; instead of going for a big gain, aim for high-probability trades. A baseball metaphor: be Rod Carew, not Harmon Killebrew.

Lastly, vertical spreads imply a degree of market direction. Consequently, it is prudent to always remember that follow-up (closing the spread or allowing exercise) is necessary for debit spreads, but no follow-up is necessary for credit spreads if all options are OTM. Otherwise, they, too, should be closed out before expiry.

Looking Forward

We will now continue our journey through the world of options by exploring calendar spreads, also known as horizontal spreads. In contrast to vertical spreads—which expire at the same time but feature different strikes—calendar spreads have the same strike but expire at different times. As such, they represent "pure theta" plays.

Problems on Vertical Spreads

1. You're pretty convinced that the price of TSLA stock is going lower. What type(s) of vertical spread would you use? Explain.

   a. Bull put spread or bull call spread.

   b. Bear call spread or bear put spread.

   c. Bull call spread only.

   d. Bear put spread only.

   e. Any of these.

2. Look at the following option quotes for a stock at $45.80. Suppose you decide to write a bull call spread. Which one would have the lowest cost, and how much would the cost be per spread? (Ignore the cost of commission for now.)

CALLS		STRIKE	PUTS	
BID	ASK		BID	ASK
14.00	17.70	30	0.00	0.75
9.40	12.80	35	0.00	0.90
5.60	7.00	40	0.05	1.00
2.05	3.50	45	1.50	2.95
0.35	1.65	50	4.70	5.90
0.20	0.60	55	8.80	10.20
0.10	0.50	60	13.50	15.00

3. Refer to the quotes in Problem 2. You are now looking at the same stock, but consider writing a bull put spread. Which one provides the highest credit, and how much would you receive per spread? (Ignore the cost of commission for now.)

4. Suppose these options expire in five days, and stock only has a 20% chance of rising $5 over that time, but a 50% chance of rising $2 over the same period. Which spread would you select?

   a. 40–45 bull call spread.

   b. 45–50 bull call spread.

   c. 45–40 bull put spread.

   d. 50–45 bull put spread.

5. Based on your selection, what price would the underlying need to attain for the spread to break even? Are the chances of reaching that price more than 50% or less than 50%?

Chapter 12

Horizontal and Diagonal Spreads

Introduction

> - Horizontal (Calendar) Spreads: Horizontal spreads are option strategies whereby a long and short *pair of calls or puts share the same strike price but have different expiries.*
> - Diagonal Spreads: Diagonal spreads are a form of option strategy whereby a long and short *pair of calls or puts are arranged such that they have neither the same strike price nor the same expiries.*

Chapter 11 discussed vertical spreads, which are a limited-risk and efficient means of exploiting expected moves in the market. In contrast, calendar spreads (also called horizontal spreads) are a form of *neutral option strategy* that exploit the different rates of premium erosion between two options of equal strike price but different expiry dates. By *neutral*, we mean that its structure does not necessarily advocate for bullish or bearish markets. These spreads have similar characteristics as vertical spreads in that they *feature limited risk and are flexible*, meaning their structure has infinitely many variants. Indeed, as we will soon see, it is possible that a calendar spread can start as a simple calendar spread and then evolve into a diagonal spread and even a vertical spread.

The common theme for both diagonal and horizontal (calendar) spreads is the use of different rates of theta manifested by options of different expiries. Horizontal and diagonal spreads specifically profit from different time decay rates. This chapter will examine the theory and practices of writing horizontal and diagonal spreads.

Time Premium Behavior

Chapter 8 looked at the nature of extrinsic value, and Chapter 10 discussed the theta statistic, which is a measure of expected time premium decay over time. Because both horizontal and diagonal spreads are strategies that rely on the differential of time premium decay rates, a review of important attributes of time premium is prudent. Here is a review of some of their more relevant facts.

Time Premium Erosion (aka Time Decay) as a Function of Expiry

To understand the rationale behind calendar spreads, we must first understand the nature of option time premium erosion. As we know, in all cases, for options of the same strike price, time premium rises as option expiration moves further away in time. We can see this whenever we look at option chains. The critical feature for calendar spreads is that the *rate of time premium erosion is not constant*; it accelerates as expiration nears. Note the following table (Table 12.1) taken from actual data.

TABLE 12.1 A comparison of extrinsic value behavior over time—SPY, WMT, AAPL.

| DAYS-TO-EXPIRY | SPY 435 | | | WMT 140 | | | AAPL 145 | | |
	EXTVAL	THETA	IV	EXT VAL	THETA	IV	EXT VAL	THETA	IV
23	$8.40	0.15	20.32%	$1.39	0.05	20.13%	$3.00	0.07	27.75%
58	$10.56	0.10	21.77%	$3.51	0.04	24.29%	$5.90	0.05	33.19%
86	$13.31	0.08	23.12%	$4.16	0.03	23.38%	$7.15	0.04	32.53%
121	$16.89	0.07	23.56%	$4.91	0.02	22.92%	$8.58	0.04	33.50%
149	$19.46	0.06	23.68%	N/A	N/A	N/A	$9.98	0.03	32.97%
177	$20.29	0.06	24.81%	$6.56	0.02	25.80%	$10.92	0.03	32.44%
268	$27.41	0.05	25.48%	$8.36	0.02	24.85%	$13.90	0.03	34.84%
485	$37.89	0.04	24.66%	$11.83	0.01	23.70%	$19.30	0.02	34.17%
849	$50.64	0.03	23.46%	$16.41	0.01	22.12%	$25.72	0.01	31.67%

When the extrinsic values in Table 12.1 are plotted as a graph, we see the full effect of decay acceleration. Note that the rate of time premium decay varies because theta increases; it is a function of the nominal size of time premium. This is logical, since theta is defined as the rate of decay: the larger the premium, the higher the rate of the "decayer" (for lack of a better word).

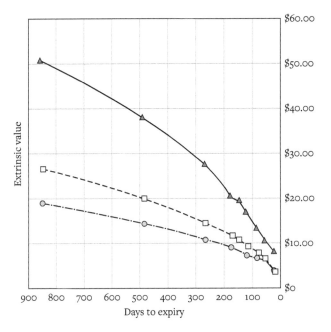

FIGURE 12.1 Extrinsic values showing rate of time premium erosion.

- <u>Time Premium Decay Accelerates as Expiry Approaches</u>: Furthermore, the acceleration is geometric and *shows extreme acceleration during the final 45 calendar days to expiry.*

Time Premium as a Function of Underlying Price

It should be no surprise that (in Table 12.1) the theta for SPY is the highest compared to the other two issues; it has the most premium to erode. But also notice that of the three sample assets, SPY has the highest underlying price. What if the underlying price is even higher? Does this contribute to higher time premiums? To find out, Table 12.2 shows the addition of two very pricey assets in addition to SPY—Tesla (TSLA) and Amazon (AMZN).

TABLE 12.2 Comparison of high-priced underlying time premium over time—TSLA, AMZN.

DAYS-TO-EXPIRY	SPY 435			TSLA 750			AMZN 3420		
	EXTVAL	THETA	IV	EXTVAL	THETA	IV	EXTVAL	THETA	IV
23	$8.40	–0.15	20.32%	$25.15	–0.60	46.90%	$68.28	–1.50	23.64%
58	$13.42	–0.10	21.77%	$49.83	–0.44	53.89%	$136.80	–1.21	29.02%
86	$16.17	–0.08	23.12%	$60.73	–0.36	52.99%	$169.43	–0.98	28.44%
121	$19.75	–0.07	23.56%	$76.38	–0.31	52.75%	$186.90	–0.83	28.60%
149	$22.32	–0.06	23.68%	$82.45	–0.29	50.77%	$223.13	–0.79	29.22%
177	$23.15	–0.06	24.81%	$92.08	–0.26	53.43%	$258.73	–0.73	32.44%
268	$30.27	–0.05	25.48%	$114.90	–0.22	54.08%	$326.65	–0.60	29.59%
485	$40.75	–0.04	24.66%	$162.38	–0.17	59.74%	$452.75	–0.46	29.85%
849	$53.50	–0.03	23.46%	$212.00	–0.12	52.39%	$620.00	–0.36	27.68%

Not surprisingly, the time premiums are indeed weighted by price of the underlying: AMZN carries a much higher time premium than either TSLA or SPY (and therefore the highest theta).

- Underlying Value Leads to Higher Time Premiums: *As the price of the underlying increases*, ceteris paribus, *time premium also rises.*

IV and Time Premium

But there is another critical element in play. When we calculate time premium *as a percent of underlying price* (Figure 12.2), a new and different story emerges. We already recognize that underlying price and time premium are positively highly correlated. If premiums are measured as a percent of the underlying price, shouldn't all premiums be equally proportionate? Mathematically, if time premium was a constant, then it should constitute the same proportion of the underlying price. The inquiry is expanded by adding two very pricey assets to the analysis. What's different?

As it so happens, the trajectory of time premium erosion is the same. AAPL call time premium (thick dashed line) is hefty, as much as 18% of the underlying price, while SPY (solid line) has a time premium of almost 12% of the underlying. Tables 12.1 and 12.2 tell part of the story. Apple is about 10% more volatile than the S&P and therefore has generated more premium. Further, this proportionately larger time premium remains throughout the option calendar. The rest of the story is clear from Figure 12.2: IV plays a compelling role in the size of time premium.

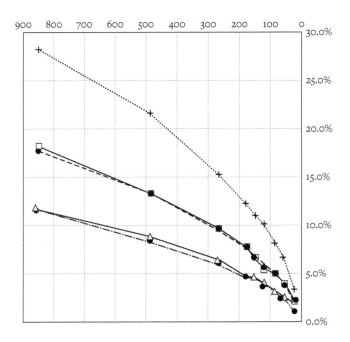

FIGURE 12.2 Time premium as % of stock price—erosion rates still geometric.

Interestingly, even though AMZN seems to have an enormous time premium, it is *proportional* to what Apple carries—and *its IV is coincidentally very close* to Apple. Tesla, on the other hand, has a truly enormous time premium, almost twice as large as Apple and Amazon and almost three times larger than the S&P. Is price of the underlying, therfore, a factor in premium size? The answer is yes—and no. *Ceteris paribus*, an underlying with a higher market price will indeed have a larger time premium. But implied volatility, a function of investor perception of risk/return, is a significant factor as well. *An underlying with a higher IV will have a higher premium*, ceteris paribus. Tesla carries an IV almost twice the size of Amazon.

> • IV Is a Factor in Time Premium Size: IV is a factor, and it has an impact across all strikes and expiries; *the higher the IV, the larger the time premium.*

Why does any of this matter? It matters very much to the horizontal spread writer because the purpose of the spread is to profit from the differential of the rate of decay between two different options. Clearly, the more premiun that exists, the greater the potential rate of return. We summarize attributes of time premium as follows:

TABLE 12.3 Plain vanilla calendar spreads.

FACTOR	IMPACT ON PREMIUM
• Time to Expiry	• **DECREASE** as time to expiry nears.
• Underlying Price	• **INCREASE** as underlying rises in value.
• Implied Volatility	• **INCREASE** as IV increases.

Plain vanilla spreads are just simple, regular spreads, nothing fancy. (In fact, *anything* "plain vanilla" is just regular, nothing fancy.) The structure of a plain vanilla calendar spread is constructed with either all calls or all puts, one which expires in two months (BTO), and one which expires in the closest month (STO) with both at the same strike. The profit is collected at the time of expiry of the closest-month option (also called the *forward-month leg*) when both options are closed out. The profit consists of the difference between the erosion of the time premium of the forward-month option, which has collapsed to zero, and the time premium of the farther-expiry option (the *back-month leg*), which will still have time premium remaining. Table 12.3a shows an example:

TABLE 12.3A Plain vanilla calendar spread (time = 0)—Caterpillar (CAT) $196.82 / share.

TYPE	ACTION	EXPIRY	STRIKE	PRICE	INT VALUE	EXT VALUE	DELTA	THETA
Call	STO 5	Oct. 15	$195.00	$5.90	$1.82	–$4.08	–.48	.12
Call	BTO 5	Nov. 19	$195.00	$9.15	$1.82	$7.33	.54	–.07
					Net Debit:	$3.25		

In this example, five of the forward-month 195 calls are sold to open, and five of the back month (November monthlies) are purchased. The net debit in the spread is $325 per spread, so the cost of this spread in total is $325 × 5 = $1,625. Notice that the theta for the forward-month leg (October) is almost twice as fast as the theta of the back-month leg (November). Not only that, but the delta for the back month is slightly higher than the forward month. These difference are what make this spread work.

To see, let us move the clock up to expiry day in October. For the sake of simplicity, we will assume that the price of CAT ended the same. The spread looks like this:

TABLE 12.3B Plain vanilla calendar spread (ending position, $t = 1$)—Caterpillar (CAT).

TYPE	ACTION	EXPIRY	STRIKE	PRICE	INT VALUE[1]	EXT VALUE	DELTA	THETA
Call	BTC 5	Oct. 15	$195.00	$5.90	$1.84	$0	–	–
Call	STC 5	Nov. 19	$195.00	$9.15	$1.82	$4.06	.48	–.12
				Net:	–$0.04	+$4.08		

Because the theta was higher for the forward-month leg, its time premium eroded faster than the farther expiry option. In fact, at expiry, the near-month option has zero time premium. When the spread is closed out, the profit for the spread is equal to the liquidation price of the November option minus the initial cost of the spread, or $404 – $325 = $79 per spread times five, for a total profit of $395.

Regarding this example, if the underlying increases in value, the calendar spread investor incurs no capital loss. Since the investor is long and short, these options at the same strike price, both the forward- and back-month options will increase intrinsic value at the same rate. However, *the time premium for the forward option will nonetheless erode to zero as expiration approaches*. Meanwhile, the back-month option time premium will also erode at its usual rate. Thus, the optimal profit condition would be stable price structure through the life of the spread.

However, if prices move much higher, *you might see an increase in time premium in the back month due to expansion of volatility*. This is a good thing because the back-month leg may, in fact, not suffer any erosion at all! This situation is rare but not impossible.

It is not unusual for stocks to end up at the same price *at some point* in a one- or even a two-month period, in which case the spread writer also reaps a profit. On the other hand, if prices decline considerably, the back-month leg will lose time premium *and* intrinsic value. Closing out the spread will probably incur losses, with the maximum risk being the initial cash outlay. If prices decline, it is often prudent to allow the front month leg to expire worthless and weigh the possibility of price improvement before selling the back-month leg. Since time can still pass before expiration of the back-month leg, the price of the underlying may improve sufficiently to improve the profit structure of the spread. Another possibility is to "roll" forward (discussed below).

---

1   Difference in Intrinsic Value is due to the bid-ask spread.

Profit/Loss Analysis

The total return for this spread is equal to $395 against a total investment of $1,625. This translates to a 24.3% return against risk (in a month!). The next question is, how risky is this trade? (This is a debit call calendar spread and has a neutral-to-bullish orientation.) We have considered what happens if the stock rises in price—or stays the same—during the holding period. If that occurs, the investor is perfectly hedged and the maximum profit is realized, with perhaps some minor adjustments if, for example, the bid-ask spread becomes wider for some reason.

However, *there is risk if the stock moves down more than the difference in the time premium erosion of the two options.* Theoretically, the inherent risk for this position is 50%; either the stock rises (or stays flat), or it declines in price. One could make the case that the expected return is either 24.3% if the stock rises or stays the same, or a loss tops out at a maximum of something *less than $325 if the stock declines.* The maximum loss would not be the full cost of the spread because the back-month leg would still retain some time premium, even if the option is OTM. The loss depends on how much the underlying declines but in no event would exceed the cost of the spread.

A determination of the amount and probability of loss requires the calculation of the underlying historic volatility, weighted for time the position is to be held (say, 30 calendar days). This amount adjusts the expected value of the back-month leg, which becomes the basis when closed out. Then, the profit/loss equals the credit attained from the erosion of time premium of the forward-month leg minus the capital loss of value of the back-month leg, as illustrated here (Table 12.3c):

TABLE 12.3C Plain vanilla calendar spread estimated profit/loss analysis.

HISTORIC VOLATILITY	HOLDING PERIOD VOL[2]	MAX EXPECTED NEGATIVE PRICE MOVE[3]	ADJUSTED BACK MONTH LEG PRICE	BACK MONTH LEG PRICE, $T = 1$	EXPECTED LOSS
36.7%	3.02%	$5.94	$2.35	$4.06	–$1.71
Risk Adj % Gain:	$162.5	Risk Adj % Loss:	–$85.50 (E)	R/Adj R/L Ratio:	1.90(E)

Unlike vertical spreads, where it is possible to accurately assess profit and loss, calendar spreads can only be estimates based on probabilities of outcome.

---

2 Holding Period Volatility: Historic Volatility X Holding Period/365
3 Maximum Expected Negative Price Move: Underlying Price @ t=0 X Holding Period Volatility

Rolling the Spread

If the underlying price moves against a horizontal spread, the loss can be at least partially mitigated by "rolling" the forward leg. Rolling is a process where the forward-month leg is closed out and a new option is opened in its place. For example, instead of closing out the example (above, Tables 12.3a, b, and c), suppose the forward-month leg was rolled forward. The spread investor has several choices. It could buy-to-close the October 195 call and simultaneously sell-to-open the 190 November 19 call, which would transform the calendar spread into a vertical spread, as follows (Table 12.3d):

TABLE 12.3D "Rolled" to new vertical spread (CAT).

TYPE	ACTION	EXPIRY	STRIKE	PRICE	INT VALUE[4]	EXT VALUE	DELTA	THETA
Call	BTC 5	Oct. 15	$195.00	$5.90	$1.84	$0	–	–
Call	STO 5	Nov. 19	$190.00	–$3.35(E)	–	–$3.35		
Call	5	Nov. 19	$195.00	$9.15	$1.82	$4.06	.48	–.12
				Net:	–$0.04	+$4.08		

Moreover, the spread investor could also decide to roll forward only a week, harvest that time premium, then roll again to the next week, and so on until the spread becomes vertical for the week of November 19. Obviously, this level of flexibility can only occur for an underlying with several weekly expiries offered in addition to the usual monthlies.

Margin Requirements

Another consideration for a plain vanilla calendar spread is that there is no margin required because the spread constitutes a perfect hedge: the long and short options have the same strike. There is no risk to the broker/dealer in the event of default.[5] This will remain the case unless the investor elects to diagonalize the spread (see below).

---

4   Difference in Intrinsic Value is due to the bid-ask spread.
5   There is no risk because, regardless of direction, the short option offsets any gain for the long option and vice versa.

Calendar Spreads Using LEAPS

- Calendar Spreads with LEAPS: Calendar spreads with LEAPS *use LEAPS as the back-month option*. Usually, these spreads *evolve to diagonal spreads* and are subject to *repeated writing of near-month options* as each expires.

When calendar spreads are written using LEAPS, the back month is a LEAP. The capture of premium from sale of a forward month option can be used to lower the cost of the LEAP. In fact, theta is usually so low for LEAPS with a year before expiry that the time premium captured in the sale of a near-month call is often equal to almost three months of time decay for the LEAP. For those with patience, this strategy can yield excellent results. First, there is enough time to roll several times during the holding period, providing enough opportunity to completely pay off the cost of the LEAP. Second, the amount of time affords the spread writer ample flexibility should it be needed. For example, Table 12.4 shows actual results of a LEAP-based calendar spread for AT&T (T). This particular sequence features an assignment, an additional LEAP purchase during the year, as well as poor price behavior of the underlying with three months left. Yet the spread writer only needs to recapture an average of $0.24 per month per option to break even on the trade. This is hardly stellar, but also shows that even adverse conditions yield reasonable performance.

Indeed, by repeating the process with skill, it is not unusual that the LEAP could eventually be a "free trade"; that is, basis for the LEAP would be zero. If the price of the underlying rises in the interim, one could still buy back the front month with capture of diminished time premium.

"Diagonalizing" the Calendar Spread

As can be seen in the example above, the strikes of the forward-month leg changes over time. When a calendar spread writer uses LEAPs as the back-month leg, this frequently happens, especially if the underlying price rises. This process is known as *diagonalizing* the spread and introduces another concept.

As prices rise, it no longer makes sense to write a forward month at a strike equal to the LEAP. Instead, the spread is "diagonalized" by writing an option that has a higher strike price in the forward month. The example in Table 12.5 provides another real experience, warts and all. Note that the stock price has risen over the course of this spread's holding period, with upswings followed by considerable periods of price consolidation (see Figure 12.3).

TABLE 12.4 LEAP Calendar Option Transactions—AT&T (T)

DATE		BOT	SLD	DESCRIPTION	QTY	PRICE	COMMISSION	AMOUNT	REG FEE
3/10/2021	**1**	X		BTO Jan 21 2022 30.0 Call	10	$2.11	$6.50	$(2,116.51)	$0.01
3/10/2021	**1a**		X	STO Mar 19 2021 31.0 Call	10	$0.18	$6.50	$173.49	$0.01
3/22/2021				EXPIRATION (Mar 19 31.0 Call)	10	$ –	$	$ –	$ –
3/22/2021	**1b**		X	STO Apr 16 30.0 Call	10	$0.36	$6.50	$353.49	$0.01
4/8/2021				ASSIGNMENT (Apr 16 30.0 Call)	10	$ –	$	$ –	$ –
4/8/2021	**1**	X		BTOT Jan 21 2022 30.0 Call	10	$1.80	$6.50	$(1,806.51)	$0.01
4/8/2021	**1c**		X	STO Apr 16 30.5 Call	-20	$0.14	$13.00	$266.97	$0.03
4/19/2021				EXPIRATION (Apr 16 30.5 Call)	20	$ –	$	$ –	$ –
4/30/2021	**1d**		X	STO May 21 2021 31.5 Call @ 0.3	-20	$0.30	$13.00	$586.97	$0.03
5/24/2021				EXPIRATION (May 21 2021 31.5 Call)	20	$ –	$	$ –	$ –
5/24/2021	**1e**		X	STO Jun 18 2021 30.0 Call @ 0.57	-20	$0.57	$13.00	$1,126.97	$0.03
6/21/2021				EXPIRATION (Jun 18 2021 30.0 Call)	20	$ –	$	$ –	$ –
6/28/2021	**1f**		X	STO Jul 16 2021 29.0 Call @ 0.2	-20	$0.20	$13.00	$386.97	$0.03
7/16/2021				EXPIRATION (Jun 18 2021 30.0 Call)	20	$ –	$	$ –	$ –
7/19/2021	**1g**		X	STO Aug 20 2021 29.0 Call	-20	$0.17	$13.00	$323.77	$0.03
8/21/2021				EXPIRATION (Aug 20 2021 29.0 Call)	20	$ –	$	$ –	$ –
8/23/2021	**1h**		X	STO Oct 15 2021 30.0 Call	-20	$0.06	$13.00	$106.98	$0.02
					0		**$91.00**	**$(704.39)**	**$0.19**

TABLE 12.5 Rolls and Expiries—Horizontal evolving to diagonals. Pfizer (PFE)

DATE		BOT	SLD	DESCRIPTION	QTY	PRICE	COMMISSION	AMOUNT	REG FEE	ROLLS	EXPIRIES
4/22/2021	1	X		BTO Jan 20 2023 40.0 Call	10	$3.35	$6.50	$(3,356.51)	$0.01		
4/22/2021	1a		X	STO May 7 2021 39.5 Call	-10	$0.44	$6.50	$433.49	$0.01		
5/7/2021	1b		X	STO May 21 2021 40.0 Call	-10	$0.30	$6.50	$293.49	$0.01		
5/7/2021	1a	X		BTC May 7 2021 39.5 Call	10	$0.03	$6.50	$(35.51)	$0.01	$396.98	
5/7/2021	1	X		BTO Jan 20 2023 40.0 Call	10	$3.47	$6.50	$(3,476.51)	$0.01		
5/7/2021	1d		X	STO Jun 18 2021 40.0 Call	-10	$0.83	$6.50	$823.49	$0.01		
5/20/2021	1c		X	STO May 28 2021 40.5 Call	-10	$0.27	$6.50	$263.49	$0.01		
5/20/2021	1b	X		BTC May 21 2021 40.0 Call	10	$0.26	$6.50	$(266.51)	$0.01	$26.98	
6/1/2021	1c			EXPIRATION (May 28 2021 40.5 Call)	10	$ –	$ –	$ –	$ –		$263.49
6/1/2021	1d		X	STO Jun 18 2021 40.0 Call	-10	$0.23	$6.50	$223.49	$0.01		
6/21/2021	1d			EXPIRATION (Jun 18 2021 40.0 Call)	20	$ –	$ –	$ –	$ –		$1,046.98
6/28/2021	1e		X	STO Jul 16 2021 39.5 Call	-20	$0.40	$13.00	$786.98	$0.02		
7/15/2021	1e	X		BTC Jul 15 2021 39.5 Call	20	$0.47	$13.00	$(953.03)	$0.03	$(166.05)	
7/15/2021	1f		X	STO Jul 30 2021 40.0 Call	-20	$0.63	$13.00	$1,246.97	$0.01		
7/27/2021	1f	X		BTC Jul 30 2021 40.0 Call	20	$0.47	$13.00	$(953.01)	$0.03	$293.96	
8/24/2021	1g		X	STO Sep 17 2021 50.0 Call	-20	$1.08	$13.00	$2,146.99	$0.01		
9/13/2021	1g	X		BTC Sep 17 2021 50.0 Call	20	$0.01	$13.00	$(33.01)	$0.01	$2,113.98	
9/13/2021	1h		X	STO Oct 21 2021 46.0 Call	-20	$0.67	$13.00	$1,326.99	$0.01		
10/17/2021	1h			EXPIRATION (Oct 21 2021 46.0 Call)	20	$ –	$ –	$ –	$ –		$1,326.99
					20		$149.50	$(1,529.71)	$0.21	$2,665.85	$2,637.46

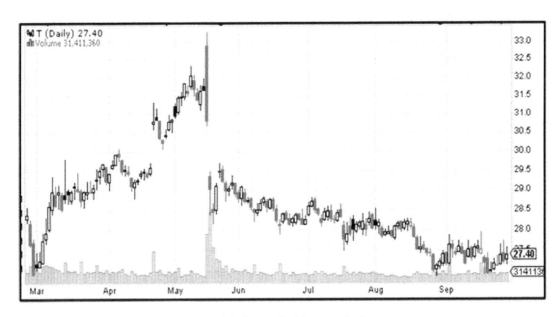

FIGURE 12.3 Price action for AT&T (T) during holding period.

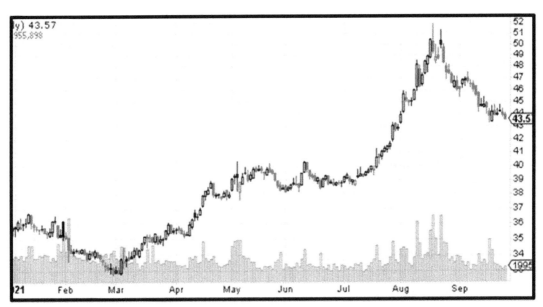

FIGURE 12.4 Price action for Pfizer (PFE) during holding period.

Since future prices are unknown, the LEAP becomes the benchmark against which strategies are considered. What the spread writer needs to consider is: (1) potentially, how many times can this spread be rolled over the life of the LEAP, such that the LEAP can be fully recompense, (2) how long should the holding period return be, and (3) how much return per option roll must be made to satisfy (1) and (2). This example calendar spread was made more complicated because the number of diagonal spreads increased (since the mechanics of the spread seemed propitious). The final result of this endeavor is not complete as of this writing, but it appears to be on its way to success. With 15 months to go, the writer needs only $1.53 in total time premium to break even—an average of about 10 cents a month per share per option—with the original option having been paid in full.

One goal for a LEAP-based debit calendar spread would be sufficient gain in the underlying to allow cashless exercise of a few of the contracts, with sale of the remainder. A cashless exercise means that shares are purchased because ample equity was earned in the option to enable exercise by use of either the margin power of the exercised shares, or from the profits earned by the sale of the non-exercised LEAPS. For example, consider this trade, with options fully reimbursed, and the underlying at $50 at expiry. The intrinsic value would be $10 per share ($1,000 per option). The ten contracts would yield a total profit of $10,000. Thus, if two of the contracts were exercised at $40 per share, costing $8,000, the entire purchase would be covered by the profits generated by the sale of the remaining eight contracts.

Diagonal Spreads

- Diagonal Spreads: Diagonal spreads consist of a long and short option, transacted simultaneously, where *both the expiry and the strike are different.*

Diagonal spreads feature options of the same type that have dissimilar expiration dates as well as dissimilar strike prices. Diagonal spreads frequently use LEAPS as the back-month option, as discussed above. There is no requirement that the front-month option be an immediately adjacent strike (i.e., forward-month leg at 45 strike, back-month leg at 45.5 strike). The single great advantage to a diagonal spread is its enormous flexibility. Indeed, when using LEAPS as the back-month leg, it is a given that the front-month leg will be rolled several times during the holding period of the back-month LEAP. Further, the strike of the forward-month option is likely to change during the holding period; if the underlying price trends, the front-month option could ultimately be several strikes away from the LEAP strike.

Many diagonal spreads evolve from calendar spreads, but obviously, it is also possible to create a diagonal spread initially. This has certain advantages. First, it allows the potential for an increase in the value of the back-month option. Second, odds are enhanced that the front-month option will expire worthless, especially if its strike is out-of-the-money. Since the strategy with LEAPS as a back-month option is to capture premium each time a new front-month option is written, the primary objective is to capture at least enough to pay off the initial premium of the LEAP over time. Therefore, the objective is to write a new front-month option with $\frac{P_L}{n}$ premium, where n is the number of expiries in the holding period and P_L is the premium of the front-month LEAP.

If the price trend moves against the spread, such as what has occurred in the AT&T example (Table 12.3 and Figure 12.4), then the writer may need to write the front-month option with a strike resembling a credit spread[6] (see Figure 12.5).

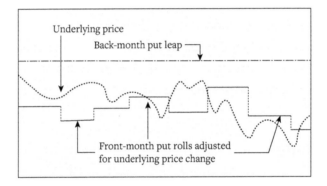

FIGURE 12.5 Diagonal spread with monthly strike adjustments dependent on underlying price moves. STO roll of front month to attain at least enough premium to recompense for cost of the LEAP over time.

Double Diagonal Spreads

- <u>Double Diagonal Spreads</u>: A spread whereby *two diagonal spreads*, one with calls and one with puts, *are simultaneously written*.

These spreads are employed when the underlying is expected to move in a range. The procedure is to simultaneously write two diagonal spreads, one for puts and one for calls, on

---

6 For a call diagonal, the front-month leg would have a strike lower than the LEAP. For a put diagonal, the front-month leg strike would be above the strike of the LEAP.

the same underlying—hence the name *double diagonal*. Any back-month LEAPS, if used in the spreads, do not necessarily have to share the same strike.

Double diagonals are often written as income-generating option strategies by undertaking the same mechanics that were shown in Figure 12.5 for a diagonal spread with LEAPS. However, if the underlying shows directional bias, the spread writer must adjust both front-month strikes so that adequate premium is captured. Therefore, these spreads require maintenance, depending on the volatility of the underlying.

Legging into a Double Diagonal Spread

Legging into any option spread means that the investor only enters into one of the options, with the intent of building the spread over time. As in calendar spreads and ordinary diagonals, it is possible to leg into a double diagonal. Indeed, if the investor has already written a simple diagonal using LEAPS, it may evolve into a double diagonal if the underlying price moves away from the original diagonal spread.

For example, consider that a 140/145 call diagonal spread on AAPL had been written, with the following transactions subsequent (Table 12.6):

TABLE 12.6 LEAP Diagonal Transactions—Apple (AAPL)

DATE		BOT	SLD	DESCRIPTION	QTY	PRICE	COMMISSION	AMOUNT	REG FEE
7/20/2021	1	X		BTO Jan 21 2023 140.0 Call	5	$20.70	$3.25	$(10,353.33)	$0.08
7/20/2021	1a		X	STO Aug 19 2021 145.0 Call	-5	$4.75	$3.25	$2,371.69	$0.06
8/19/2021		X		BTC Aug 19 2021 145.0Call	5	$2.65	$3.25	$(1,328.33)	$0.08
8/22/2021	1b		X	STO Sep 19 150.0 Call	-5	$3.85	$3.25	$1,921.69	$0.06
9/17/2021				EXPIRATION (STO Sep 19 150.0 Call)	5	$ –	–	$ –	–
9/20/2021	1c		X	STO Oct 15 145.0 Call	-5	$3.55	$3.25	$1,771.74	$0.01
					0		$16.25	$(5,616.54)	$0.29

But now the spread writer is concerned about headwinds in the future. She writes a new diagonal using puts, by buying to open the 140 June 2022 back month and selling to open a 135 October 15 put. The spread writer is hedging by legging into a diagonal put spread of shorter duration. This maneuver has changed the plain vanilla diagonal spread into a double diagonal. The outcome now looks like this (Table 12.7):

TABLE 12.7 Positions After Legging into Double Diagonal—Apple (AAPL)

DATE		BOT	SLD	DESCRIPTION	QTY	PRICE	COMMISSION	AMOUNT	REG FEE
7/20/2021	*1*	X		BTO Jan 21 2023 140.0 Call	5	$14.78	$3.25	$(7,391.63)	$0.08
7/20/2021	*1c*		X	STO Oct 15 145.0 Call	−5	$3.55	$3.25	$1,771.69	$0.06
9/20/2021	*2*	X		BTO Mar 18 2022 140.0 Put	5	$9.50	$3.25	$(4,753.33)	$0.08
8/22/2021	*2a*		X	STO Oct 19 135.0 Put	−5	$3.85	$2.51	$1,922.43	$0.06
					0		**$12.26**	**$(8,450.84)**	$0.28

In Table 12.7, notice that the cost basis for the Jan 2023 140 LEAP has already been reduced by $2,961.70 through time premium recapture, three months into the diagonal. The new spread has added only $1,059.21 of additional basis because of more premium capture from the sale of the October 135 put and the October 145 call. This position can now benefit whether the stock rises or falls between now and six months from now, after which the writer has additional choices to make.

Iron Butterflies

These are actually a species of double diagonal and are composed of a set of puts and calls, with one of the puts and one of the calls sharing a strike. These will be discussed in more detail in Chapter 13.

Summary and Conclusion

This chapter explores the most popular and risk-balanced methods to capitalize on the single, greatest, uncontestable truth in investing; that extrinsic value always erodes to zero. First, we reviewed some of the salient points regarding time premium erosion, since this phenomenon plays a central role in the construction of calendar spreads and its variants.

The rest of the chapter was devoted to a discussion of "plain vanilla" calendar spreads and their variants. Considerable verbiage was dedicated to the discussion of calendar spreads using a LEAP as the back-month leg; they offer the skilled investor unparalleled flexibility. To broaden the perspective, the mechanics of legging into other spreads were discussed, with examples in tabular and graph form.

Looking Forward

In the next chapter, we will continue our adventure by exploring the world of "neutral" spreads, straddles, strangles, and butterfly spreads.

Problems on Calendar Spreads

1. What feature of time premium is the fundamental logic behind calendar spreads?

    a. Time premium is the same across all time periods.

    b. Volatility is reduced as option expiry lengthens.

    c. Time premium erodes more quickly as expiry increases.

    d. The difference in time premium erosion between long-term and short-term options is exploited.

2. What is a LEAP?

    a. It is a sporting event in the Summer Olympics.

    b. It is something you do when you make assumptions, particularly in regard to religious belief.

    c. It is an acronym for Long-term Equity Anticipation Securities and refers to options that were issued with one year or more to expiry.

    d. It is a type of bond option issue.

3. You buy a January 2020 65 call and you sell a June 2019 65 call. What is the purpose of this spread?

4. You sell a 288 May call for $2.88 (really!) and then you buy a January 2020 288 call for $14.71. Do you still make a profit if SPY rises to 290? Explain.

5. You sell a May 2019 QQQ 185 call for $2.16 and you buy a July 185 QQQ call for $6.04. What happens if QQQ falls to 183? Explain.

Chapter 13

Neutral Option Strategies

> - <u>Neutral Option Strategies</u>: So-called "neutral" option strategies do not necessarily rely on underlying price direction to be profitable.

A "neutral" strategy is one that does not necessarily rely on underlying directional trends to attain profits. However, some do rely on range-bound underlying price behavior. All neutral strategies involve some combination of long and short puts and calls, and most neutral strategies tend to rely on the erosion of premium for profit. They tend to be more complex and therefore involve more transactions with attendant increases in transaction costs than either bull or bear strategies. Neutral strategies include butterfly spreads, condor spreads, collars, strangles, straddles, and in some instances, ratio and calendar spreads. We have already discussed vertical and calendar spreads. Here we discuss strangles, straddles, collars, butterfly spreads, and iron condors.

Straddles and Strangles

> - <u>Straddle</u>: An option strategy composed of a put and call pair (either both long or short) with the same strike and expiry.
> - <u>Strangle</u>: An option strategy composed of a put and call pair (either both long or short) with different strikes but the same expiry.

Straddles and strangles are both composed of a call and put, both long or both short. The difference between a straddle and a strangle is straightforward. Straddles are composed of a call and a put of the same strike and the same expiry (both long or both short). Strangles are the same as a straddle, except that the strikes are not the same.

Long Straddles and Strangles

Table 13.1 provides an example of both a long straddle and a long strangle. The most important feature of these spreads is that one of the options will always be profitable—*if* the underlying moves sufficiently in one direction or another. Thus, the largest (and very real) risk for either strangles or straddles is that the underlying price move is not sufficient to offset the high cost of entry.

TABLE 13.1 Example of a Long Straddle and Strangle

DATE	BOT	SLD	DESCRIPTION	QTY	PRICE	COMMISSION	AMOUNT	REG FEE
STRADDLE—JOHNSON & JOHNSON (JNJ) $160.47/SHARE								
10/1/2021	X		BTO Nov 19 2021 160 Call	2	$5.20	$1.30	$(1,041.32)	$0.02
10/1/2021	X		BTO Nov 19 2021 160 Put	2	$4.50	$1.30	$(901.32)	$0.02
						TOTAL COST OF STRADDLE:	**$(1,942.64)**	
STRANGLE—JOHNSON & JOHNSON (JNJ) $160.47/SHARE								
10/1/2021	X		BTO Nov 19 2021 165 Call	2	$2.74	$1.30	$(549.32)	$0.02
10/1/2021	X		BTO Nov 19 2021 150 Put	2	$2.75	$1.30	$(551.32)	$0.02
						TOTAL COST OF STRANGLE:	**$(1,100.64)**	

In the example shown in Table 13.1, JNJ would need to move at least $19.50 in either direction for the straddle to be profitable, a move of 12.19%. With the options carrying an IV of slightly more than 20%, the likelihood of a profit for this straddle is remote, indeed. The picture is bleak for the strangle as well, since JNJ would need to move at least $11.25 below $150 ($139.75), or $11.25 above $165 ($176.25), to be profitable. Since the volatility smile tells us that these OTM options will carry an even higher IV than the straddle, a high probability exists that the strangle will incur losses to the investor as well.

Consequently, these positions are to be used only when market-moving news is about to be released and high volatility in one direction or the other is anticipated and the investor wants to capitalize on what will either be great news or unwelcome news.

Payoff of a Long Straddle or Strangle

We can see Figure 13.1a and Figure 13.1b show the payoffs of straddles and strangles. To determine break-even points, the math is rudimentary. For a straddle, if the cost of the put and call are V_p and V_c, respectively, and the strike for both options is K, then the break-even point to the upside is $BE_{up} = V_p + V_c + K$ and for the downside is $BE_{dn} = K - (V_p + V_c)$. Simply stated, the strike price plus or minus the sum of the option premiums is the loss range: profits can only be made if the move in the underlying is greater than the combined cost of the options.

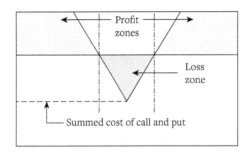 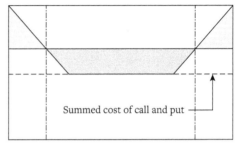

FIGURE 13.1A Payoff of a straddle: Profit occurs only if the underlying moves enough to offset the sum of the initial cost of both options. **Figure 13.1B:** Payoff of a strangle: Profit occurs only under similar conditions as a straddle.

Short Straddles and Strangles

A different configuration consists of selling-to-open a put and a call to construct a straddle or strangle. The logic is well placed: if premiums are too high to profit from long straddles, then perhaps shorting a put and call will deliver enough premium to overcome any expected move in the underlying. These strategies are pure theta plays: their success is directly a function of how much time premium is captured as a function of how much volatility an underlying will experience.

For the same reasons that long straddles and strangles rarely work, short straddles and strangles tend to work out better. The critical factor is the IV of the combined options compared to the historic volatility of the underlying. If the underlying has a lower historic volatility than the combined volatility of the options, there is a better-than-50% chance that the short strangle or straddle will be successful. What needs to happen is that the underlying must only move so that: (1) with the straddle, the move is less than the value of the combined options sold with the optimum profit attained if the underlying closes at exactly $160 at expiry; and (2) with the strangle, the move is less than the value of the combined options sold with the optimum profit attained if both options expire OTM.

However, it is important to discuss other risks—in particular, the risk of assignment—and their impact on the risk/return dynamics of short straddles and strangles. Consider a short strangle on JNJ, with inputs from that example. The positions are indicated as Table 13.2:

TABLE 13.2 Example of Short Straddle and Strangle

DATE	BOT	SLD	DESCRIPTION	QTY	PRICE	COMMISSION	AMOUNT	REG FEE
STRADDLE—JOHNSON & JOHNSON (J NJ) $160.47/SHARE								
10/1/2021		X	STO Nov 19 2021 160.0 Call	−2	$4.85	$1.30	$968.68	$0.02
10/1/2021		X	STO Nov 19 2021 160.0 Put	−2	$4.30	$1.30	$858.68	$0.02
					TOTAL PREMIUM FROM OPTION SALES:		**$1,827.36**	
STRANGLE—JOHNSON & JOHNSON (JNJ) $160.47/SHARE								
10/1/2021		X	STO Nov 19 2021 165.0 Call	−2	$2.58	$1.30	$514.68	$0.02
10/1/2021		X	STO Nov 19 2021 155.0 Put	−2	$2.75	$1.30	$548.68	$0.02
					TOTAL PREMIUM FROM OPTION SALES:		**$1,063.36**	

As we see in Table 13.2 above, a profit of no more than $1,827.36 is possible for the short straddle, while no more than $1,063.36 is possible for the short strangle. In both cases, margin is required because the short options expose exercise risk to the account holder. What happens if either one is exercised? (Only one is at risk of assignment because if one is ITM, the other must be OTM.)

Payoff of a Short Straddle

Consider what happens if the straddle is in place and the 160 call is exercised. The option writer must deliver the shares immediately, creating a net short position of 200 shares of JNJ at $160 per share, or -$32,000 liability. Assuming there is adequate equity in the account (the trade would not have happened if not), the position account holder is also carrying a 160 put, so that an additional amount of equity of $32,000 is required for that contingent purchase if exercised. The short 160 puts do not help the situation. Exercise of the naked call requires the call writer to purchase JNJ in the open market for delivery at $160 per share to the counterparty who exercised their option. Provided that JNJ has not moved more than $9.14 above $160 (or a closing price of $169.14),[1] then the account

---

1   The $1,827.36 is for 200 shares so that the break-even price would be $1,827.36/200 = $9.14.

holder buys the shares in the open market to satisfy the delivery terms of the short call and keeps any profit, which is the arithmetic difference between the share price and the total premium earned.

Now consider what happens if the 160 put is exercised. The option writer buys JNJ at $160, but its basis is $160 minus $9.14, or $151.86. If JNJ is trading above this break-even point, then the account holder can decide to either keep the shares or sell the shares, with the profit equal to the difference between the price of JNJ and the total premium earned by the straddle writer.

Payoff of a Short Strangle

The difference in profits is solely a function of the different strikes in the strangle. For the strangle, if the 165 call is exercised, the option writer must deliver the shares at $165 per share, or -$33,000 liability, with an additional amount of margin equity equal to -$31,000 required as cover for the 155 put. As in the case of the straddle, the strangle writer must purchase JNJ in the open market for delivery at $165 per share to the counterparty who exercised their option. Provided that JNJ has not moved more than $5.32 above the $165 (or a closing price of $170.32),[2] then the account holder buys the shares in the open market to satisfy the delivery terms of the short call and keeps any profit, which is the arithmetic difference between the share price and the total premium earned.

Now consider what happens if the 155 put is exercised. The option writer buys JNJ at $155 with a basis of $155 minus $5.36, or $149.64. If JNJ is trading above this break-even point, then the account holder can decide to either keep the shares or sell the shares with the profit equal to the difference between the price of JNJ and the total premium earned by the straddle writer.

Return on Risk

The risk-return profile is not as favorable as vertical spreads or calendar spreads due to the imposition of margin requirements for the trade. Depending on the margin policy of the firm, the straddle writer will need to have either the higher of the margin to cover the short call or short put, or enough to cover both short options in the event of exercise. Assuming the best-case scenario (and assuming the actual historic vol of only 22.06% for JNJ), the risk/return is as follows:

---

2 The $1,063.36 is for 200 shares so that the break-even price would be $1,053.36/200 = $5.32.

STRATEGY	CASH AT RISK	MARGIN REQUIRED	MAX PROFIT[3]	RETURN ON RISK
LONG STRADDLE	$1,942.64	$0.00	–$1,230	–63.3%
LONG STRANGLE	$1,100.64	$0.00	–$1,100.54	–100%
SHORT STRADDLE	$0.00	$36,000.00	$1,827.36	5.08%
SHORT STRANGLE	$0.00	$31,000.00	$1,063.36	3.43%

Even though overall IV for equity and index options is higher today than in the recent past, neither short straddles nor short strangles compare favorably to other option strategies. (In fact, the long straddle and strangle have a *negative* expected return.) Short strategies require too much margin offsets to promote adequate returns. Similarly, because IV is high in today's markets—resulting in high option prices—long straddles and strangles are low probability positions. Option premiums are so high today, they require too much investment to promote adequate returns on risk. Other combinations show more promise, and we move now to a discussion of butterfly spreads, which provide a better risk-adjusted return than strangles and straddles.

Butterfly Spreads

- Butterfly Spreads: Butterflies are a limited-risk, neutral options strategy with a high probability of earning a small profit. They consist of three positions of one type of option, with the middle position having twice as many options as the other two.

Besides evoking poetry, grace, and elegance, butterfly spreads are a fully hedged quintessential neutral option strategy. Butterfly spreads are so named because they feature a proportionate ratio of long and short options that balance fully. Butterflies (by which name they are usually referred) feature three separate positions of the same type of option: two equal "wings" and a heavier "body." Plain vanilla butterflies are written with only calls or only puts, with strikes equidistant to each other.

Short Butterfly Spreads
Short butterfly spreads can be established either with all calls or with all puts. A short call butterfly is a credit spread. An example will be used and is shown on Table 13.3.

---

3 Assumes historic volatility for JNJ of 22.06%.

TABLE 13.3 Short Call Butterfly Spread—United Therapeutics (UTHR) –*$185.90/Share*

DATE	BOT	SLD	DESCRIPTION	QTY	PRICE	COMMISSION	AMOUNT	REG FEE
			INITIAL POSITION: NET TRADE CREDIT: $286.77					
10/1/2021		X	STO Nov 19 2021 180.0 Call	–5	$13.60	$3.25	$6,796.69	$0.06
10/1/2021	X		BTO Nov 19 2021 185.0 Call	10	$9.80	$6.50	$(9,806.61)	$0.11
10/1/2021		X	STO Nov 19 2021 190.0 Call	–5	$6.60	$3.25	$3,296.69	$0.06
			TOTAL COST OF SPREAD:				**$286.77**	

The middle strike options (the body) are usually ATM options; the lower wing is ITM; and the upper wing is OTM. The idea in this spread is to hope the price of the stock will be beyond the wing strikes (on either side) at expiry, at which time the spreader captures its initial credit since extrinsic value erosion is complete, and either the options have expired worthless, or, as explained in more detail below, only the profit from erosion of extrinsic value remains.

Now consider what happens if UTHR closes at exactly $185 per share at expiration: (1) the short 190 calls expire worthless, and the other options lose all extrinsic value; (2) at expiry, the spread writer will need to close both the 10 short 180 calls and the 20 long 185 calls.[4] The loss, before any small price adjustments and commissions, would be maximized because of the need to close out the 185- and 190-strike calls. The total loss is –$4,013.23 (see Table 13.4). A close at $185 represents the worst possible outcome.

Suppose UTHR declines in value such that all the options expire worthless (all are OTM at expiry). This happens if the stock closed at $179.99 or less, and the gain would equal the total initial credit, or $286.77. This represents the best-case scenario.

Now we explore what the profit situation would be if UTHR closes higher than $185, say, $200. What is the profit profile? First, none of the options expire worthless, but time premium has completely eroded away. And intrinsic value? Note that the two wings of the spread—the ten short 180 calls and the ten short 190 calls—have an average strike of 185. Thus, the wings of the spread are composed of 20 short calls with an average strike of 185—the exact reciprocal of the spread body—20 long 185 calls; the gain of the long; calls offset the losses of the short calls. The spread losses are maximized and are equal to the initial cost of the spread. The generic profit/loss profile for a short call butterfly looks like the configuration in Figure 13.2 (above). The risk profile outlined on Table 13.4 and Figure 13.2 also visualizes the dynamics of a short put butterfly spread. The short put butterfly is characterized by

---

4 If shares close at the strike at expiry, there is a possibility that the options would be exercised. It is prudent to close them out before the close of the last trading day.

TABLE 13.4 Short Call Butterfly Spread—United Therapeutics (UTHR)—*Theoretical Close*

DATE	BOT	SLD	DESCRIPTION	QTY	PRICE	COMMISSION	PR/LOSS	REG FEE
CLOSING POSITION—UTHR = < $180.00/SHARE								
11/19/2021			EXP Nov 19 2021 180.0 Call	−5	$ −	$ −	$6,796.69	$ −
11/19/2021			EXP Nov 19 2021 185.0 Call	10	$ −	$ −	$(9,806.61)	$ −
11/19/2021			EXP Nov 19 2021 190.0 Call	−5	$ −	$ −	$3,296.69	$ −
						TOTAL PROFIT OF SPREAD:	$286.77	
CLOSING POSITION—UTHR = $185.00/SHARE								
11/19/2021	X		BTC Nov 19 2021 180.0 Call	−5	$5.00	$3.25	$2,496.69	$0.06
11/19/2021			EXP Nov 19 2021 185.0 Call	10	$ −	$ −	$(9,806.61)	$ −
11/19/2021			EXP Nov 19 2021 190.0 Call	−5	$ −	$ −	$3,296.69	$ −
						TOTAL LOSS OT SPREAD:	$(4,013.23)	
CLOSING POSITION—UTHR ⇒ $190.00/SHARE								
11/19/2021	X		BTC Nov 19 2021 180.0 Call	−5	$10.00	$3.25	$1,796.69	$0.06
11/19/2021		X	STC Nov 19 2021 185.0 Call	10	$5.00	$6.50	$(4,806.61)	$0.11
11/19/2021			STO Nov 19 2021 190.0 Call	−5	$ −	$ −	$3,296.69	$ −
						TOTAL PROFIT OF SPREAD:	$286.77	

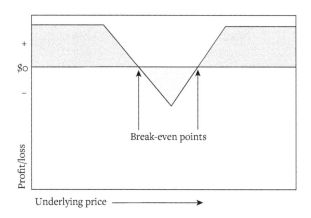

FIGURE 13.2 Profit/loss profile for short call butterfly spread. Dark tone: loss. Light tone: profit.

the same **–1 : 2 : –1** symmetry of the short call butterfly. In fact, if the same underlying and strikes were used as in the example shown above, except that put options would be used instead of calls, then the payoff and risk would be identical to the short call butterfly spread (a demonstration of put-call parity). In the interests of brevity (and to avoid repetition), we elucidate no further.

Long Butterfly Spread

In contrast, we see in Table 13.5 the mechanics of the long put butterfly. This spread is created by a ratio of **1:-2:1**, buying one OTM put option with a lower strike and one ITM put option with a higher strike, and then also selling two ATM puts. A **net** debit is created when entering the position.

TABLE 13.5 Long Put Butterfly Spread—AbbVie Inc. (ABBV) –*$111.18/Share*

DATE	BOT	SLD	DESCRIPTION	QTY	PRICE	COMMISSION	AMOUNT	REG FEE
			INITIAL POSITION: NET COST OF TRADE –$718.20					
10/1/2021	X		STO Nov 19 2021 105.0 Put	5	$1.91	$3.25	$(958.30)	$0.05
10/1/2021		X	BTO Nov 19 2021 110.0 Put	–10	$3.60	$6.50	$3,593.40	$0.10
10/1/2021	X		STO Nov 19 2021 115.0 Put	5	$6.70	$3.25	$(3,353.30)	$0.05
			TOTAL COST OF SPREAD:				$(718.20)	

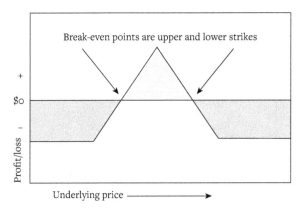

FIGURE 13.3 Generic payoff of a long put butterfly spread.

This position has a maximum profit when the underlying is at the strike price of the middle options at expiry. This is true because of the erosion of extrinsic value from the sold middle-strike options, less transaction costs. The generic profit/loss profile for a long butterfly looks like the configuration in Figure 13.3.

The maximum loss of the trade is limited to the initial premiums and commissions paid.[5] Table 13.6 shows the dynamics of the maximum profit and loss for this butterfly variant:

TABLE 13.6 Long Put Butterfly Spread—AbbVie Inc. (ABBV) *–$111.18/Share*

DATE	BOT	SLD	DESCRIPTION	QTY	PRICE	COMMISSION	CASH FLOW	PR(LS)
			CLOSING POSITION: ABBV <= $105.00/SHARE (ASSUME $100)					
10/1/2021		X	STC Nov 19 2021 105.0 Put	–5	$5.00	$3.25	$2,496.70	$1,545.05
10/1/2021	X		BTC Nov 19 2021 110.0 Put	10	$10.00	$6.50	$(10,006.60)	$(6,413.20)
10/1/2021		X	STC Nov 19 2021 115.0 Put	–5	$15.00	$3.25	$7,496.70	$4,143.40
			TOTAL PR/LOSS FINAL POSITION:					$(724.75)
			CLOSING POSITION: ABBV = $110.00/SHARE					
10/1/2021			EXP Nov 19 2021 105.0 Put	EXP	$ –	$ –	$ –	$(958.30)
10/1/2021			EXP Nov 19 2021 110.0 Put	EXP	$ –	$ –	$ –	$3,593.40
10/1/2021	X		STO Nov 19 2021 115.0 Put	5	$15.00	$3.25	$7,496.70	$4,143.40
			TOTAL PR/LOSS FINAL POSITION:					$6,778.50
			CLOSING POSITION: ABBV => $115.00/SHARE					
10/1/2021			EXP Nov 19 2021 105.0 Put	EXP	$ –	$ –	$ –	$(958.30)
10/1/2021			EXP Nov 19 2021 110.0 Put	EXP	$ –	$ –	$ –	$3,593.40
10/1/2021			EXP Nov 19 2021 115.0 Put	EXP	$ –	$ –	$ –	$(3,353.30)
			TOTAL PR/LOSS FINAL POSITION:					$(718.20)

Meanwhile, a long butterfly can also be created with calls: buying one OTM call option with a low strike price, writing two ATM calls, and buying an ITM call option at a higher strike price. The strategy echoes the familiar **1 : –2 : 1** symmetry of the long put butterfly. Indeed, if the option were written with calls at the same strikes and underlying as the long put butterfly spread, then the payoff and risk would be identical to the long put butterfly spread (put-call

---

5 In some cases, if the middle strike is ITM, the maximum loss is slightly distorted because, when all issues expired worthless, intrinsic value is lost.

parity). Thus, an examination of Figure 13.3 provides an accurate portrayal of this strategy's risk profile. Further, by virtue of put-call parity, a substitution of the puts with calls in Table 13.6 produces very similar—if not identical—results. Again, in the interests of brevity (and to avoid repetition), we elucidate no further.

Return on Risk

The risk-return profile for butterflies is interesting because of their extremes. Probabilities of success for a long butterfly are very small—around 5% if narrowly constructed[6]—but gains would be exceptionally large, frequently equal to ten times the risk. But the opposite is true for short butterflies, where probabilities for success could be as high as 90% for narrowly constructed butterflies, but with gains being paltry. Assuming the best-case/worst-case scenarios, risk/return is as follows in Table 13.7:

TABLE 13.7 Butterfly spreads: Risk/return attributes.

STRATEGY	CASH AT RISK	MAX LOSS	MAX PROFIT	P_x OF PROFIT	RET ON RISK
LONG BUTTERFLY	$718.00 (Debit)	–$718.00	$6,778.50	8.5%	944.1%
SHORT BUTTERFLY	$286.77(Credit)	–$4013.23	$286.77	91.5%	7.1%

The key to success with butterflies is the adjustment of the width of the spread. In these examples, there is only a one-strike distance between the various options. If the width were two or three strikes between options, the range of profitability greatly improves, as does the probability of success. However, once again, there is no free lunch: the spread writer must accept higher amounts at risk (higher cost of the spread or higher chance of loss) as a trade-off.

General Observations—Butterfly Spreads

This overview allows the luxury of some general observations, to wit:

- For debit butterflies (short butterflies), losses are limited to the initial cost of the spread. This explains why wider spreads have more potential loss: wider spreads reduce the amount of premium for the written options, since they are further OTM.

---

6 Narrowly constructed: Only one-strike distance between top, middle, and bottom options.

- There is a tradeoff between payoff range and probability of profits at expiry. The wider the range, the higher the probability that the spread will be profitable, and vice versa, but profit maxima are reduced. The following example illustrates this dynamic:

DATE	BOT	SLD	DESCRIPTION	QTY	PRICE	BREAK-EVEN	MAX LOSS	PROB OF LOSS	MAX PROFIT	RET ON RISK
		10	SPY 13 JUN 409 CALL	–10	7.83	408.58				
30-May	20		SPY 13 JUN 410 CALL	20	7.29	&	($747.66)	6%	$30.00	94%
		10	SPY 13 JUN 411 CALL	–10	6.67	410.97				
		10	SPY 13 JUN 395 CALL	–10	17.88	400.92				
30-May	20		SPY 13 JUN 410 CALL	20	7.29	&	($8,907.00)	40%	$5,800.00	60%
		10	SPY 13 JUN 425 CALL	–10	1.14	419.24				

- Reciprocal pairs of butterflies are a direct application of put-call parity. Accordingly, erosion of extrinsic value is key to the success of all short butterflies.

Condor Spreads

> - <u>Condors</u>: Condors are similar to butterflies, except that the middle strike, instead of being one strike, has different strikes so that the profit zone is also wider.

Condors are like butterflies, but with wider "wings." This is accomplished by creating a range in the middle strikes, as opposed to a single-strike value. Thus, there are four options in a condor spread, all of the same type. The result is a wider payoff range. As in plain vanilla butterflies and iron butterflies, there are long and short condor spreads, which can be constructed with either all puts or all calls.

Long Condor Spreads

Here, we analyze a typical long condor (with calls). A ***long condor*** is arranged like this:

- Low strike—STO CALL
- Middle strike—BTO CALL

- Middle strike—BTO CALL
- High strike—STO CALL

You can also view a long condor as a combination of a bull and bear call spread:

- **Short 195 call, long 200 call (bear call spread)**

+

- **Long 205 call, short 210 call (bull call spread).**

The maximum profit occurs if the underlying price is at or beyond the outside strikes, similar to a typical short butterfly. The spread is a credit spread and relies on high vol to be profitable. An example is shown in Table 13.8:

TABLE 13.8 Long Condor Spread—Caterpflar, Inc., *−$204/Share*

DATE	BOT	SLD	DESCRIPTION	QTY	PRICE	COMMISSION	AMOUNT	REG FEE
			INITIAL POSITION: NET DEBIT OF TRADE −$638.24					
10/5/2021		X	STO Nov 19 2021 195.0 Call	−5	$11.45	$3.25	$5,721.69	$0.06
10/5/2021	X		BTO Nov 19 2021 200.0 Call	5	$8.65	$3.25	$(4,328.31)	$0.06
10/5/2021	X		BTO Nov 19 2021 205.0 Call	5	$6.25	$3.25	$(3,128.31)	$0.06
10/5/2021		X	STO Nov 19 2021 210.0 Call	−5	$3.75	$3.25	$1,871.69	$0.06
							$136.76	

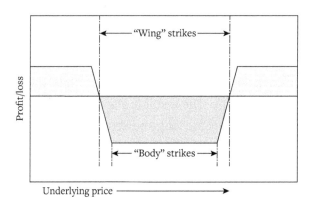

FIGURE 13.4 Generic payoff of a long condor spread.

If CAT settles below the lowest strike, all of the options expire worthless, and the initial credit is the maximum return possible. Therefore, the maximum gain on this position is exactly what was generated at the spread's inception. Maximum losses occur in the body range, and profits again emerge as prices move outside the highest strike. The long condor profit profile is shown as Figure 13.4, above.

Table 13.9 shows the final positions and actions to be taken under three alternative scenarios: a close in the middle range and a close beyond either wing.

TABLE 13.9 Long Condor Spread—Caterpillar, Inc., –*$204/Share*

DATE	BOT	SLD	DESCRIPTION	QTY	PRICE	COMMISSION	CASH FLOW	PR(LS)
			OPTION CLOSING POSITION: CAT = $195/SHARE					
10/5/2021			BTC Nov 19 2021 195.0 Call	5	$ –	$ –	$ –	$5,721.69
10/5/2021			STC Nov 19 2021 200.0 Call	–5	$ –	$ –	$ –	$(4,328.31)
10/5/2021			STC Nov 19 2021 205.0 Call	–5	$ –	$ –	$ –	$(3,128.31)
10/5/2021			BTC Nov 19 2021 210.0 Call	5	$ –	$ –	$ –	$1,871.69
			TOTAL PR/LOSS FINAL POSITION:				$136.76	
			OPTION CLOSING POSITION: CAT = $202.50/SHARE					
10/5/2021			STO Nov 19 2021 195.0 Call	5	$7.50	$3.25	$(3,753.25)	$1,968.44
10/5/2021			BTO Nov 19 2021 200.0 Call	–5	$2.50	$3.25	$1,246.75	$(3,081.56)
10/5/2021			BTO Nov 19 2021 205.0 Call	EXP	$6.25	$ –	$ –	$(3,128.31)
10/5/2021			STO Nov 19 2021 210.0 Call	EXP	$3.75	$ –	$ –	$1,871.69
			TOTAL PR/LOSS FINAL POSITION:				$(2,369.74)	
			OPTION CLOSING POSITION: CAT = $210/SHARE					
10/5/2021	X		BTO Nov 19 2021 195.0 Call	5	$15.10	$3.25	$(7,553.25)	$(1,831.56)
10/5/2021		X	STC Nov 19 2021 200.0 Call	-5	$10.00	$3.25	$4,996.75	$668.44
10/5/2021		X	STC Nov 19 2021 205.0 Call	-5	$5.00	$3.25	$2,496.75	$(631.56)
10/5/2021			EXP Nov 19 2021 210.0 Call	EXP	$ –	$ –	$ –	$1,871.69
			TOTAL PR/LOSS FINAL POSITION:				$77.01	

Note again that this spread is not directional: neither it nor the investor cares whether the market moves up or down, provided it moves up or down *enough*. We can now make these general observations about condors:

- A condor is basically a "butterfly with a wider body." This is actually why condors are so named. (Some Wall Street wise-guy recognized the payoff relationship to butterflies and thought it was a clever take.) Therefore, the payoff structure is similar, except that the returns are smaller but more likely in the body.

- Just like butterfly spreads, the payoff range of any condor can be widened or narrowed. In the case of condors, this can be done by widening or narrowing the strike gap between the middle strike and the outer edges. Wider gap widens the range of profitability but lowers return, and narrower gap narrows the range of profitability but increases return.

- Condors have limited risk and limited returns so that accuracy in vol calculations is essential. However, an underlying with low vol will also have commensurately low premiums, thus lowering profit potential. There are no free lunches in the investment world.

- Condors are frequently positions that have evolved from either a strangle or from a vertical call or put spread. It therefore can be used to advance returns if the spread writer deems that a new market direction is in the offing.

Short Condor Spreads

A short condor is the reciprocal of the long condor: profits are generated if the underlying price moves inside the "body" range. This spread is therefore conceived to profit from low vol markets. A ***short condor*** is arranged like this:

- Low strike—BTO CALL
- Middle strike—STO CALL
- Middle strike—STO CALL
- High strike—BTO CALL

You can also view a short condor as a combination of a bull and bear call spread. In this example, this is the combination:

- **Long 195 call, short 200 call (bull call spread)**

  +

- **Short 205 call, long 210 call (short call spread).**

The maximum profit occurs if the underlying price is lower than the lowest strike and higher than the highest strike, similar to a typical long butterfly. The spread is a debit spread that relies on higher volatility for profitability. Positions at spread initiation are shown in Table 13.10:

TABLE 13.10 Long Condor Spread—Caterpillar, Inc., *–$204/Share*

DATE	BOT	SLD	DESCRIPTION	QTY	PRICE	COMMISSION	AMOUNT	REG FEE
			INITIAL POSITION: NET DEBIT OF TRADE –$638.24					
10/05/2021	X		BTO Nov 19 2021 195.0 Call	5	$11.45	$3.25	$(5,728.31)	$0.06
10/05/2021		X	STO Nov 19 2021 200.0 Call	–5	$8.65	$3.25	$4,321.69	$0.06
10/05/2021		X	STO Nov 19 2021 205.0 Call	–5	$6.25	$3.25	$3,121.69	$0.06
10/05/2021	X		BTO Nov 19 2021 210.0 Call	5	$3.75	$3.25	$(1,878.31)	$0.06
							$(163.24)	

Let us see the results of this spread by fast-forwarding to expiry. Maximum profits will occur if the underlying moves beyond the "body" strike range in either direction at expiry. This becomes evident when we see Table 13.11, which shows the final positions and actions to be taken under three alternative scenarios: a close in the middle range, and a close beyond either wing.

TABLE 13.11 Long Condor Spread—Caterpillar, Inc., *–$204/Share*

DATE	BOT	SLD	DESCRIPTION	QTY	PRICE	COMMISSION	CASH FLOW	PR(LS)
			OPTION CLOSING POSITION: CAT = $195/SHARE					
10/5/2021			EXP Nov 19 2021 195.0 Call	EXP	$ –	$ –	$ –	$(5,728.31)
10/5/2021			EXP Nov 19 2021 200.0 Call	EXP	$ –	$ –	$ –	$4,321.69
10/5/2021			EXP Nov 19 2021 205.0 Call	EXP	$ –	$ –	$ –	$3,121.69
10/5/2021			EXP Nov 19 2021 210.0 Call	EXP	$ –	$ –	$ –	$(1,878.31)
			TOTAL PR/LOSS FINAL POSITION:				$(163.24)	
			OPTION CLOSING POSITION: CAT = $202.50/SHARE					
10/5/2021	X		STC Nov 19 2021 195.0 Call	–5	$7.50	$3.25	$3,746.75	$(1,981.56)
10/5/2021		X	BTC Nov 19 2021 200.0 Call	5	$2.50	$3.25	$(1,253.25)	$3,068.44
10/5/2021			EXP Nov 19 2021 205.0 Call	EXP	$ –	$ –	$ –	$3,121.69
10/5/2021			EXP Nov 19 2021 210.0 Call	EXP	$ –	$ –	$ –	$(1,878.31)
			TOTAL PR/LOSS FINAL POSITION:				$2,330.26	
			OPTION CLOSING POSITION: CAT = $210/SHARE					
10/5/2021	X		BTO Nov 19 2021 195.0 Call	–5	$15.00	$3.25	$7,496.75	$1,768.44
10/5/2021		X	STO Nov 19 2021 200.0 Call	5	$10.00	$3.25	$(5,003.25)	$(681.56)
10/5/2021		X	STO Nov 19 2021 205.0 Call	5	$5.00	$3.25	$(2,503.25)	$618.44
10/5/2021			EXP Nov 19 2021 210.0 Call	EXP	$ –	$ –	$ –	$(1,878.31)
			TOTAL PR/LOSS FINAL POSITION:				$(172.99)	

The table shows a maximum return for the spread when prices stay within the body strikes. The greatest component of profit is driven by extrinsic value erosion, with complete gains of the upper-strike options, which more than offset any gains from premium remaining on the lower-strike options.

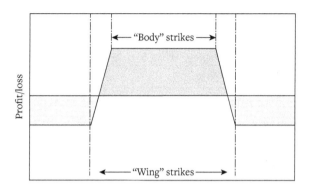

FIGURE 13.5

If, on the other hand, CAT closes either at or above the 210-strike or at or below the 195-strike, losses are incurred. First, at $210, all of the options that are ITM must be closed out. And although extrinsic value has eroded to zero, the options have plenty of extrinsic value remaining. Therefore, the initial debit, less minor costs, will be the profit. On the other hand, if CAT is below $195, all of the options are OTM and expire worthless. The loss is the debit paid at the initiation of the spread. Thus, we demonstrate that losses for a short condor are equal to no more than the initial debit.

This analysis demonstrates the profit dynamics of a short condor spread. Its structure is designed for markets with light volatility, but the profit/loss ratios are highly favorable. Unfortunately, few markets today exhibit the low vol.

Generalized Performance Expectations: Multi-Leg Strategies

Keeping track of butterfly and condor profit/loss attributes is not easy. The structure and idiomatic language are often easy to confuse. This chart provides some much-needed clarity:

SPREAD TYPE	# LEGS	DESIRED VOL	CREDIT OR DEBIT	PROFIT PROFILE
Long Straddle	2	VERY HIGH	Debit	Underlying price must move more than combined cost of spread.
Short Straddle	2	LOW	Credit	Underlying price CANNOT move more than credit earned.
Long Strangle	2	VERY HIGH	Debit	Same as long straddle.
Short Strangle	2	LOW	Credit	Same as short straddle.
Long Butterfly	3	LOW	Debit	Underlying price at middle strike.
Short Butterfly	3	HIGH	Credit	Underlying price outside wing strikes.
Long Iron Butterfly	4	LOW	Debit	Same as long butterfly.
Short Iron Butterfly	4	HIGH	Credit	Same as short butterfly.
Long Condor	4	LOW	Credit	Same as long butterfly—wider profit range.
Short Condor	4	HIGH	Debit	Same as short butterfly.
Long Iron Condor	4	LOW	Credit	Same as short condor.
Short Iron Condor	4	HIGH	Debit	Same as long butterfly—wider profit range.
Collars	2	NEUTRAL	NEUTRAL	Very small arbitrage profit in any direction.

Collars

The average investor doesn't usually think about employing collars, but fund managers do. Fist, a collar is a result and is legged in; it is not something conceived *ex nihilo*. That sounds odd, but it is a fact. What is a collar? A collar consists of a long underlying, a short OTM call, and a long ATM or OTM put. The overall purpose is to hedge gains without spending much, if anything.

Consider an investor who has been fortunate enough to gain considerably on a stock short-term but wants to hold the position long-term. The investor faces a dilemma because the underlying (say, a stock) looks "tired" and has all the appearances of a price decline. Does the investor sell the shares? What if the investor doesn't want to take on the capital gain tax burden? What if the investor isn't quite sure when or how far the decline will go?

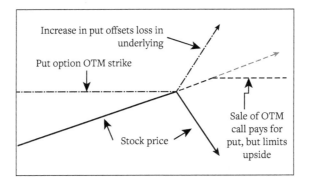

FIGURE 13.6 Collar: Designed to hedge against decline in the underlying.

This investor plays it safe: it sells an OTM call and uses the proceeds to buy a protective put. The stock is now "collared." If it continues to rise, the call will be exercised and the stock intrinsic gain (this may represent the "worst case" from the investor's standpoint). If the stock declines, the put protects against price erosion. Gains or losses are not the objective; the objective is maintenance of the status quo.

Summary and Conclusion

Wow. What a chapter. These spreads "up the ante" as far as complexity is concerned. But there are a number of important takeaways buried in the mechanics of the strategies imparted in this chapter, and the previous one as well.

First, these spreads demonstrate that an almost limitless range of strategies are available to the investor. In fact, these are the most common multi-leg "neutral" strategies, but they are by no means the only ones. For example, butterfly spreads need not be symmetric. The distance between the body and wings do not have to be equal on both sides. The same is true for condors, iron butterflies, and iron condors. The wide variety of option combinations is great for raising profit potential in any type of market.

More importantly, the strategies outlined here could become the means by which a failing trade can be either reversed or in the least improved. This can be accomplished by "legging into a trade." This refers to a practice where a simple vertical spread is transformed into a more complex spread by adding additional option legs to the original. Suppose a spread writer entered into a bear call spread but has second thoughts based on market action. The spread writer could turn the spread into a butterfly by writing a new bull call spread so that the lower long option strike is the same as the upper long strike of the existing spread. The obvious takeaway from this is to never panic with spreads. Instead, think of a way to either reduce exposure or to even turn the bad trade into a good one.

We also note that the old adages of finance play out with these more complex spreads. First, as mentioned in the text, don't ever expect a free lunch. These spreads have a habit of providing either high probability of small returns or low probability of high returns. Clearly, because of both limited gain and limited loss, these spreads have appeal, but the problem lies in the narrowness of the profit zone. The probability of a profit diminishes as the spread narrows. Unfortunately, the amount of profit potential also diminishes as the spread widens, which usually more than offsets the probability of success.

Payoff charts for these spreads have commonality among long and short spreads. For example, long iron butterflies are identical to those of long butterflies. This relationship is based on the truism that the only real difference is that butterflies are created with only one type of option, while iron butterflies use both calls and puts.

The long condor can be a great strategy to use when you feel neutral on a stock—you sense it will trade in a narrow range. Like the butterfly, the condor is a limited-risk, limited-reward strategy that profits in stagnant markets. Where it differs from a butterfly is the width of the profit zone. And the wider the spread, the greater the likelihood of success; unlike butterflies and iron butterflies, the maximum payoff range can be much wider.

The reader has now been introduced to a whole universe of potential spreads, and the only limitations each spread writer has are (1) imagination; (2) ability to see opportunity; and (3) account size.

Looking Forward

The next chapter focuses on the so-called "iron" spread strategies, which are similar to their less metallic cousins except that the spreads employ puts and calls together. The spreads are not much different, but keeping them confined in the same chapter as the regular butterflies and condors is simply too confusing for the average reader (and to the author).

Problems on Neutral Spreads

For all the problems below, refer to this option chain:

CALLS		STRIKE	PUTS	
BID	**ASK**		**BID**	**ASK**
9.55	9.85	**245**	1.35	1.45
7.50	7.75	**247.5**	1.85	1.96
5.70	5.90	**250**	2.62	2.72
5.00	5.25	**251**	2.99	3.05
4.40	4.30	**252**	3.35	3.5
4.05	4.20	**253**	375	385
3.70	3.90	**254**	4.25	4.35
3.20	3.35	**255**	4.65	4.90
2.69	2.78	**256**	5.25	5.45
1.50	1.59	**257**	5.85	6.10
1.20	1.28	**258**	6.55	6.80

1. You are looking at an option chain for DIA and you know DIA always moves at least one-half percent from week-to-week. You decide to write an iron condor.

    a. Which one would be beyond the 0.5% range for the week?

    b. How much credit would be received?

    c. If the trade had a 90% success probability, would it be worth it? Explain.

2. What is the break-even point(s) for the spread enumerated above?

3. What are the maximum loss and maximum gain on the spread enumerated in Problem 1?

4. You are looking at the data and you are also considering a short butterfly spread.

    a. Is there any meaningful difference in return for the put or call butterflies?

    b. How much credit would be received?

    c. If the trade had a 90% success probability, would it be worth it? Explain.

    d. Would a long butterfly be better? Explain.

5. What is the break-even point(s) for the spread enumerated above?

6. What are the maximum loss and maximum gain on the spread enumerated in Problem 4?

7. You are looking at the data and you are also considering a long iron butterfly spread. Is there any meaningful difference in return for the put or call butterflies?

    a. How much credit would be received?

    b. If the trade had a 90% success probability, would it be worth it? Explain.

    c. Would a short iron butterfly be better? Explain.

8. What is the break-even point(s) for the spread enumerated above?

9. What are the maximum loss and maximum gain on the spread enumerated in Problem 4?

10. Comparing the three trades above, which one looks more attractive to you? Explain. (No correct answer—looking for logic in your comments.)

Chapter 14

Iron Spreads

Introduction

It isn't entirely clear why these strategies are "iron." They could just as well be copper, or tin, or zinc, or steel spreads. A spread is an iron spread if it uses both puts and calls in its construction. Accordingly, there are iron butterflies and iron condors, both of which will be discussed in this chapter. Usually, iron butterflies or condors are constructed at the initial date, but it is not at all unusual for a spread writer to convert a plain vanilla vertical spread into an iron spread over time if the writer is looking to hedge or if market conditions shift.

Iron Butterflies

> • <u>Iron Butterflies</u>: A neutral spread *similar to a butterfly, but composed of puts and calls.*

Iron butterflies are a variety of butterfly spread done with a combination of puts and calls. Similar to regular butterflies, iron butterflies maintain an average strike price between long and short options. Also similar to butterflies, there are long iron butterflies and short iron butterflies. (*Caution is advised here because terminology is easily confused. Indeed, an internet search will find competing websites saying opposite things regarding the terminology of "long" or "short" butterflies, iron butterflies, condors, or iron condors.*) The convention in this text—and for most money managers—is that *a long multi-positioned spread (more than two options) is one where the middle strikes are long options, and vice versa.*

Long Iron Butterfly Spread

A **long iron butterfly** is arranged like this (an example also is shown as Table 14.1):

- Low strike—STO PUT
- Middle strike—BTO PUT
- Middle strike—BTO *CALL*
- High strike—STO *CALL*

TABLE 14.1 Long Iron Butterfly Spread—SPDR DJIA Trust (DIA) *–$340.10/Share*

DATE	BOT	SLD	DESCRIPTION	QTY	PRICE	COMMISSION	AMOUNT	REG FEE
			INITIAL POSITION: NET CREDIT OF TRADE ($1,713.12)					
10/01/2021		X	STO Nov 19 2021 337.0 Put	−5	$8.10	$3.25	$4,046.69	$0.06
10/01/2021	X		BTO Nov 19 2021 340.0 Put	5	$9.45	$3.25	$(4,728.31)	$0.06
10/01/2021	X		BTO Nov 19 2021 340.0 Call	5	$9.15	$3.25	$(4,578.31)	$0.06
10/01/2021		X	STO Nov 19 2021 343.0 Call	−5	$7.10	$3.25	$3,546.69	$0.06
							$(1,713.24)	

These spreads are essentially the combination of a bull call spread (debit) and a bear put spread (debit) jammed together. Long iron butterflies are therefore debit spreads that rely on volatility to be profitable. Consider the net results of the example illustrated above. Maximum profits for this position occur beyond the wings, while maximum loss occurs in the middle range:

TABLE 14.2 Long Iron Butterfly Spread—SPDR DJIA Trust (DIA) *–$340.10/Share*

DATE	BOT	SLD	DESCRIPTION	QTY	PRICE	CASH FLOW	PR(LS)
			CLOSING POSITION : DIA <= $337/SHARE (I.E., $336)				
10/1/2021	X		BTC Nov 19 2021 337.0 Put	5	$1.00	$(503.30)	$1,918.39
10/1/2021		X	STC Nov 19 2021 340.0 Put	−5	$4.00	$1,196.70	$(1,756.61)
10/1/2021			EXP Nov 19 2021 340.0 Call	EXP	$9.15	$ –	$
10/1/2021			EXP Nov 19 2021 343.0 Call	EXP	$7.10	$ –	$
			TOTAL PR/LOSS FINAL POSITION:				$161.78

(continued)

TABLE 14.2 Long Iron Butterfly Spread—SPDR DJIA Trust (DIA) –*$340.10/Share*

DATE	BOT	SLD	DESCRIPTION	QTY	PRICE	CASH FLOW	PR(LS)
			CLOSING POSITION : DIA = $340/SHARE				
10/1/2021			EXP Nov 19 2021 337.0 Put	EXP	$ –	$ –	$2,421.69
10/1/2021			EXP Nov 19 2021 340.0 Put	EXP	$ –	$ –	$(2,953.31)
10/1/2021			EXP Nov 19 2021 340.0 Call	EXP	$ –	$ –	$(3,003.31)
10/1/2021			EXP Nov 19 2021 343.0 Call	EXP	$ –	$ –	$2,196.69
			TOTAL PR/LOSS FINAL POSITION:				$(1,338.24)
			CLOSING POSITION : DIA >= $343/SHARE (I.E., $344)				
10/1/2021			EXP Nov 19 2021 337.0 Put	EXP	$ –	$ –	$2,421.69
10/1/2021			EXP Nov 19 2021 340.0 Put	EXP	$ –	$ –	$(2,953.31)
10/1/2021		X	STC Nov 19 2021 340.0 Call	–5	$4.00	$1,996.70	$(1,006.61)
10/1/2021	X		BTC Nov 19 2021 343.0 Call	5	$1.00	$496.70	$1,699.99
			TOTAL PR/LOSS FINAL POSITION:				$161.76

Because this is a debit spread, the worst-case scenario is if DIA closes at exactly $340 per share at expiry. All options will be worthless, with the net result a loss of –$1,338.24, equal to the original cost of the spread. The best-case scenario occurs if vol is higher, and the shares drop either below the 337 strike or above the 343 strike. These occurrences (either one—can't be both!) mean that three of the four options expire worthless; only one need be closed, being ITM. The payoff, however, is comparatively small, only $161.76. The small return and the large potential loss pose a conundrum. Why even bother with this spread? The answer is not complicated. Those who write these spreads realize that the chances of the large loss being larger than the meager gain is less than 10%. Consider your decision if you determined that the historic vol of the Dow Jones Average was such that at expiry, the price of the underlying is 90%+ *likely to move into full payoff territory.* Therefore, *those who write these spreads believe it is a low-return, high-probability trade.* Of course, not everyone is sanguine with these odds and simply will not enter these trades.

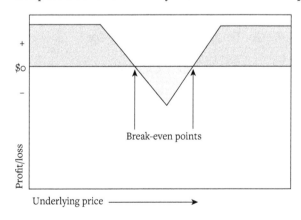

FIGURE 14.1 Profit profile for a long iron butterfly spread. Darker tone, profit; lighter tone, loss.

Short Iron Butterfly

By contrast, we note the short iron butterfly. The best way to visualize this spread is to think of it as a combination of a bear call spread (credit) together with a bull put spread (credit). A short iron butterfly[1] is arranged like this:

- Low strike – BTO PUT
- Middle strike – STO PUT
- Middle strike – STO *CALL*
- High strike – BTO *CALL*

Thus, the result is a trade with a net credit that is *best suited for low-volatility scenarios*. The *maximum profit occurs if the underlying stays at the middle strike*, with profits occurring in the range between the wings of the short iron butterfly. An example is indicated in Table 14.3:

TABLE 14.3 Short Iron Butterfly Spread—SPDR DJIA Trust (DIA) –*$340.10/Share*

DATE	BOT	SLD	DESCRIPTION	QTY	PRICE	COMMISSION	AMOUNT	REG FEE
			INITIAL POSITION: NET CREDIT OF TRADE $1,161.88					
10/1/2021	X		BTO Nov 19 2021 337.0 Put	5	$8.25	$3.25	$(4,128.31)	$0.06
10/1/2021		X	STO Nov 19 2021 340.0 Put	–5	$9.25	$3.25	$4,621.69	$0.06
10/1/2021		X	STO Nov 19 2021 340.0 Call	–5	$8.80	$3.25	$4,396.69	$0.06
10/1/2021	X		BTO Nov 19 2021 343.0 Call	5	$7.45	$3.25	$(3,728.31)	$0.06
							$1,161.76	

The best-case scenario would occur if DIA closes at exactly $340 per share at expiry (the middle strike). All of the options will be worthless, and in direct contrast to the long iron butterfly, the net result is a comparatively large profit of over $1,100. This best-case scenario occurs if vol is very low, with prices more or less unchanged over the lifespan of the spread. The worst case—not as likely as the situation with a butterfly—is not a disaster: losses are small and occur if DIA either falls below the lower strike or rises above the upper strike. The reciprocal symmetry of the long and short iron butterfly is striking (no pun intended): a short iron butterfly has a small chance of a large gain, and a large chance of a small loss. The profit range of the short iron butterfly is shown in Figure 14.2 and Table 14.4.

---

1 Long iron butterflies are also called *reverse iron butterflies* for reasons not entirely clear.

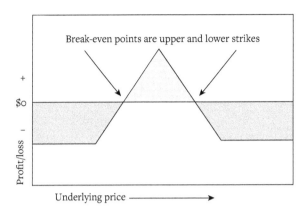

FIGURE 14.2 Profit profile, short iron condor.

TABLE 14.4 Short Iron Butterfly Spread—SPDR DJIA Trust (DIA) *at Expiry*

DATE	BOT	SLD	DESCRIPTION	QTY	PRICE	CASH FLOW	PR(LS)
CLOSING POSITION : DIA <= $337/SHARE (I.E., $336)							
10/1/2021		X	STC Nov 19 2021 337.0 Put	−5	$1.00	$496.70	$(3,631.61)
10/1/2021	X		BTC Nov 19 2021 340.0 Put	5	$4.00	$(2,003.30)	$2,618.39
10/1/2021			EXP Nov 19 2021 340.0 Call	EXP	$ –	$ –	$4,396.69
10/1/2021			EXP Nov 19 2021 343.0 Call	EXP	$ –	$ –	$(3,728.31)
			TOTAL PR/LOSS FINAL POSITION:				$(344.84)
CLOSING POSITION : DIA = $340/SHARE							
10/1/2021			EXP Nov 19 2021 337.0 Put	EXP	$ –	$ –	$(4,128.31)
10/1/2021			EXP Nov 19 2021 340.0 Put	EXP	$ –	$ –	$4,621.69
10/1/2021			EXP Nov 19 2021 340.0 Call	EXP	$ –	$ –	$4,396.69
10/1/2021			EXP Nov 19 2021 343.0 Call	EXP	$ –	$ –	$(3,728.31)
			TOTAL PR/LOSS FINAL POSITION:				$1,161.76
CLOSING POSITION : DIA >= $343/SHARE (I.E., $344)							
10/1/2021			EXP Nov 19 2021 337.0 Put	EXP	$ –	$ –	$(4,128.31)
10/1/2021			EXP Nov 19 2021 340.0 Put	EXP	$ –	$ –	$4,621.69
10/1/2021	X		BTC Nov 19 2021 340.0 Call	5	$4.00	$1,996.70	$2,399.99
10/1/2021		X	STC Nov 19 2021 343.0 Call	−5	$1.00	$496.70	$(3,231.61)
			TOTAL PR/LOSS FINAL POSITION:				$(338.24)

General Insights on Iron Butterflies

The most noticeable difference between a long and short iron butterfly is the huge difference in credit and debit and their respective gains and losses. This raises key points about iron butterflies and their uses and suggests these general observations:

- The payoff range[2] of any iron butterfly (or any butterfly) can be widened or narrowed by widening or narrowing the gap between the middle strike and the outer edges. *Wider gap widens the range of profitability, and narrower gap narrows the range of profitability.*

- As in plain vanilla butterflies, losses are limited to the initial cost of the spread. This explains why wider spreads offer more loss potential: wider spreads reduce the amount of premium for the written options, since they are further OTM.

- Risk-adjusted risk/return ratios improve as payoff ranges increase, but nominal losses also increase. For example, consider the calculations in the following table. By widening a DIA spread from 338-340-342 to 330-340-350 strikes, chance of profit decreases to 76% from 91% while profit rises from $60 to $845. Losses also widen, from about $600 to about $1,660. Table 14.5 compares results:

TABLE 14.5 Iron butterfly—Probability of profit and size of profit is inversely proportionate

STRIKE RANGE	PROFIT	PR	ADJ PROFIT	AVG LOSS	PR	ADJ LOSS	R/R RATIO
A	B	C	B × C	D	E	D × E	|(B × C)/(D × E)|
330–340–350	$845	76.5%	$646.43	–$1658	23.5%	–$389.63	1.66
332–340–348	$510	80.2%	$409.02	–$1406	19.8%	–$301.95	1.47
334–340–346	$270	84.0%	$226.80	–$1350	16.0%	–$216.00	1.38
336–340–344	$110	89.0%	$97.9	–$850	11.0%	–$93.50	1.05
337–340–343	$60	90.8%	$54.48	–$604	9.2%	–$55.59	0.98
338–340–342	$25	94.3%	$23.58	–$465	5.7%	–$55.58	0.94

- Iron butterflies are superior to strangles and straddles for use in exploiting pending large moves in the underlying because, unlike straddles and strangles, their likelihood of success is higher and total costs are lower.

---

2 Payoff range: the width of price range wherein the spread is profitable at expiry.

- There is *a tradeoff between payoff range and probability of profits at expiry*. The wider the range, the lower the probability that the spread will be profitable, and vice versa.

- Short iron butterflies are a direct application of put-call parity. Accordingly, erosion of extrinsic value is key to their success.

Iron Condor Spreads

> - <u>Iron Condors</u>: A neutral spread *similar to a condor, but composed of puts and calls.*

Just when you thought the worst was over, we introduce iron condors. This strategy is "iron" because like iron butterflies, they are composed of both puts and calls. And just like butterflies, there are short and long iron condors.

Long Iron Condor

The idea in a long iron condor is to profit from a volatile market regardless of expected direction. A ***long iron condor*** is arranged like this:

- Low strike – STO PUT
- Middle strike – BTO PUT
- Middle strike – BTO *CALL*
- High strike – STO *CALL*

Or consider a long iron condor as a combination of a bull call and bear put spread:

- **Short 337 put, long 340 put (bear put spread)**

+

- **Long 345 call, short 348 call (bull call spread).**

An example of this spread variation is shown on Table 14.6:

TABLE 14.6 Long Iron Condor Spread—SPDR DJIA Trust (DIA) –$343.10/Share

DATE	BOT	SLD	DESCRIPTION	QTY	PRICE	COMMISSION	AMOUNT	REG FEE
			INITIAL POSITION: NET CREDIT OF TRADE ($1,713.12)					
10/1/2021		X	STO Nov 19 2021 337.0 Put	–5	$8.10	$3.25	$4,046.69	$0.06
10/1/2021	X		BTO Nov 19 2021 340.0 Put	5	$9.45	$3.25	$(4,728.31)	$0.06
10/1/2021	X		BTO Nov 19 2021 345.0 Call	5	$8.10	$3.25	$(4,053.31)	$0.06
10/1/2021		X	STO Nov 19 2021 348.0 Call	–5	$5.50	$3.25	$2,746.69	$0.06
							$(1,988.24)	

The maximum profit occurs if the underlying price is either at or lower than the lowest strike, or at or higher than the highest strike. As in long condors, the spread is a debit spread and relies on volatility for profitability. Initiation of this spread results in a debit; the debit represents the worst-case loss, occurring if all the options in the spread expire worthless. And reciprocal to the short iron condor, the worst case is also not a disaster: losses are small, and occur if the price of the underlying stays within the range of the inside strikes. Also, like a long iron butterfly, this spread has a small chance of a large loss, and a large chance of a small gain. The profit range of the long iron condor is shown in Figure 14.3 and Table 14.7.

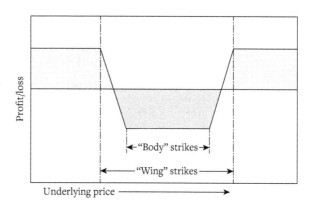

FIGURE 14.3 Profit profile of the long iron condor.

Short Iron Condor

This spread is the reciprocal of a long iron condor and profits from a volatile market regardless of expected direction. A ***short iron condor*** is arranged like this:

- Low strike – BTO PUT
- Middle strike – STO PUT
- Middle strike – STO *CALL*
- High strike – BTO *CALL*

TABLE 14.7 Long Iron Condor Spread—SPDR DJIA Trust (DIA) *at Expiry*

DATE	BOT	SLD	DESCRIPTION	QTY	PRICE	CASH FLOW	PR(LS)
			CLOSING POSITION: DIA <= $337/SHARE (I.E., $336)				
10/1/2021	X		BTC Nov 19 2021 337.0 Put	−5	$ –	$ –	$4,046.69
10/1/2021		X	STC Nov 19 2021 340.0 Put	5	$3.00	$1,496.70	$(3,231.61)
10/1/2021			EXP Nov 19 2021 340.0Call	EXP	$ –	$ –	$(4,053.31)
10/1/2021			EXP Nov 19 2021 343.0Call	EXP	$ –	$ –	$2,746.69
			TOTAL PR/LOSS FINAL POSITION:				$(491.54)
			CLOSING POSITION: DIA = $340/SHARE				
10/1/2021			EXP Nov 19 2021 337.0 Put	EXP	$ –	$ –	$4,046.69
10/1/2021			EXP Nov 19 2021 340.0 Put	EXP	$ –	$ –	$(4,728.31)
10/1/2021			EXP Nov 19 2021 340.0Call	EXP	$ –	$ –	$(4,053.31)
10/1/2021			EXP Nov 19 2021 343.0 Call	EXP	$ –	$ –	$2,746.69
			TOTAL PR/LOSS FINAL POSITION:				$(1,988.24)
			CLOSING POSITION: DIA >= $343/SHARE (I.E., $344)				
10/1/2021			EXP Nov 19 2021 337.0 Put	EXP	$ –	$ –	$4,046.69
10/1/2021			EXP Nov 19 2021 340.0 Put	EXP	$ –	$ –	$(4,728.31)
10/1/2021		X	STC Nov 19 2021 340.0Call	5	$3.00	$1,496.70	$(2,556.61)
10/1/2021	X		BTC Nov 19 2021 343.0 Call	−5	$ –	$ –	$2,746.69
			TOTAL PR/LOSS FINAL POSITION:				$(491.54)

And a short iron condor as a combination of a bull put and bear call spread with an initial credit:

- **Short 337 put, long 340 put (bear put spread)**

  +

- **Long 345 call, short 348 call (bull call spread).**

An example of this spread variation is shown in Table 14.8:

TABLE 14.8 Short Iron Condor Spread—SPDR DJ IA Trust (DIA) –*$343.10/Share*

DATE	BOT	SLD	DESCRIPTION	QTY	PRICE	COMMISSION	AMOUNT	REG FEE
			INITIAL POSITION: NET CREDIT OF TRADE $1,686.76					
10/1/2021	X		BTO Nov 19 2021 337.0 Put	5	$8.20	$3.25	$(4,103.31)	$0.06
10/1/2021		X	STO Nov 19 2021 340.0 Put	–5	$9.25	$3.25	$4,621.69	$0.06
10/1/2021		X	STO Nov 19 2021 345.0 Call	–5	$8.00	$3.25	$3,996.69	$0.06
10/1/2021	X		BTO Nov 19 2021 348.0 Call	5	$5.65	$3.25	$(2,828.31)	$0.06
							$1,686.76	

A short condor as the reciprocal of the long condor: profits are generated if the underlying price remains within the "body" range. This spread is therefore conceived to profit from low vol markets. Like the long condor and butterflies, the short condor is a limited-risk, limited-reward strategy.

The maximum profit occurs if the underlying price is between the lowest strike and the highest strike. The spread is a credit spread that relies on low volatility for profitability. Also, like a short iron butterfly, this spread has a small chance of a large loss and a large chance of a small gain. The profit range of the long iron butterfly is shown in Figure 14.4.

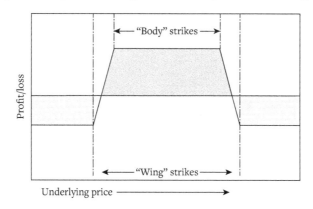

FIGURE 14.4 Profit profile of the short iron condor.

Payoff of the Short Iron Condor

First, it is clear that if the underlying price stays within the condor body, all options expire worthless. This represents the best case—the spread writer captures all sold time premium. In this regard, short iron condors have payoffs that are like short iron butterflies. Table 14.9 shows the potential results of the example in Table 14.7, at various prices.

The potential profit is the difference between the debit and the profit earned on either the call side or the put side. Therefore, this strategy relies on relatively high volatility, and, as might have been surmised, the returns are small compared to potential losses. Further, also consistent with the relationship between profit and losses in these spreads, the probabilities of small profits are high, while the probability of loss is small.

Legging into Iron Spreads

The very nature of these spreads invites the possibility that a spread writer can "leg" into an iron butterfly or an iron condor. "Legging" into a spread is a practice whereby one part is entered into first, and later, another part of the spread is consummated. Thus, any vertical spread can be turned into an iron butterfly or an iron condor by trading into the proper vertical spread. Under what circumstances should this be done?

Legging into any iron spread should only be done if either risk is reduced, profits expanded, or both. For example, suppose the spread writer wrote an out-of-the-money bear call spread, and the market obliges and the underlying declines in value. The decrease in market value has created a new opportunity: *writing a bull put spread* on the same underlying. The writer has now created a long iron butterfly—or a long iron condor, depending on the strikes of the bull put spread. The spread writer, in the very least, has reduced risk by opening an opportunity for a profit on at least one of the legs. If the profit of the bull put spread is large enough, the spread writer may have created a risk-free trade.

Summary and Conclusions

This chapter concludes our discussion of option spreads. We have discussed three- and four-option positions containing both puts and calls, the so-called iron spreads. These particular types of spreads are usually constructed positions as the spread writer either tries to improve the performance of previous option spread positions or sees additional opportunities by writing an additional credit spread.

It has been the practice of some to use iron condors as "brackets" around an expected range in market indexes. Under these circumstances, the width of the body is determined by a statistical measure of likely ranges over a specific timeframe. These strategies therefore adapt well to algorithmic trading.

Looking Forward

The journey continues as we examine important issues pertaining to trade follow-up in the next and last chapter. The upcoming chapter should be regarded as parting advice given by someone who has traveled this road before. You ignore those words at your financial peril.

Chapter 15

Looking Forward

Introduction

Some knowledge can be a bad thing, if the person possessing it believes it is "complete" and all encompassing. Those people will lose money because futures and options are not without their risks, a fact commonly ignored when charging forth into "battle"; ignoring these risks will lead to self-destruction. Equally dangerous is a trader who lacks self-awareness. Unfortunately, self-awareness is a rarely taught field of knowledge, particularly in finance.

The use of futures and options is not a video game; it is a means of building wealth and disposable income over time. Unfortunately, the type of adrenaline rush that occurs during trading is the kind of high that many "traders" cherish, but it is the type that needs to be avoided. This sounds prudish but is actually sound advice. This is particularly true for younger traders or older plebians just starting out. Generally speaking, younger traders quickly get ahead of their skis, just for the thrill. Older traders face the risk of early success, which promptly builds ego, or conversely feel the impending need to "make it back" all at once. Neuroscientists suggest this amygdala-based "fast thinking" emerged evolutionarily as a "fight-or-flight" reaction to risk. A place at the trading table cannot be set for this type of thinking.

It's All About Risk Management

An old adage that still holds true stipulates that any gain, even $1, is better than any loss. That is the function of risk management. However, the random nature of the investment world (and life, generally) prevents anyone from achieving a batting average of 1.000. That is not the point of risk management. Given that risk exists, the idea is to *minimize losses and maximize the probability of gain.*

The Role of Probability

To avoid the pitfalls of impulse decision-making, understand that when all is said and done, both futures and options trading rely on probabilities: the Black-Scholes model demonstrates this fully, considering the context of the variables d_1 and d_2. Yet a PhD in mathematics is not required to assess the likelihood of achieving desired results: for options, calculate the asset's historic volatility to obtain a sense of the asset's price capability before entering a trade; wishful thinking will not work. Once an approximate outcome probability is realized, calculate expected returns by multiplying the probability of success of the trade by the maximum return. Then, compare this result to an expected loss multiplied by the probability of loss. The decision can be stated as:

If $E(P) > E(L)$, **proceed.** Otherwise, do not proceed.

Where $\mathbf{E(P)} = p * \max(\text{Return})$ and $E(\mathbf{L}) = (1 - p) * \max(\text{Loss})$.

As an example, consider the folly of one who purchases a deep OTM call with a delta of .01. It has a 99% chance of being in-the-money at expiry and costs perhaps $5. The expected return must be discounted by roughly 99% before determining if the risk is worth the return.

Futures demand more attention. First, as stated previously, futures trading requires advanced knowledge concerning the fundamental forces that manifest supply and demand. Second, leverage of futures suggests that even market noise has an amplified effect on account equity. Most futures brokers/dealers permit direct electronic tie-ins to their trading platforms. A serious futures trader would be well advised to develop an algorithm for day trading, a subject well beyond the scope of this text.

Curiously, though, many *mature* investors only consider the upside without due consideration for what can go wrong. This is particularly dangerous with futures, whose leverage can destroy equity faster than it can be earned back.

The Role of Planning

Calculation of risk-weighted return ratios, historic volatility, or a probability distribution implies the obvious: avoidance of impulse trading yields better risk management. Further, trades require advance planning; a trade that is planned in advance—exit plans and what to do if things don't go as expected—means that the trader has no need for impulse trading. An "exit plan" consists of an analysis of *logical exit points* based on either performance of the asset price-wise or performance as moderated by impactful news and events that modify initial trade criteria.

Option flexibility offers a variety of alternatives if prices move against a trade, and the investor should think through all alternatives to find the best one before deciding to dissolve the spread ahead of expiry. Circumstances are individual, but in general, alternative exit strategies can be summarized as follows:

- **Vertical Spreads:** Vertical spreads can be rolled forward. For those who believe an unfavorable price trend is temporary, rolling the spread forward is frequently the best option, especially for credit spreads. Very often, if selected properly, the spreader may be able to roll the spread into the direction of the unfavorable trend, change strikes, and receive additional premium. Or a vertical spread can be transformed into a calendar spread, a butterfly, condor, or any other combination.

- **Calendar Spreads:** Calendar spreads are designed to exploit the theta differentials between long- and short-term options. If the long end of the calendar is far enough away (at least a year is recommended), then the spread writer can rewrite a new short option (as the new short-term leg) when the original expires. Care must be taken, however: if the strike of the short-term leg wanders too far away from the long-term leg, it is very difficult to unwind when the underlying price reverses.

- **Diagonal Spreads:** These positions are self-hedged and are usually transformed from other types of spreads. However, they, too, can be transformed into either verticals or straight calendar spreads if conditions require. Always try to attain credits first when adjusting these spreads.

- **Butterfly and Condor Spreads:** All butterflies, condors, and their "iron" cousins feature either high probability of small gain with low probability of large loss, or low probability of large gain with high probability of small loss. They are inherently static and are almost never altered over time except in the closing days before expiry. The usual alteration would be the removal of the short positions to emphasize a direction. This not frequently done.

Revisit the plan if it is a long-term trade (i.e., greater than three months) and moderate strategy and/or trade exit accordingly. It is possible that no changes are required. If so, do nothing. Doing nothing is free of charge.

The Role of Analysis

Analysis provides an overarching reality check. On a macro level, analysis of the overall market may be arduous but provides a depth of understanding that only improves over time;

on a micro level, a firm's overall financial health and future prospects. *Analysis* is a broad term that encompasses much, most of it beyond the scope of this text. But analysis should not be shortcut or ignored altogether. At the very least, for the options investor, understand the fundamentals of the underlying. The best source of information is attainable from the SEC EDGAR Company Search website. The site offers investors downloadable data in Excel format for further analysis. Consider listening to archived corporate earnings webcasts, paying particular attention to the Q&A if available, and reading two years of annual reports. Assume all information is not at hand; being curious is a virtue in the investment world.

Part of the analysis means the trader keeps detailed records of all trades, including the rationale for entering the trade. This contemporaneously composed record is an invaluable tool when referenced for future trades.

The Role of Information

Decisions are rash if they are based on false information. This is not the same as believing in no information (that is simply laziness). However, in trading as in any other decision, consider the source of the information and how much the source could or should know. If necessary, research the source to determine if it is even credible. Then, consider the logic of the information. What assumptions underlie it? Does it make sense?

The Right Frame of Mind

Leave Your Ego at the Door

No investor should believe that their unique personhood relies on the success of the next trade. Emotion and ego have zero place in this game anymore than they would at a chess table or in an operating room. Investors usually don't fret if losses are incurred; losses are an inevitable part of the game. Investors tend to be solitary creatures (if not managing OPM[1]). There is no audience jeering when a judgment error is made, nor kudos when a good trade is consummated. Further, investing is not an activity for engendering bragging rights. Consider this: boasting about one's success invites others to ask about your "trade secrets," and each boasted success raises the pressure for more success. Who needs that stress?

---

1   OPM: "other people's money."

It's Not a Contest

Irony: the primitive urge for wealth and power *undermines the discipline* required to attain trade success. Super Lotto tickets offer a more likely path to sudden wealth than even the least prudent option or future speculation. It's not a contest—even against oneself. It is a means of building wealth, one brick at a time. For those who lack confidence, open an account and "paper trade" until a sufficient reservoir of confidence and experience builds up.

Meanwhile, for those interested in winning stock-picking contests, try sponsored, free contests offered online (just search "free stock contests" online).

It Is Impossible to Know It All

Be flexible if new information changes the outlook of the trade, but don't be rash and impulsive. Maturity and experience bring level-headed decisions to mind. What does knowledge bring? Knowledge means exposure to situations and conditions not likely to be encountered in real time. This increases awareness of alternatives, an important thing to have when confronted by challenges. "Those who don't know, but think they know, are fools," to paraphrase the sages. And those who are closed to ideas, or too lazy to consider them, end up in a rut that will ultimately prove disastrous: the world does not ask permission to change.

Stay Healthy

Get plenty of rest; do not fuss over trades. Keep alert and fit. Relax.

Avoiding Common Traps and Errors—Futures

Failure to Use Stops

A speculator who opens too many contracts repeats the single most common mistake in futures trading. There is no rule of thumb as to how much excess equity to keep dormant in an account. However, it is urgently critical that the futures trader be well grounded and aware of the impact of changes in commodity value per tick and its overall impact on the account. But adequate equity—whether it is two or three times the size of the required contract margin—is only part of the story. Institute stop-loss orders immediately upon entering a trade; whether it be at a "resistance level" (if these things exist) or a specific dollar or point amount is irrelevant. What is important is that a stop-loss level be instituted and *never moved*, unless a "trailing stop" has been initiated.[2]

Pyramiding a Position

Pyramiding is a popular strategy that increases the number of futures contracts using unrealized gains from previously added positions of the same commodity. The error occurs if the speculator becomes overwhelmed by the size of the position, begins to trade on impulse, or overreaches risk.

All of these point to the same issue: a willingness to accept ever-greater risk over time, despite the obvious truism that all price trends end and reverse. Therefore, pyramiding increases risk (more contracts) as the likelihood of price reversal increases. There are a few ways to keep this activity in check: (1) use Bollinger bands[3] with two- and three-standard deviation widths. Any move outside these points suggests caution and eventually reversal; (2) use RSI to gauge "overbought" or "oversold" conditions. Pyramiding should cease as these levels are breached.

Overtrading

Overtrading is the constant in-and-out of trades during the course of a day. Those who do this habitually are probably addicted to the act of trading; no market features that many opportunities in a day. Exceptions include algorithmic "scalping." Scalping is a trading strategy that relies on small moves and large positions for profits. For those who wish to scalp a point here and there, develop an algorithm that can integrate into the trading platform of a reliable broker/dealer and back-test thoroughly.

Avoiding Common Traps And Errors—Options

Naked Long Option Position

The question of purchasing long puts or calls has been discussed from time to time in this text. The market is sufficiently "efficient" to usually make long purchases of calls and puts

---

2   Trailing stop: "A trailing stop order is a stop or stop limit order in which the stop price is not a specific price. Instead, the stop price is either a defined percentage or dollar amount, above or below the current market price of the security ("trailing stop price"). As the price of the security moves in a favorable direction the trailing stop price adjusts or "trails" the market price of the security by the specified amount." Source: SEC.gov. Investor Bulletin: Stop, Stop-Limit, and Trailing Stop Orders.

3   Bollinger bands denote the range of price distribution of an asset over a given timespan. For more about bollinger bands, see: Bollinger, John, *Bollinger on Bollinger bands* (New York : McGraw-Hill), 2002. 227 pages.

losing propositions. The single most common error made by investors is the purchase of short-term OTM calls and puts. These rarely earn a profit. Consider the reasons: (a) the largest extrinsic value is always for ATM options; (b) the largest amount of trade activity is ATM or near-the-money options for the nearest expiry; (c) near-the-money and ATM options are the least volatile; (d) theta is usually high and expanding quickly, and (e) deltas for these options are approximately 50. The risk-return for these options is generally unfavorable. For example, assume an investor is considering the purchase of an ATM call. The only way to profit from this trade at expiry is if the stock price is greater than the option strike, plus cost of the option. If the investor buys the ATM option, it has already stacked the bet against it by purchasing the option with the highest cost possible combined with a rapidly rising theta.

If the investor must speculate—and no one is forcing it to—the logical thing to do would be to purchase the option one or two strikes OTM. First, they are much cheaper, and second, if the speculator is right, and the stock does rise, then the purchased OTM option becomes the ATM option with the extreme extrinsic value. (Under these circumstances, the speculator shouldn't be greedy: close the long position.) Any comparison between a naked long option position and a spread reveals that spreads inherently have less risk and greater percent return potential than a stand-alone option. Consider these two alternatives (Table 15.1):

TABLE 15.1

ON SEMICONDUCTOR—BULL CALL SPREAD			ON SEMICONDUCTOR—CALL		
COST		RETURN	COST		RETURN
BTO 17 Dec 47.0 Call	$200.00	$300.00	BTO 17 Dec 47.0 Call	$880.00	$1,300
STO 17 Dec 50.0 Call					
Total Return on Capital		**50%**	**Total Return on Capital**		**50%**

The maximum return per spread is $100 (three-point spread minus $200 cost of spread), achieved if the stock reached $50 or more by expiry. There is theoretically no maximum return on the long 47 call, but the option would need to have a value of $1,300 at expiry *to achieve the same proportionate result*. This would require the underlying asset to rise from $47 per share to $60 per share, or 27.6% over a month; possible, but certainly less likely than the stock rising to $50 per share from $47 per share.

Naked Short Call Position

Spread writing offers a superior alternative to naked call writing, with a much better risk profile and return attributes. Consider a naked call on a $50 stock. Margin requirement would be approximately $2,500, and the premium—assuming the nearest option expiry—would be between $150 and $300, depending on asset volatility or strike. At best, the call expires worthless, which yields a return of between 6% and 12% for the period, with potentially unlimited risk.[4] Assume, however, that the stock has an 85% chance of rising no more than 15%, or $7.50 per share. If it does so, the option would be bought-to-close for a loss of between $450 and $600. Furthermore, short call option holders face the potential risk of an early exercise, as discussed in Chapter 5.

Now assume the alternative, an example 50–55 bear call spread harvests a credit between $175 and $215, depending on underlying vol. To maximize returns, the underlying needs to only decline to $50 or less per share, which results in the expiration of both option legs. The return on risk is between 35% and 43% for the period. Percent returns are better than a naked call, and risk is capped at the strike spread less credit received. For those seeking higher nominal returns, more spreads can be written, and the attendant increase in risk remains less than a naked call write.

Naked Short Put Position

Some investors sell naked puts to harvest premium, with the specific intention of allowing the put to expire OTM. For these individuals, the same logic applies on the naked put side as on the naked call side: bull put spread works as well or better with less risk. Furthermore, as discussed in Chapter 5, there is risk of assignment, against which a bull put spread is hedged.

As discussed, an assigned put writer must have adequate cash or margin power to buy the underlying at the strike, even if the investor does not intend to own the underlying after exercise. However, *if the put writer is interested in buying the underlying, it makes sense to use the sale of naked puts*: in essence, naked puts are equivalent to a limit order, except the investor receives premium for it. (And the premium can be an offset of the underlying price if exercised.)

Using the Greeks

A final word on the use of the Greeks: a worthwhile effort involves careful examination of the use of the Greeks on spreads, but it is not necessary to be caught in the details. The

---

4 In theory, no upper limit exists on stock prices.

important consideration is that the impact of the Greek statistics on *spreads* is best *stated in net terms*. For example, consider the establishment of a bull call spread, expiring in a month. The component and composite Greeks are as follows (Table 15.2):

TABLE 15.2

OPTION	PRICE	DELTA	GAMMA	THETA	VEGA
BTO BA 3 DEC 2021 210	−$9.55	.59	.02	−.13	.24
STO BA 3 DEC 2021 215	$6.65	.48	.02	.12	.23
COMPOSITE DEBIT RESULTS	**−$3.00**	**.11**	**.04**	**−.01**	**.47**

The chart above demonstrates that debit spreads neutralize theta while lowering delta at the time it is constructed. But what happens if the underlying moves up or down? The spread becomes more volatile if the underlying also becomes more volatile. Some consider this increase in gamma to be dangerous, but this is not necessarily true for near-month spreads of any kind, since theta increases proportionately to dissolve excess premium. Indeed, the decline in *net delta* is considered by many traders as a positive, since it suggests that the overall response of spreads to underlying price change is reduced to negligible amounts. For spreads, both credit and debit verticals, the implication is that the Greeks become almost irrelevant; the objective becomes modest *movement of the underlying for the benefit of the spread*. Indeed, for credit spreads, because the Greeks become almost irrelevant (even theta!), the objective becomes modest *movement of the underlying away from the spread*.

For calendar spreads, we observe the following (Table 15.3):

TABLE 15.3

OPTION	PRICE	DELTA	GAMMA	THETA	VEGA
STO BA 3 DEC 2021 210	$9.25	.59	−.02	.13	.24
BTO BA 21 JAN 2022 210	−$14.85	.57	.01	−.08	.39
COMPOSITE CREDIT RESULTS	**+$2.30**	**.02**	**-.01**	**.05**	**.15**

The chart above demonstrates that calendar spreads tend to neutralize delta and theta, but exposure to volatility exists. Consider what happens to this spread if a sharp *decline* occurs. First, the shorter-term option will depreciate faster than the longer-term option (but not by much) due to the slower erosion of time premium for the further month. In a short calendar spread (such as the one above), theta is net negative, meaning that overall, *erosion of time premium will proceed as expected, but at a slower rate.* However, the negative gamma and positive vega suggests that short calendar spreads have some exposure to increases in volatility because of impact on the price of the shorter-term leg of the spread. If implied vol rises, it affects all contracts, but more so the near short contract, and the position will take a hit.

We already know that butterflies are almost delta neutral. What about the remaining Greeks? Consider Table 15.4:

TABLE 15.4

OPTION	QTY	PRICE	DELTA	GAMMA	THETA	VEGA
BTO BA 3 DEC 2021 210	1	−$9.25	.59	.02	−.13	.24
STO BA 3 DEC 2021 215	−2	$13.90	−.98	.04	+.26	.23
BTO BA 3 DEC 2021 220	1	−$4.85	.38	.02	−.08	.39
COMPOSITE CREDIT RESULTS		**−$0.20**	**.11**	**.00**	**−.01**	**−.01**

Similar to calendars, the negative gamma engenders some risk. But short butterflies are by nature highly unlikely to pose large losses, since that would necessitate the underlying to occupy a very narrow price zone. Similarly for long butterflies, which pose minor losses at expiry with a small chance for a large return. For short straddles and short strangles, however, gamma risk can be extreme, as recently demonstrated in the year 2021 by GameStop, Avis, AMC, and others caught in a gamma squeeze.

And finally, any position with a net positive theta will have a net negative gamma, and vice versa. This implies that spread writers can either benefit from a price move, as in the case of bull call spreads or bear put spreads, or by time erosion, as in the case of short iron condors, and all credit spreads.

Concluding the Conclusion

Those who embark on the turbulent waters of options can find calm in the storm by using spreads rather than straight long or short positions. Unlike commodities, whose values counterpoint so closely to the fundamentals of supply and demand, option values react to price pressures not necessarily related to supply and demand. Instead, price pressure comes from the passage of time, from market-makers themselves, and even from random events unrelated to the value of the underlying. For those who embark on the hurricane waters of commodities: be a student of the commodity's fundamentals. Build an understanding of the factors that affect supply and demand, since that dynamic, more than any other, drives price in commodities. Commodities become a lifelong endeavor. Go forth in peace, and enjoy exploring.

References

Abd Wahab, M. A., Mohamad, A., & Sifat, I. (2019). On contango, backwardation, and seasonality in index futures. *The Journal of Private Equity*, 22(2), 69–82.

Admati, A. R., & Pfleiderer, P. (1988). A theory of intraday patterns: Volume and price variability. *The Review of Financial Studies (1986–1998)*, 1(1), 3–40.

Admati, A. R., & Pfleiderer, P. (1989). Divide and conquer: A theory of intraday and day-of-the-week mean effects. *The Review of Financial Studies (1986–1998)*, 2(2), 189–223.

Aldridge, I. E. (2013). *High-frequency trading: A practical guide to algorithmic strategies and trading systems* (2nd ed.). Wiley.

Aitken, M., Cumming, D., & Zhan, F. (2015). High frequency trading and end-of-day price dislocation. *Journal of Banking & Finance*, 59, 330.

Aït-Sahalia, Y., Mykland, P. A., & Zhang, L. (2011). Ultra-high frequency volatility estimation with dependent microstructure noise. *Journal of Econometrics*, 160(1), 160.

Amadori, M. C., Bekkour, L., & Lehnert, T. (2014). The relative informational efficiency of stocks, options and credit default swaps during the financial crisis. *The Journal of Risk Finance*, 15(5), 510–532.

Amihud, Y., & Mendelson, H. (1980). Dealership market: Market making with inventory. *Journal of Financial Economics*, (8), 31–53.

Ariely, D. (2008). *Predictably irrational*. Harper-Collins.

Arnuk, S., & Saluzzi, J. (2012). *Broken markets: How high frequency trading and predatory practices on Wall Street are destroying investor confidence and your portfolio*. FT Press.

Avellaneda, M. (2004). A look ahead at options pricing and volatility. *Quantitative Finance*, (4)C51–C54.

Back, K. (1993). Asymmetric information and options. *The Review of Financial Studies (1986–1998)*, 6(3), 435.

Bagehot, W. (pseud.) (1971). The only game in town. *Financial Analysts Journal*, (27)2, 12–14; 22.

Barberis, N. (2013). The psychology of tail events: Progress and challenges. *American Economic Review*, 103(3), 611–616.

Barberis, N., Shleifer, A., & Vishny, R. (1997). *A model of investor sentiment.* National Bureau of Economic Research.

Barberis, N., & Thaler, R. (2002). *A survey of behavioral finance.* National Bureau of Economic Research.

Barnea, A. (1974). Performance evaluation of New York Stock Exchange specialists. *Journal of Financial and Quantitative Analysis,* (9), 511–535.

Barnea, A., & Logue, D. (1975). The effect of risk on the market-maker's spread. *Financial Analysts Journal* (31), Nov./Dec., 45–49.

Bartram, S., Fehle, F., & Shrider, D. G. (2008). *Does adverse selection affect bid-ask spreads for options? The Journal of Futures Markets, 28*(5), 417.

Baylis, J. *October's market demons: The '87 stock market crash and likelihood of a recurrence.*

Beissner, P. (2017). Equilibrium prices and trade under ambiguous volatility. *Economic Theory, 64*(2), 213–238.

Benninga, S., Eldor, R., & Zilcha, I. (1984). The optimal hedge ratio in unbiased futures markets. *Journal of Futures Markets, 4*(2), 155–159.

Benston, G., & Hagerman, R. (1978). Risk, volume, and spread. *Financial Analysts Journal, Jan./Feb. 1978, 34*(1), 46–49.

Bernstein, P. L. (1996). *Against the gods: The remarkable story of risk.* John Wiley & Sons.

Biais, B., & Hillion, P. (1994). Insider and liquidity trading in stock and options markets. *The Review of Financial Studies (1986–1998), 7*(4), 743.

Black, F., & Scholes, M. (1972). The valuation of option contracts and a test of market efficiency. *Journal of Finance, 27*(2), 399–417.

Brenner, M., & Subrahmanyam, M. (1988). A simple formula to compute the implied standard deviation. *Financial Analysts Journal, 44*(5), 80–83.

Brody, D., Davis, M., Friedman, R., & Hughston, L. (2008). *Informed traders.* Working Paper, Department of Mathematics, Imperial College, London. 17 Nov. 2008.

Chaboud, A., Chiquoine, B., Hjalmarsson, E., & Vega, C. (2009). *Rise of the machines: Algorithmic trading in the foreign exchange market.* Federal Reserve Bank of St. Louis.

Chan, L., Jegadeesh, N., & Lakonishok, J. (1999). The profitability of momentum strategies. *Financial Analysts Journal, 55*(6), 80–90.

Chang, E. C., Cheng, J. W., & Khorana, A. (2000). An examination of herd behavior in equity markets: An international perspective. *Journal of Banking & Finance, 24*(10), 1651–1679.

Chen, N-F., Roll, R., & Ross, S. (1986). Economic forces and the stock market. *Journal of Business, 59*(3), 383–403.

Chen, S. S., Lee, C. F., & Shrestha, K. (2003). Futures hedge ratios: A review. *The Quarterly Review of Economics and Finance*, 43(3), 433–465.

Cho, Y-H., & Engle, R. (1999). Modeling the impacts of market activity on bid-ask spreads in the option market. NBER. Working Paper No. 7331.

Chordia, T., Roll, R., & Subrahmanyam, A. (2005). Evidence on the speed of convergence to market efficiency. *Journal of Financial Economics*, 76(2), 271–292.

Chordia, T., Roll, R., & Subrahmanyam, A. (2001). Market liquidity and trading activity. *The Journal of Finance*, 71(6), 501–530.

Cochrane, J. H. (1996). A cross-sectional test of an investment-based asset pricing model. *Journal of Political Economy*, 104(3), 572–621.

Cohen, G. (2005). *The Bible of option strategies*. FT Press-Pearson.

Cohen, K. J., Maier, S. F., Schwartz, R. A., & Whitcomb, D. K. (1981). Transaction costs, order placement strategy, and existence of the bid-ask spread. *The Journal of Political Economy*, 89(2), 287.

Constantine, D. M., Tymerski, R., & Greenwood, G. (2020). Differential evolution optimization of the broken wing butterfly option strategy. *Technology and Investment*, 11(3), 23–45.

Copland, T., & Galai, D. (1983). Information effects on the bid-ask spread. *Journal of Finance*, (38)5, 1457–1469.

Cordier, J., & Gross, M. (2009). *The complete guide to option selling* (2nd ed). McGraw-Hill.

Corgnet, B., Kujal, P., & Porter, D. (2013). Reaction to public information in markets: How much does ambiguity matter? *The Economic Journal*, 123(569), 699–737.

Corrado, C. J., & Miller Jr., T. W. (1996). A note on a simple, accurate formula to compute implied standard deviations. *Journal of Banking & Finance*, 20(3), 595–603.

Degutis, A., & Novickyte, L. (2014). EMH: A critical review of literature and method. *Ekonomika*, 93(2), 7–23.

DeJong, F., & Rindi, B. (2009). *The microstructure of financial markets*. Cambridge University Press.

Demsetz, H. (1968). The cost of transacting, *Quarterly Journal of Economics*, 82, 33–52.

Douglas, G., & Yorulmazer, T. (2011). Liquidity hoarding. *IDEAS Working Paper Series from RePEc*, (488).

Drehmann, M., Oechssler, J., & Roider, A. (2005). Herding and contrarian behavior in financial markets. *The American Economic Review*, 95(5), 1403–1426.

Dugast, J., & Foucault, T. (2016). *Data abundance and asset price informativeness*. Federal Reserve Bank of St. Louis.

Easley, D., & O'Hara, M. (1987). Price, trade size, and information in securities markets. *Journal of Financial Economics, 19*(1), 69–90.

Easley, D., & O'Hara, M. (2004). Information and the cost of capital. *The Journal of Finance, 59*(4), 1553–1583.

Easley, D., & O'Hara, M. (2010). Microstructure and ambiguity. *The Journal of Finance, 65*(5), 1817–1846.

Easley, D., O'Hara, M., & Srinivas, P. S. (1998). Option volume and stock prices: Evidence on where informed traders trade. *The Journal of Finance, 53*(2), 431–465.

Eberlein, E., Glau, K., & Papapantoleon, A. (2010). Analysis of Fourier transform valuation formulas and applications. *Applied Mathematical Finance, 17*(3), 211–240.

Egginton, J. F., Van Ness, B., & Van Ness, R. A. (2016). Dealers and changing obligations: The case of stub quoting. *Review of Quantitative Finance and Accounting, 47*(4), 919–941.

Einhorn, H. J., & Hogarth, R. M. (1986). Decision making under ambiguity. *Journal of Business, 59*(4), S225–S250.

Epstein, L. (2001). Sharing ambiguity. *American Economic Review, 91*(2), 45–50.

Epstein, L., & Ji, S. (2013). Ambiguous volatility and asset pricing in continuous time. *The Review of Financial Studies, 26*(7), 1740–1786.

Epstein, L., & Schneider, M. (2008). Ambiguity, information quality, and asset pricing. *The Journal of Finance, 63*(1), 197–228.

Epstein, L., & Schneider, M. (2010). *Ambiguity and asset markets.* National Bureau of Economic Research.

Fama, E. F. (1965). The behavior of stock-market prices. *Journal of Business, 38*(1), 34–105.

Fama, E. F. (1998). Market efficiency, long-term returns, and behavioral finance. *Journal of Financial Economics, 49*(3), 283–306.

Fama, E. F. (2014). Two pillars of asset pricing. *American Economic Review, 104*(6), 1467–1485.

Fama, E. F., & French, K. R. (1992). The cross-section of expected stock returns. *The Journal of Finance, 47*(2), 427.

Feng, Y. (2013). *The trading efficiency on options market: Essays on stock options market.*

Figuerola-Ferretti, I., & Gonzalo, J. (2010). Modelling and measuring price discovery in commodity markets. *Journal of Econometrics, 158*(1), 95–107.

Fleming, J., Ostdiek, B., & Whaley, R. E. (1996). Trading costs and the relative rates of price discovery in stock, futures, and option markets. *The Journal of Futures Markets, 16*(4), 353.

Foucault, T., Pagano, M., & Röell, A. (2013). *Market liquidity: Theory, evidence, and policy.* Oxford University Press.

Füllbrunn, S., Rau, H. A., & Weitzel, U. (2014). Does ambiguity aversion survive in experimental asset markets? *Journal of Economic Behavior & Organization*, 107, 810–826.

Gârleanu, N., Pedersen, L. H., & Poteshman, A. M. (2009). Demand-based option pricing. *The Review of Financial Studies*, 22(10), 4259.

Geman, H. (2002). Pure jump Lévy processes for asset price modelling. *Journal of Banking & Finance*, 26(7), 1297–1316.

Gerig, A. (2012). High-frequency trading synchronizes prices in financial markets. Federal Reserve Bank of St. Louis.

Ghosh, A. (1993). Hedging with stock index futures: Estimation and forecasting with error correction model. *Journal of Futures Markets*, 13(7), 743–752.

Gider, J., Schmickler, S. N., & Westheide, C. (2016). *High-frequency trading and fundamental price efficiency*. Working paper.

Givoly, D., & Lakonishok, J. (1987). Aggregate earnings expectations and stock market behavior. *Journal of Accounting, Auditing & Finance*, 2(2), 117–137.

Glosten, L., & Harris, L. (1988). Estimating components of the bid-ask spread. *Journal of Financial Economics*, 21, 123–142.

Glosten, L., & Milgrom, P. (1985). Bid, ask, and transaction prices in a specialist market with heterogeneously informed traders. *Journal of Financial Economics*, (14), 75–100.

Graham, J. R., Harvey, C. R., & Huang, H. (2009). Investor competence, trading frequency, and home bias. *Management Science*, 55(7), 1094–1106.

Grossman, S. (1976). On the efficiency of competitive stock markets where trades have diverse information. *The Journal of Finance*, 31(2), 573–585.

Grossman, S. J., & Stiglitz, J. E. (1980). On the impossibility of informationally efficient markets. *American Economic Association*, 70(3), 393–408.

Guéant, O., Lehalle, C., & Tapia, J. (2013). *Dealing with the inventory risk*. IDEAS Working Paper Series from RePEc.

Gulley, A., & Tilton, J. E. (2014). The relationship between spot and futures prices: An empirical analysis. *Resources Policy*, 41, 109–112.

Gupta, N. J., Kurt, M., & White, R. (2016). The Buffett critique: Volatility and long-dated options. *Journal of Economics and Finance*, 40(3), 524–537.

Hasbrouck, J. (1988). Trades, quotes, inventories, and information. *Journal of Financial Economics*, 22(2), 229–252.

Hasbrouck, J. (1993). Assessing the quality of a security market: A new approach to transaction-cost measurement. *Review of Financial Studies*, 6(1), 191–212.

Hasbrouck, J. (2007). *Empirical market microstructure*. Oxford University Press.

Hatemi-J, A., & Morgan, B. (2009). An empirical analysis of the informational efficiency of Australian equity markets. *Journal of Economic Studies*, 36(5), 437–445.

Haug, E. P. (2007). *The complete guide to option pricing formulas*. McGraw-Hill.

Hautsch, N., & Huang, R. (2012). The market impact of a limit order. *Journal of Economic Dynamics & Control*, 36(4), 501.

Hellwig, M. (1979). On the aggregation of information in competitive markets. *Journal of Economic Theory*, 22(3), 477–498.

Hendershott, T., Jones, C., & Menkveld, A. (2011). Does algorithmic trading improve liquidity? *Journal of Finance*, 66(1) 1–33.

Hens, T., Herings, J.-J., & Predtetchinskii, A. (2006). Limits to arbitrage when market participation is restricted. *Journal of Mathematical Economics*, 42(4–5), 556–564.

Hirschleifer, D. (2001). Investor psychology and asset pricing. *The Journal of Finance*, 56(4), 1533–1597.

Hirschleifer, D. (2011). Short arbitrage, return asymmetry, and the accrual anomaly. *The Review of Financial Studies*, 24(7), 2429–2461.

Ho, T., & Macris, R. (1984). Dealer bid-ask quotes and transaction prices: Empirical study of some AMEX options. *Journal of Finance*, 39, 23–45.

Ho, T., & Stoll, H. (1983). The dynamics of dealer markets under competition. *Journal of Finance*, 38(4), 1053–1074.

Hsieh, D. (1991). Chaos and nonlinear dynamics: Application to financial markets. *Journal of Finance*, 46(5), 1839–1879.

Hull, J. C. (2010). *Options, futures, and other derivatives* (7th ed.). Pearson.

Illeditsch, P. K. (2011). Ambiguous information, portfolio inertia, and excess volatility. *The Journal of Finance*, 66(6), 2213–2247.

In, F., & Kim, S. (2006). The hedge ratio and the empirical relationship between the stock and futures markets: A new approach using wavelet analysis. *The Journal of Business*, 79(2), 799–820.

Ivanenko, Y., & Pasichnichenko, I. *Uncertainty and absence of arbitrage opportunity*. http://arxiv.org/pdf/1307.5602v1.

Jarrow, R. (2013). Option pricing and market efficiency. *The Journal of Portfolio Management*, 40(1), 88–94.

Jordan, J., & Radner, R. (1982). Rational expectations in microeconomic models: An overview. *Journal of Economic Theory*, 26(2): 201–223.

Jung, H. M. (2010). Perfect regular equilibrium. *MPRA* (26534).

Kahnemann, D., & Tversky, A. (1979). Prospect theory: An analysis of decision under risk. *Econometrica, 47*(2), 263–292.

Kahnemann, D., & Tversky, A. (1982). *Judgment under uncertainty: Heuristics and biases.* Cambridge University Press.

Kaizoji, T. (2010). A route to speculative chaos in a heterogeneous agent model of the financial market. *IUP Journal of Behavioral Finance, 7*(3), 29–37.

Kandelousi, A. S., Alifiah, M. N., & Karimiyan, A. (2016). Investigation of the association between disclosure and asymmetric information. *Journal of Business Studies Quarterly, 7*(3), 39–46.

Kenmoe, R. N., & Sanfelici, S. (2014). An application of nonparametric volatility estimators to option pricing. *Decisions in Economics and Finance, 37*(2), 393–412.

Kumar, R., et al. (1992). The behavior of option price around large block transactions in the underlying security. *Journal of Finance, (47)*3 879–889.

Kyle, A. S. (1985). Continuous auctions and insider trading. *Econometrica (Pre-1986), 53*(6), 1315–1336.

Kyle, A. S. (1989). Informed speculation with imperfect competition. *The Review of Economic Studies, 56*(187), 317.

Labadie, M., & Lehalle, C.-A. (2010). Optimal algorithmic trading and market microstructure. Federal Reserve Bank of St. Louis.

Lakonishok, J. (1980). Stock market return expectations: Some general properties. *The Journal of Finance, 35*(4), 921–931. https://doi.org/10.2307/2327210

Lakonishok, J., Vishny, R., & Shleifer, A. (1993). *Contrarian investment, extrapolation, and risk.* National Bureau of Economic Research.

Lee, C. I., Rosenthal, L., & Gleason, K. (2004). Effect of regulation FD on asymmetric information. *Financial Analysts Journal, 60*(3), 79–89.

Lee, J. W., & Zhang, Y. (2009). Evidence on normal backwardation and forecasting theory in futures markets. *Journal of Derivatives & Hedge Funds, 15*(2), 158–170.

Lewis, M. (2015). *Flash Boys: A Wall Street Revolt.* W. W. Norton.

Lin, B.-H., Hung, M.-W., Wang, J.-Y., & Wu, P.-D. (2013). A lattice model for option pricing under GARCH-jump processes. *Review of Derivatives Research, 16*(3), 295–329. https://doi.org/10.1007/s11147-012-9087-8

Linton, O., & Mahmoodzadeh, S. (2018). *Implications of high-frequency trading for security markets.* Federal Reserve Bank of St. Louis.

Liu, H., & Wang, Y. (2016). Market making with asymmetric information and inventory risk. *Journal of Economic Theory, 163*, 73–109.

Lo, A. W. (2012). Adaptive markets and the New World Order. *Financial Analysts Journal*, 68(2), 18–29.

Lo, A. W., & MacKinlay, A. C. (1988). Stock market prices do not follow random walks: Evidence from a simple specification test. *The Review of Financial Studies*, 1(1), 41–66.

Lowenstein, R. (2000). *When genius failed: The rise and fall of long-term capital management* (1st trade paperback ed.). Random House Trade Paperbacks.

Lucas, R. (1978). Asset prices in an exchange economy. *Econometrica (Pre-1986)*, 46(6), 1429–1446.

Madan, D. B., Carr, P. P., & Chang, E. C. (1998). The variance gamma process and option pricing. *Review of Finance*, 2(1), 79–105.

Madhavan, A. (2002). Market microstructure: A practitioner's guide. *Financial Analysts Journal*, (58)5, 28–42.

Madhavan, A., & Smidt, S. (1991). A Bayesian model of intraday specialist pricing. *Journal of Financial Economics*, 30, 99–134.

Madhavan, A., & Smidt, S. (1993). An analysis of changes in specialist quotes and inventories. *Journal of Finance*, 48(5), 1595–1628.

Magiera, F. T. (1997). Accounting principles and practices. *CFA Digest*, 27(1), 14–16.

Malkiel, B. G. (2003). The efficient market hypothesis and its critics. *Journal of Economic Perspectives*, 17(1), 59–82.

Manahov, V., Hudson, R., & Gebka, B. (2014). Does high frequency trading affect technical analysis and market efficiency? And if so, how? *Journal of International Financial Markets, Institutions and Money*, 28, 131–157.

Miu, P., Chung, D. Y., & Hrazdil, K. (2013). Speed of convergence to market efficiency in the ETFs market. *Managerial Finance*, 39(5), 457–475.

Moskowitz, T. J., Ooi, Y. H., & Pedersen, L. H. (2012). Time series momentum. *Journal of Financial Economics*, 104(2), 228–250.

Mozumder, S., Sorwar, G., & Dowd, K. (2013). Option pricing under non-normality: A comparative analysis. *Review of Quantitative Finance and Accounting*, 40(2), 273–292.

Myers, R. J., & Thompson, S. R. (1989). Generalized optimal hedge ratio estimation. *American Journal of Agricultural Economics*, 71(4), 858–868.

Nyström, K., Aly, S. M. O., & Zhang, C. (2014). Market making and portfolio liquidation under uncertainty. *International Journal of Theoretical & Applied Finance*, 17(5), 1.

O'Brien, T. J., & Schwarz, P. M. (1982). Ex ante evidence of backwardation/contango in commodities futures markets. *The Journal of Futures Markets (pre-1986)*, 2(2), 159.

O'Hara, M. (1997). *Market microstructure theory*. Blackwell Business Press.

O'Hara, M., & Oldfield, G. (1986). The microeconomics of market making. *Journal of Financial and Quantitative Analysis*, 27(4), 361–376.

Park, T. H., & Switzer, L. N. (1995). Bivariate GARCH estimation of the optimal hedge ratios for stock index futures: A note. *The Journal of Futures Markets (1986–1998)*, 15(1), 61.

Paroush, J., & Wolf, A. (1989). Production and hedging decisions in the presence of basis risk. *Journal of Futures Markets*, 9(6), 547–563.

Paulos, J. A. (2003). *A mathematician plays the stock market*. Basic Books.

Peterson, P. E. (2015). Contango and backwardation as predictors of commodity price direction. https://ageconsearch.umn.edu/record/285844.

Poterba, J., & Summers, L. (1984). *The persistence of volatility and stock market fluctuations*. National Bureau of Economic Research.

Poterba, J. M., & Summers, L. H. (1988). Mean reversion in stock prices. *Journal of Financial Economics*, 22(1), 27–59.

Roll, R. (1984). A simple implicit measure of the effective bid-ask spread in an efficient market. *The Journal of Finance*, 39(4), 1127–1139.

Romer, P. (2016). The trouble with macroeconomics: Commons Memorial Lecture.

Ruan, J., & Ma, T. (2017). Bid-ask spread, quoted depths, and unexpected duration between trades. *Journal of Financial Services Research*, 51(3), 385–436.

Rubinstein, M. (1974). An aggregation theorem for securities markets. *Journal of Financial Economics*, 1(3), 225–244.

Santoni, G. J. (1988). The October crash: Some evidence on the cascade theory. *Review—Federal Reserve Bank of St. Louis*, 70(3), 18–34.

Sarkar, S., & Tripathy, N. (2002). An empirical analysis of the impact of stock index futures trading on securities dealers' inventory risk in the NASDAQ market. *Review of Financial Economics*, 11(1), 1–17.

Scholtus, M., Van Dijk, D., & Frijns, B. (2014). Speed, algorithmic trading, and market quality around macroeconomic news announcements. *Journal of Banking & Finance*, 38, 89–105.

Sewell, M. V. (2012). The efficient market hypothesis: Empirical evidence. *International Journal of Statistics and Probability*, 1(2).

Sharpe, W. (1970). *Portfolio theory and capital markets*. McGraw-Hill.

Shiller, R. J. (2003). From efficient markets theory to behavioral finance. *Journal of Economic Perspectives*, 17(1), 83–104.

Shleifer, A., & Vishny, R. W. (1997). The limits of arbitrage. *The Journal of Finance*, 52(1), 35.

Slezak, S. L. (2003). On the impossibility of weak-form efficient markets. *The Journal of Financial and Quantitative Analysis*, 38(3), 523.

Smidt, S. (1979). *Continuous versus intermittent trading on auction markets.* Paper presented at the Western Finance Association.

Smith, H. (2011). Test of a theory: An empirical examination of the changing nature of investor behavior. *Journal of Management Policy and Practice*, 12(3), 49–68.

Srinivasan, P. (2011). Modeling and forecasting the stock market volatility of S&P Index using GARCH models. *IUP Journal of Behavioral Finance*, 8(1), 51–69.

Stefanova, J. (2018). *High-speed technology trading innovations and capital market performance in Bulgaria. Financial Studies*, 22(2), 6–37.

Stoikov, S. (2006). Pricing options from the point of view of a trader. *International Journal of Theoretical & Applied Finance*, 9(8), 1245–1266.

Stoikov, S., & Saĝlam, M. (2009). Option market making under inventory risk. *Review of Derivative Research*, 12, 55–79.

Stoll, H. (1976). Dealer inventory behavior: An empirical investigation of NASDAQ stocks. *Journal of Financial and Quantitative Analysis*, 356–380.

Stoll, H. (1978a). The supply of dealer services in securities markets. *Journal of Finance, (33)*, 1133–1151.

Stoll, H. (1978b). The pricing of security dealer services: An empirical study of the NASDAQ stocks. *Journal of Finance (33)*, 1153–1172.

Stoll, H. (1989). Inferring the components of the bid-ask spread: Theory and empirical tests. *Journal of Finance*, 1(44), 115–134.

Subrahmanyam, A. (1991). Risk aversion, market liquidity, and price efficiency. *The Review of Financial Studies (1986–1998)*, 4(3), 417–442.

Sundaram, R., & Das, S. (2011). *Derivatives principles and practice.* McGraw-Hill.

Symeonidis, L., Prokopczuk, M., Brooks, C., & Lazar, E. (2012). Futures basis, inventory and commodity price volatility: An empirical analysis. *Economic Modelling*, 29(6), 2651–2663.

Taleb, N. (2010). *The black swan: The impact of the highly improbable* (2nd ed.). Random House Trade Paperbacks.

Taleb, N. N. (2005). *Fooled by randomness: The hidden role of chance in life and in the markets* (2nd ed., updated). Random House.

Tangman, D. Y., Gopaul, A., & Bhuruth, M. (2008). Exponential time integration and Chebychev discretisation schemes for fast pricing of options. *Applied Numerical Mathematics*, 58(9), 1309–1319.

Thaler, R. (1991). *Quasi-rational markets.* The Russell Sage Foundation.

Thijssen, J. J. (2011). Incomplete markets, ambiguity, and irreversible investment. *Journal of Economic Dynamics and Control, 35*(6), 909–921.

Tinic, S. (1972). The economics of liquidity services. *Quarterly Journal of Economics, 86*(2), 79–93.

Tripathy, N., & Peterson, R. (1991). The relationship between OTC bid-ask spreads and dealer size. *Journal of Financial Research, 14*(2), 117–127.

Vayanos, D., & Woolley, P. (2008). *An institutional theory of momentum and reversal.* National Bureau of Economic Research.

Vijh, A. (1990). Liquidity of CBOE equity options. *Journal of Finance, 45*(4), 1157–1179.

Willems, B. (2004). *Cournot competition, financial options markets and efficiency.* IDEAS Working Paper Series from RePEc.

Zhang, F. (2010). The effect of high-frequency trading on stock volatility and price discovery. SSRN eLibrary.

Zovko, I. I. (2008). *Topics in market microstructure.* Amsterdam University Press.

Index

CPSIA information can be obtained
at www.ICGtesting.com
Printed in the USA
LVHW060107051022
729968LV00002B/33